MAGOSAHA

Cliff,

Maybe this will recall some memories of those special days we spent on the Sulu Sea in those faraway days of our youth.

Best wishes,

Barry

MAGOSAHA
An Ethnology of the
Tawi-Tawi Sama Dilaut

H. Arlo Nimmo

ATENEO DE MANILA UNIVERSITY PRESS

ATENEO DE MANILA UNIVERSITY PRESS
Bellarmine Hall, Katipunan Avenue
Loyola Heights, Quezon City
P.O. Box 154, 1099 Manila, Philippines
Tel.: 426–59–84 / FAX: (632) 426–59–09
email: unipress@admu.edu.ph

Cover and book design by J.B. dela Peña

The National Library of the Philippines CIP Data

Recommended entry:

Nimmo, H. Arlo
    Magosaha : an ethnography of the Tawi-Tawi Sama
Dilaut / by H. Arlo Nimmo. – Quezon City : ADMU
Press, c2000.
    I v

1. Sama Dilaut (Philippine people). 2. Sama
Dilaut – Social life and customs. 3. Ethnology –
Philippines. I. Title.

DS666.S35 305.9921 2000 P004000007
ISBN 971-550-369-1 (pbk.)

To
the Sama Dilaut of Tawi-Tawi
who taught me a new way to view the world

ACKNOWLEDGEMENTS

Many people and organizations facilitated the research that resulted in this book.

Friend and fellow anthropologist Richard Stone first convinced me I should conduct fieldwork among the Sama Dilaut. Father Emile Laquerre and Father Henri LaVallee, Oblates of Mary Immaculate priests in Bongao during the 1960s, frequently fed me and bedded me at their convento when I was ill, soaked from stormy seas, or weary of anthropological fieldwork. During my first days in the field, Tarabasa Idji acted as friend, assistant, and interpreter and helped me survive those difficult days of early fieldwork.

Among the Sama Dilaut, Masarani, Hadjulani, Timpa, Landisani, Mastarani, Palasia, Lajima, Hadjira, and Musulaini were especially good friends who shared their homes with me as they taught me their culture. They and all the other Sama Dilaut who contributed to this book helped make my stay in Tawi-Tawi one of the great experiences of my life.

Over the years I have benefited greatly from the writings and personal correspondence of Clifford Sather. I am fortunate to have shared my research interests with such a fine, competent anthropologist. Also through the years, Marc Scruggs has offered insights into my data during our many conversations about Sulu and the Sama Dilaut. Without his support and companionship, I am not sure I could have handled the Tawi-Tawi I discovered when I returned in 1977 and 1982. Gerard Rixhon has been another constant during my years of researching and writing about the Sama Dilaut. His great knowledge of Sulu cultures has provided an invaluable sounding board for my ideas and interpretations since I first met him in 1963. Frank Lynch, S. J., directed my first research among the Sama Dilaut and taught me much about field methods. At the University of Hawaii, Katharine Luomala set standards of excellence in research and writing that shall always be goals for me. Certain chapters of this book benefited from the critical readings of Ronald Himes, Jean Treloggen Peterson, Gerard Rixhon, and Marc Scruggs.

Others who contributed directly and indirectly to this book include Doug Bond, Shawn Brown, Bevery DeLong-Tonelli, Alice Dewey, Audrey Greenberg, Charles Langlas, Jo Lonam, Doris Lutzky, Seymour Lutzky, Falak Thaver, Ricardo Trimillos, Warren Peterson, and Robert Youngblood.

Financial support for this research came from the East-West Center, Honolulu; the National Science Foundation, Washington, D. C.; the Wenner-Gren Foundation for Anthropological Research, New York; the Carnegie Foundation, New York; and the National Defense Graduate Fellowship Program, Washington, D. C. I gratefully acknowledge these institutions for their support.

CONTENTS

PROLOGUE

Magosaha is the word the nomadic boat-dwelling Sama Dilaut of Tawi-Tawi use to explain their movements throughout the seas of the southern Philippines. When asked why they travel so much, a Sama Dilaut invariably replies, "Aku magosaha," which literally translated means "I am seeking a livelihood." But as with most literal translations, this is insufficient, for "magosaha" means more than simply seeking a livelihood.

Frequently I met Sama Dilaut families who had recently returned to their home moorage with fish-laden boats. When asked how long they would stay at the moorage, they replied they would not travel again for some time since they had resources to last several weeks. In a few days, they were gone. All my questions concerning their whereabouts elicited the same response from their neighbors: "Magosaha." When Sama Dilaut families abandoned house living and left the moorage for several months of life in their houseboats, "magosaha" was again the explanation. And when Sama Dilaut youth joined fishing expeditions to distant Palawan even though nearby fishing grounds were equally profitable, "magosaha" was their reason. "Magosaha" then does not mean simply looking for a livelihood. Perhaps it can best be defined as wanderlust conditioned by a lifetime of travel, as well as a very real necessity to continuously search the seas for sustenance.

This book is a description of the nomadic boat-dwelling Sama Dilaut of the Tawi-Tawi islands in the southern Philippines, their need for magosaha, and how that need shapes their culture. Some of the discussions have appeared in somewhat different form in my earlier publications, but others have not been published before. I have used the ethnographic present to describe the Sama Dilaut culture I observed in the 1960s.

From the time the Sama Dilaut first appeared in the literature, confusion has reigned regarding their name. Their autonym is "Sama" and if they need to distinguish themselves from the shore-dwelling Sama people, they call them-

1

selves "Sama Dilaut" ("Sama of the sea"). In eastern Borneo, other people call all Sama people "Bajau" and the Sama Dilaut are called "Bajau Laut" ("Bajau of the sea"). "Bajau" is apparently an Indonesian name for boat-dwelling people that was transferred to the Sama people in Borneo, both land dwelling and boat dwelling. In the Sulu Archipelago, "Bajau" is commonly used by outsiders for the Sama Dilaut, but not for other Sama people. The earliest visitors to Sulu referred to the Sama Dilaut as "Bajau" and that name became established in the ethnographic literature for the full-time and part-time boat-dwelling Sama of Sulu. I followed that tradition and referred to the Sama Dilaut as "Bajau" in previous publications. I was always uncomfortable about doing so and in recent years have become increasingly so. Alain Martenot called the Sitangkai "Bajau" by their autonym Sama (Martenot 1981), and belatedly, I am doing the same. It is time for "Sama Dilaut" to become established in the ethnographic literature as the name for the sea-dwelling Sama people of the Sulu archipelago and eastern Borneo.

Literature on the Sama Dilaut of the Sulu Islands

The earliest written references to the Sama Dilaut of the Sulu archipelago are found in the journals of the first European visitors to the southern Philippines. Antonio Pigafetta accompanied Ferdinand Magellan on his voyage around the world and reported in 1521 that near present-day Zamboanga "The people of that island make their dwellings in boats and do not live otherwise" (Pigafetta 1906, 53). About a hundred and fifty years later, in 1667, Francisco Combes described a people he called "Lutaos" who lived in the waters of the Zamboanga peninsula. This name does not appear elsewhere in the literature, but almost certainly these people were Sama Dilaut. Combes (1904) described them as sea-dwelling people involved in trade with land-based people. In 1773, the British explorer Thomas Forrest described boat-dwelling people in the waters around present-day Semporna. Brief references to the Sulu Sama Dilaut are found in other early writings, but it was not until the 1930s that the first significant descriptions of them appeared.

In the late 1920s, Carl Taylor traveled throughout the Philippines, including the Sulu islands, where he encountered Sama Dilaut. He spent several days at Sitangkai in the Sibutu islands, where he participated in curing ceremonies and made observations about Sama Dilaut boats. He eventually wrote four somewhat redundant articles about his experiences in Sulu among the Sama Dilaut (Taylor 1930a, 1930b, 1931, 1932), which later became part of his book *Odyssey of the Islands* (1936). Taylor was not an anthropologist and his writing tends toward the "Great White Explorer" genre, but nonetheless he provided important early documentation of the Sama Dilaut of Sulu.

The first anthropological research among the Sama Dilaut did not occur until the summer of 1962, when anthropology graduate students from the Ateneo de Manila participated in the Coordinated Investigation of Sulu Culture co-sponsored by the Ateneo de Manila and the Notre Dame of Jolo College. Four important papers resulted from that research. Richard L. Stone investigated the nature of intergroup relations among the Tausug, Sama, and Bajau (Sama Dilaut) in the Siasi area. His investigation explored the hierarchical relationships of the three groups and how members change group identity (especially women) as they marry into the group above them (Stone 1962). Nena Eslao studied child-rearing practices in Manubul, Siasi, a village comprised of both Sama Dilaut living in houses over the sea- and land-dwelling Sama living in houses on shore. She explored the different child-rearing practices of the two groups in terms of the "differences in certain socialization ideas, attitudes, and practices associated with geographical and residential differences" (Eslao 1962, 81). Dolores Ducommun researched the village of Sisangat, a Sama Dilaut community near Siasi and described its "marriage practices, care and education of children, political organization, worldview, and out-group relations" (1962, 91). Jose Arong was the first to conduct field research among the boat-dwelling Sama Dilaut near Sanga-Sanga island in Tawi-Tawi. His short but ambitious paper included "a description of the Badjaw [Sama Dilaut] communities in Sulu, an exposition of the concept of Badjaw nomadism, an estimate of the population, and a brief survey of their material culture, modes of interpersonal relations and their religious beliefs and rites" (Arong 1962, 137). Anthropologist Frank Lynch directed these studies, which were all six weeks long, except Stone's, which was somewhat longer. The studies yielded important data about the Sama Dilaut and illustrate that properly directed, short-term field research can produce important results. Stone returned for additional field research on the same subject in 1963 for his M. A. thesis at the University of Hawaii, which was never published.

Arong's paper served as a springboard for my fieldwork among the Tawi-Tawi Sama Dilaut. From June through December 1963, I conducted fieldwork among the boat-dwelling Sama Dilaut to investigate their social organization. That research resulted in my M. A. thesis, eventually published as "The Social Organization of the Tawi-Tawi Badjaw" (1965b). I returned to Tawi-Tawi in September 1965 for an additional eighteen months of fieldwork. Half that time was spent among the boat-dwelling Sama Dilaut of Tawi-Tawi and the other half among the house-dwelling Sama Dilaut of Sitangkai. My investigation was focused on the changes that occurred when the Sama Dilaut moved from boats to houses. The Tawi-Tawi boat dwellers were used as a baseline for discussing the changes that occurred when the Sitangkai Sama Dilaut moved to houses.

This research formed my Ph. D. dissertation and was published as *The Sea People of Sulu* (1972). I returned to Tawi-Tawi for short research trips during the summers of 1977 and 1982, and the fall of 1997. The bibliography of this book contains all the publications that resulted from my fieldwork among the Sama Dilaut.

The next important research among the Sama Dilaut was that of Clifford Sather, who studied the house-dwelling Sama Dilaut (he calls them "Bajau Laut") near Semporna, Sabah from October 1964 to September 1965. Although not within the current political boundaries of the Philippines, these Sama Dilaut are closely related to the Sitangkai Sama Dilaut. This initial fieldwork resulted in Sather's Ph. D. dissertation, "Marriage and Domestic Relations among the Bajau Laut of Northeastern Borneo" (1971) and several fine articles (Sather 1976, 1978, 1984, 1985). Sather returned to the field in May 1974, July and August 1979, and July 1994. He has published extensively on various aspects of Sama Dilaut culture, but the summation and capstone of his research appeared in 1997 as *The Bajau Laut: Adaptation, History, and Fate in a Maritime Fishing Society of South-Eastern Sabah*. This book is important as both ethnography and history. It contains excellent discussions of Bajau Laut economics, social organization, and religion. In addition, it traces the history of this society from the first observations of early European visitors to the most recent observations of Sather himself. Sather's complete publications on the Sama Delaut are listed in the bibliography.

In 1965, geographer David Sopher published *The Sea Nomads, A Study of the Maritime Boat People of Southeast Asia*. Sopher combed the literature for the many scattered references to boat-dwelling people in Southeast Asia to describe their distribution, culture, and history. At the time of Sopher's research, virtually no anthropological fieldwork had been conducted among the boat people. Sopher included in his book a description of the Sama Dialut of Sulu. His discussion of the various Sama groups in the Sulu Islands holds up fairly well, but his theories of origins and history have fared less well in light of subsequent research. His book is still important for anyone interested in Southeast Asia's boat people and is discussed in greater detail in chapter 2.

Linguist A. Kemp Pallesen conducted linguistic research in Siganggang, a Siasi Sama Dilaut village, from 1963 through 1970 under the auspices of the Summer Institute of Linguistics. An important publication from this research was "Reciprocity in Samal Marriage" (1972), a discussion of the network of obligations and reciprocity resulting from Sama Dilaut marriage. Even more important was Pallesen's *Culture Contact and Language Convergence*, based on his 1977 Ph. D. dissertation and published in 1985. He collected extensive data himself and utilized other linguistic studies for this historical linguistic account of the settlement of the Sulu Archipelago. His study concluded that the Sama entered Sulu from the Zamboanga area about a thousand years ago, some 300 years before the Tausug began to arrive. He detailed the dispersal of Sama speakers and their interaction with Tausug, and challenged some of Sopher's conclusions regarding Sama origins. This study's relevance to Sama Dilaut history is discussed in greater detail in chapter 2.

Alain Martenot was one of the few anthropologists to conduct fieldwork in Sulu during the 1970s, a period of great civil unrest. In 1975 and 1976 he spent eighteen months in Sitangkai, where his investigation focused on Sama Dilaut religion. He has yet to publish his findings on religion, but he published an excellent article on the boats of the Sitangkai Sama Dilaut (1981). In 1980, he and ethnomusicologist Jose Maceda produced an LP record of Sama Dilaut vocal and instrumental music with an accompanying text entitled "Sama de Sitangkai." This recording has become increasingly valuable, as the traditional music of the Sama Dilaut has changed over the years.

In the late 1970s, Talib L. Sangogot conducted research among the Tawi-Tawi Sama Dilaut that I studied in the 1960s who at the time were residing in houseboats at the community near Bongao now known as Lu'uk Bangka. His research resulted in an M.A. thesis at Marikina Institute of Science and Technology, entitled "Socio-Economic-Relgious Status and School Attendance Rate of the Badjaos (Tawi-Tawi): Implications for Educational Policies, Curricula and Management Practices Revisions" (1980). His theoretical considerations and recommendations are now a bit dated, but the thesis includes important ethnographic data on the Sama Dilaut.

In 1981, James Warren published *The Sulu Zone 1768–1898*, subtitled *The Dynamics of External Trade, Slavery, and Ethnicity in the Transformation of a Southeast Asian Maritime State*. Based primarily on library and archival data, the book is an excellent, well-written history of the Sulu sultanate, and is relevant to this context because of Warren's discussions of Sama Dilaut roles as fishermen, pearl divers, and collectors within the economic sphere of the sultanate. It is a must-read for anyone interested in Sulu or island Southeast Asia.

Saladin S. Teo's book *The Life Style of the Badjaos: A Study of Education and Culture* (1989) is an important contribution to Sama Dilaut ethnography. Teo is a Sama Dilaut who grew up in the Siasi area, and his book is the most extensive account of the Siasi Sama Dilaut available. The major part of the book is a description of Sama Dilaut subsistence activities, social organization, child rearing, ceremonies and spiritual beliefs followed by suggestions for implementing more successful education programs among the Sama Dilaut. The book is important not only because it adds significant data to the ethnographic literature of the Sama Dilaut, but also because Teo is a Sama Dilaut who grew up among the people he describes. Hopefully, more Sama Dilaut will follow his lead and offer their special insights into their culture.

In the early 1990s, Bruno Bottignolo conducted anthropological fieldwork among the same Sama Dilaut (he calls them "Badjao") I worked with in the 1960s, more specifically he worked in Lu'uk Bangka near Bongao and in Bilatan near Batu-Batu. Bottignolo's book is both interpretative and descriptive. Part one, "The Sacred," is a phenomenological interpretation of the Sama Dilaut spiritual realm, and part two, "The Celebration," is a description of the important Sama Dilaut ceremonies. Bottignolo's research was done some twenty-five years after my initial fieldwork and reveals some important changes in Sama Dilaut religion, especially the emergence of a being called "Umboh" who, he says, "dominates the entire Badjao existence" (p. 6). Neither Sather nor I found this being in our earlier research, which possibly resulted from the influence of Islam on Sama Dilaut religion. Bottignolo's book is a very significant addition to Sama Dilaut ethnography because of his phenomenological interpretation, which is an important departure from the more traditional anthropological approaches of earlier researchers.

Another important study to emerge from research in the early 1990s is the study of religious change among the Sama of Simunul island by Patricia Horvatich (1993, 1994, 1997). Horvatich conducted research from September 1989 to January 1991, focussing on Islamic reform movements at the village level. Although the Simunul people are not Sama Dilaut, Horvatich's discussions of religious change are relevant to all Sama of Tawi-Tawi.

Nicole Revel is currently involved in the collection of *Kata-Kata* epics among the Sama people, including the Sama Dilaut. These long narratives are highly regarded as sacred literature among some Sama Dilaut groups. Her research in the Philippines is part of a larger project to collect and archive Asian epics sponsored by UNESCO and the French government. The Philippine epics are archived at the Ateneo de Manila University in Quezon City and at the Centre National de Recherches Scientifique in Paris.

Wilfredo Torres recently completed field research for his M. A. thesis at Ateneo de Manila among a Sama Dilaut community near Jolo that moved from a fishing economy to an aquaculture economy. The study is important in that it explores the changing economic bases of Sama Dilaut communities with the introduction of *agalagar* (seaweed) farming.

Research among Sama Dilaut groups outside the Philippines has occurred in recent years. In 1996, Adrian B. Lapian and Nagatsu Kazufumi published "Research on Bajau Communities: Maritime People in Southeast Asia." The reader is referred to that paper for a discussion of fieldwork among Sama Dilaut (Bajau) communities outside the Philippines.

Methodology

I first learned of the Sama Dilaut as an anthropology graduate student at the University of Hawaii. Richard Stone, a fellow graduate student, arrived in Hawaii in the fall of 1962 fresh from a summer of fieldwork in the Sulu islands. We both had grants at the East-West Center that would sponsor research in Asia or the Pacific. Stone was interested in organizing a small group of Center grantees to participate in a coordinated research project in Sulu. After plying me with romantic tales of Sulu over beers at the local pubs, he talked me into joining the group. My part of the project was to study religious change among the boat-dwelling Sama Dilaut of the Tawi-Tawi islands in southern Sulu, a project I abandoned soon after I arrived in the field in favor of a survey of Sama Dilaut social organization.

As with many anthropologists of my time (and I suspect today also), my preparation for the field was limited. I had studied anthropology for about two years. My language preparation was a summer of Hawaiian and a year of Indonesian. The Sama Dilaut language had not yet been described. I read all I could find about Sulu, which was a short list in those days. The Sama Dilaut themselves were virtually unknown. Several mostly misleading journalistic articles had been written about them, but anthropologists were just beginning to explore their culture

I was in Tawi-Tawi from June through most of December 1963 and the research from that stay resulted in my M. A. thesis. After additional graduate studies, I returned to Tawi-Tawi in September 1965 and stayed through May 1967 for Ph. D. research. I made short trips to Tawi-Tawi in the summers of 1977 and 1982 and the fall of 1997, but this book is based primarily on the field trips of the 1960s.

My first field trip was spent entirely among the Tawi-Tawi Sama Dilaut and resulted in a description of their social organization (Nimmo 1965a, 1965b). The second field trip was a study of social change that compared the boat-dwelling Sama Dilaut of Tawi-Tawi to the former boat-dwelling Sama Dilaut of Sitangkai who lived in houses and were rapidly embracing Islam (Nimmo 1969, 1972). My chief interest was always with the boat-dwelling Sama Dilaut and the bulk of my field research was among them. Consequently, this book is a description of the boat-dwelling culture of the Tawi-Tawi Sama Dilaut as I observed it in the 1960s.

When I first arrived among the Sama Dilaut, most of them were suspicious, if not afraid, of me. They had suffered a great deal of abuse from outsiders throughout their history and consequently were suspicious of anyone new. A priest who had recently established a small school at the Sama Dilaut moorage of Tungkalang near Sanga-Sanga Island introduced me to that community. No one wanted me to stay in his house or houseboat, so I ended up living in an abandoned barracks at the nearby outpost of the Philippine Air Force. Each day I went to the moorage to make friends. Most children were terrified of me and ran away screaming at my approach. The women did not scream but they hurried away when they saw me coming. The men put up with my company somewhat longer, but they too usually found something else to do some distance away from me. My first friends were three teenage boys who attended the Catholic school and knew a few words of English. From them, the rest of the moorage began to realize I was harmless. At about that same time, I acquired an interpreter from one of the nearby land villages. He knew some of the Sama Dilaut and introduced me to them. Within days, a family invited me to stay in their house and I set up quarters in one of its corners. I soon attached myself to several other families, and before long was participating in their activities. My interpreter was with me during the day, but I was on my own at night, when I studied the Sama Dilaut language. I used the interpreter during my first six-month stay. When I returned for my second stay, I continued to work with him for three months and then felt comfortable enough in the language to work by myself. I always called on him for long interviews, however, especially those dealing with religion. At the end of my fieldwork, I was still learning the language. I shall always be suspicious of field workers who say they spent the first month learning the language and then conducted research on their own. Perhaps I am a bit slower than most.

During my first field trip, I spent most of my time at the moorage of Tungkalang near Sanga-Sanga island. A house in Tungkalang served as my home base, but I lived and traveled frequently with other boat-dwelling families. At the beginning of my second trip, I acquired my own houseboat and attached myself to three different boat-dwelling families and divided my time and travel among them. Much of this trip was spent in the Bilatan area of central Tawi-Tawi. It was impossible for me to study only one moorage because of the frequent movements in and out of it, so I lived with several family groups and followed their movements throughout the Tawi-Tawi waters. I soon became known to all the Tawi-Tawi Sama Dilaut and had little difficulty gaining entry to their communities when I visited them. In the beginning many of them quizzed me about my reason for living among them. I told them I was writing a book so other people would know about them. Most had no knowledge of books, but they eventually ceased to wonder about me and accepted me as *Melikan*, "the American." My research method was the traditional participant observation approach of anthropology. Because of the openness of Sama Dilaut society, it was easy for me to observe and participate in all events that occurred. I ate, fished, and sailed with the Sama Dilaut. I watched their babies born, assisted at their illnesses, attended their ceremonies, and mourned their deaths. In addition, I took censuses, collected genealogies, and conducted formal interviews.

In those days, Tawi-Tawi was incredibly beautiful and the traditional cultures were still intact. I was always aware that I was having one of the great experiences of my life while living in one of the most beautiful corners of the world with a truly unique group of people. This is not to say my research was one long idyllic affair for the two years I was in the field. At times I thought I could not stand another day in Tawi-Tawi. In the early weeks, I often became ill from the food and water, and suffered the resulting dysentery in quiet anguish at ever having left the comforts of home. As romantic as houseboat living initially seemed, the reality of the cramped quarters, hard decks, leaky roofs, foodless days, stormy seas, lack of privacy, and unsanitary conditions soon made it otherwise.*

A well-known American anthropologist once told me he always wanted to study the Sama Dilaut, but became middle aged before he was able to do so. He claimed the Sama Dilaut were for young anthropologists. He was right. As a middle-aged man, I could never have endured the rigors of fieldwork that I did as a young man. I used to wonder why most anthropologists do a major field trip at the beginnings of their careers, and thereafter do only short ones, if any. Now I know why.

Theoretical Considerations

Anthropologists have traditionally tried to collect their data objectively, but most have always realized that their research methods are less than scientific and their descriptions of culture are ultimately subjective. In recent years the claims of scientific objectivity in anthropological research have been challenged and much research is conducted today with no claim to objectivity. Such was not the case in the 1960s. Our aim at that time was to collect data objectively for descriptive and comparative purposes. We tried to do so, but of course we did not. We brought into the field our cultural backgrounds, our personal worldviews and all the experiences that color our perceptions.

My research trips were designed to investigate specific issues, but my intent was to someday write a holistic description of Sama Dilaut culture, especially the boat-dwelling culture. Even in those days, most anthropologists believed that truly holistic descriptions were impossible and not particularly desirable. Nonetheless, it was the holistic approach to the study of culture—not to mention the holistic approach of anthropology to the study of humankind—which was one of my initial attractions to the discipline. I realized the limitations and ultimate impossibility of holism, but nonetheless I tried to discover all I could about Sama Dilaut culture. I failed to do a holistic study, of course, and some of the glaring blanks in my data are embarrassing today and make me wonder how I could possibly have overlooked them in the field. For example, I have almost no data on the many herbal remedies the Sama Dilaut use for curing. I saw hundreds of dances, but I did not record the different types, not to mention the basic movements of dance. And although I have much data on the rich song traditions of the Sama Dilaut, I have almost nothing on their instrumental music. Nonetheless, I am glad I made the attempt at holism, since the culture I researched no longer exists and my descriptions, limited though they may be, are the only ones that describe that lost culture.

I do not consider my observations a description of some sort of pure, pristine boat-dwelling culture. Rather they are descriptions of the boat-dwelling culture that existed in the 1960s, which was no doubt considerably different from that observed by the first visitors to Sulu. Culture is constantly changing to adapt to new environments and Sama Dilaut culture is no exception. Among the major events in Sulu's past which surely resulted in significant changes for the Sama Dilaut were the arrival of the Tausug people in Sulu some 700 years ago; the coming of Islam and the subsequent Tausug sultanate; the penetration of Chinese, Indian, and Arab traders in search of Sulu's natural riches; the Spaniards' pursuit of souls and more empire; the arrival of the Americans and the bloody battles they fought with local Muslims before they established dominance over their Asian colony; the World War II invasion of the Japanese and the battles in their wake; and the postwar establishment of the independent Philippine national government and its plans for Sulu.

The Sama Dilaut culture I observed in the 1960s had survived these events and adapted to them. Its greatest test for survival, however, came in the 1970s with the introduction of seaweed aquaculture and the secessionist war between Sulu Muslims and the Philippine national government that resulted in massive population shifts in the archipelago. Tawi-Tawi Sama Dilaut culture did not survive the changes resulting from those events. The Sama Dilaut who fled Tawi-Tawi for eastern Borneo have retained their traditional culture for a few more years but those who remained in Tawi-Tawi are being rapidly absorbed into Sulu Islamic culture.

THE SULU REALM

Weighing anchor, we were shortly wafted by the westerly tide and a light
air towards that beautiful island, which lay in the midst of its little Archipelago;
and as we were brought nearer and nearer, we came to the conclusion that in
our many wanderings we had seen nothing to compare to this enchanting spot.
(Charles Wilkes 1844)

Thus wrote the American explorer Charles Wilkes in 1842 when he arrived
at Jolo, the capital of the Sulu archipelago, after traveling the southern Pacific
Ocean and the northern Philippine Islands. Few who visited the Sulu islands
before or since Wilkes's time would deny his claim. Although set in a part of
the world where tropical beauty is typical landscape, this small chain of islands
between Mindanao and Borneo continues to impress visitors with its varicolored reefs, misty summits, gentle seas, verdant forests, and colorful cultures.

Geography of Sulu

The Sulu islands comprise the southernmost provinces of the Republic of
the Philippines.[1] North of the equator between latitudes 4 and 6, the islands are
washed by the Sulu Sea on the north and the Celebes Sea on the south (see fig.
1). Because both seas are ringed by islands and far enough from the Asian
continent to be strongly influenced by the monsoons, they rarely experience the
violent weather sometimes typical of the South China Sea and the open ocean
of the Pacific. The Sulu islands were once part of a land bridge that connected
Borneo to Mindanao. Seas invaded and left only mountain peaks as witnesses
to past land while coral islands grew around the warm shallow shores. Much
later when humans invaded the sea in boats, the islands acted as stepping-stones
between the two large land masses at their eastern and western extremities. The
extent of prehistoric human traffic among the islands can only be surmised
since archaeological excavation has hardly begun in Sulu. However, if the his-

toric period is indicative of the past, Sulu has always been an important route for the flow of goods and ideas between Borneo and Mindanao.

The picturesque peaks of Basilan island mark the northern gateway to the Sulu archipelago. Lying only a stone's throw from the port of Zamboanga, this volcanic island is the largest in the Sulu chain. Surrounding its shores are smaller, less imposing coral islands. Although a part of the geologic formation that forms the Sulu archipelago and included in the old Sulu sultanate, Basilan is presently politically separate from the other Sulu islands and is administered as part of Zamboanga province.[2] Southwest of Basilan are the low, coral Samales islands, infamous in early Spanish annals as the stronghold of some of Sulu's most notorious pirates, especially the Sama of Balingingi island. Like most of the low islands in Sulu, these islands suffer perennial drinking water shortages and support only a sparse scrub flora and, of course, the ubiquitous coconut, the source of copra, Sulu's most important export.

West of the Samales is the Jolo group, the ancient and current capital of the archipelago. The large volcanic island of Jolo is extremely fertile and the most intensively cultivated island in the archipelago. Its capital city, also called Jolo, has a population of some thirty-thousand and is the economic and political center of the province. Northwest of Jolo are the Pangutaran islands, low coral islands not unlike the Samales. Southwest of Jolo are the Siasi islands,

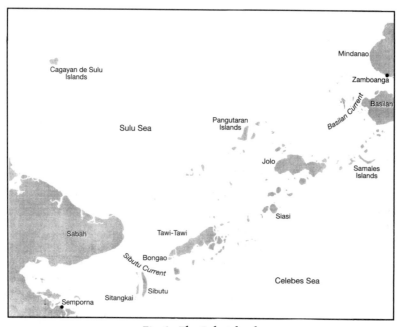

Fig. 1 The Sulu islands

12

an assortment of small volcanic islands flanked by coral atolls of varying sizes. Farmers cultivate the high islands while the low ones host fishing populations who depend on their farming neighbors for fruits and vegetables, and sometimes drinking water.

The next and largest island group in the chain is Tawi-Tawi, a long, narrow island that supports a mountain range that stretches some forty kilometers in a northeast-southwest direction. Although Tawi-Tawi's interior is sparsely inhabited, its shores and especially the many coral islands scattered about its southern and eastern reefs support heavy populations. Bongao, with a population of some 5,000, is the chief port and administrative center of the area.

The final group of islands, the Sibutu islands, were described by one unimpressed traveler as "the most God-forsaken islands of the entire archipelago" (Landor 1904, 233). These low coral islands are separated from the Tawi-Tawi group by the swift Sibutu passage that acts effectively as a barrier to the movement of small watercraft during certain seasons of the year. As a result, the islands enjoy less frequent interaction with the rest of the archipelago than the other groups. Extensive reefs characterize the area and provide it with one of the richest fishing grounds of the entire archipelago—indeed, of the entire Philippines.

The Cagayan de Sulu islands are politically a part of Sulu province, but because of their isolation, they have always been peripheral to the mainstreams of history which have shaped the other Sulu islands. Linguistic and cultural anomalies distinguish the Cagayan people from other Sulu populations and they are consequently excluded from any generalizations about the Sulu archipelago. "Sulu," then, will be used throughout this book to include the islands of Samales, Jolo, Pangutaran, Siasi, Tawi-Tawi, and Sibutu, but excluding the islands of Cagayan de Sulu which are outside the Sulu archipelago, and Basilan which is outside Sulu province.

Although the Sulu islands experience the monsoon winds, they do not have the pronounced wet and dry seasons characteristic of the monsoon lands of continental Southeast Asia. The northeast monsoon is generally well established in Sulu by November and lasts until April. These winds are more constant than winds of other months—sometimes blowing for four or five days at a stretch—and bring some of the longest periods of cool weather, rain, and rough seas. June ushers in the less predictable southwest monsoon winds that last until October. The velocity and unpredictability of these winds often endanger small craft on the open sea. The greatest amount of rain falls from June to December, whereas rainless months have been reported for February and April. Sulu's yearly average temperature is 79 degrees F. Recorded temperature extremes range from 95 degrees F. to 65 degrees F.; however, the difference between summer and winter mean temperatures does not exceed two degrees F. (*Sailing Directions for the Philippine Islands* 3:1956).

Tides are diurnal in Sulu and range from two to six feet. The strong tidal currents typical of some parts of the archipelago are due to the movement of water from the Sulu and Celebes Seas over the shelf that supports the island chain. The most noteworthy currents, some of which flow up to seven knots at the spring tides, include the Basilan current between Basilan island and Pilas island, and the Sibutu current between Bongao island and Sibutu island (*Sailing Directions for the Philippine Islands* 3: 1956). Few Sulu sailors venture into the currents at their greatest strengths, and when they do, they time their entry to take advantage of the fast flow of the water.

The high islands host dry rice farming and abound in tropical fruits, such as bananas, coconuts, papayas, mangoes, lansones, oranges, guavas, jack fruit, mangosteens, and durians. The dry, low islands have fewer varieties of fruits, and on the driest islands only coconuts are found. Cassava grows on almost all islands and is the staple food for most people of Sulu. Monkeys, wild pigs, birds, lizards, and snakes are the most common fauna of the high islands while the low islands support a much sparser population of these animals. Crocodiles were once common in certain Tawi-Tawi islands and are still rumored to live in the interior swamps of Sanga-Sanga island and Tawi-Tawi island. Jolo island once supported a small herd of elephants, a gift from a Javanese sultan to the Sultan of Sulu, but they died off long ago. Domesticated horses and cattle are not numerous but are found throughout the archipelago. By far the most important fauna in Sulu is the rich marine life that feeds most Suluanos and provides one of their chief incomes.

The History of Sulu

Most early written accounts of Sulu are about Jolo island and the Tausug people who inhabit it. Earliest reports indicate that Jolo was an important center of trade for eastern Malaysia long before the present ports of Sandakan, Ujung Pandan, Cebu, and Manila rose to power. As late as 1842, Charles Wilkes reported a brisk trade between Jolo and southern China. Earlier writers describe boats and goods in Jolo from Java, Sumatra, Malaya, eastern Borneo, Celebes, Mindanao, Cambodia, China, and even distant Japan. The central location of Jolo in island Southeast Asia, as well as the traditional commercial and sailing interests of the Sama and Tausug people, have contributed most significantly to its historic commercial role. Apparently, long before Islam arrived in the archipelago, Jolo enjoyed this commercial position; indeed, it was probably its commercial importance that attracted the first Muslim teachers and traders.

The Genealogy of Sulu, a Tausug tradition found in *The History of Sulu* (Saleeby 1963) credits the introduction of Islam to three men, namely Makdum, Raja Baginda, and Abu Bakr. Makdum, allegedly a scholar from Malacca, arrived in Sulu about 1380 and visited most of the islands to preach his faith. About ten years later, Raja Baginda arrived in Zamboanga from Menangkabau in Sumatra. From there he went to Jolo, where he succeeded in establishing himself as supreme ruler of that island. Some time later Abu Bakr arrived and married the daughter of Raja Baginda. He eventually took over his father-in-law's position and is most important in early Sulu history for reorganizing the Muslim church and the political and legal structure of the sultanate (Saleeby 1963). The line between myth and history is so thin in the *Genealogy of Sulu* that it is unwise to trust it too fully as a historical document. Other students have suggested that Islam may have been introduced to Sulu from southern China (Majul 1963, xii). The possibility is not moot, considering the extensive Muslim missionizing in southern China at that time and the frequent trade by Arab merchants between China and Sulu. But until further evidence is discovered, the origins of Sulu's Islam must rest with other unknowns, and perhaps unknowables, of Malaysia.

Spanish conflict with the Muslims occurred almost simultaneously with Spain's arrival in the Philippines. Although the stronghold of Philippine Islam was concentrated in Sulu and southern Mindanao, small enclaves of Muslims were scattered throughout the Visayas and as far north as Manila. Had the Spaniards arrived 100 years later, they probably would have found Islam firmly entrenched throughout the entire Philippines. With amazing speed, the Spaniards conquered and Christianized the lowland areas of Luzon, the Visayas, and northern Mindanao as they defeated the small Muslim settlements they encountered. With these easy victories behind them, a Spanish fleet set out in 1578 with orders to reduce Sulu and Mindanao to vassal states and to wipe out the "accursed doctrine" of Islam (Saleeby 1963, 52). The Spaniards attacked Jolo and reported the sound defeat of the Muslims; however, they established no garrison in Jolo and consequently no foothold in the archipelago. Their first attack did little more than arouse the ire of the Muslims and to set the stage for a long series of attacks and counter-attacks that lasted throughout most of the Spanish occupation of the Philippines. Several times throughout the period, the Muslims suffered devastating defeats, but because the Spaniards seldom occupied the sites of their victories, the lands immediately fell back to Muslim control.

In 1899 the Americans arrived in Jolo and soon discovered that the Muslims claimed sovereignty in Sulu and were ill disposed to relinquish it to new invaders. Before America gained control of Sulu, another bloody chapter was written in Philippine history.

Until 1913, battles between the Muslims and American troops were common. The superior weapons of the Americans brought them many victories, but the Muslims persisted with a tenacity that sometimes taxes credibility. In 1913 a decisive American victory against Muslims on Mount Bagsak on Jolo island established United States' control of Sulu. Muslim factions occasionally rebelled, but no major battles occurred during the remainder of the American occupation of the Philippines.

Prior to 1913 a military government met the Muslim defiance in Sulu. With the subjugation of the Muslims that year, the Department of Mindanao and Sulu was established with a civilian governor. In 1920 Sulu was placed under the Bureau of Non-Christian Tribes, and became a regular province in 1921. Throughout this period of peace in Sulu, American influence spread and many of the islands, especially in the south, were visited for the first time by Westerners. However, with the Japanese invasion of Luzon in 1942, war again returned to Sulu. Japanese bases were established at Jolo and Tawi-Tawi, and during the final months of the war the Sulu Sea was the scene of several battles. Throughout the war, Muslim guerilla troops resisted the Japanese and offered immediate support to the returning liberation forces. In 1946 the Philippines gained independence from the United States, but it was not until 1957 that Sulu had its first elected governor.

Following the war, most of Sulu's prewar economy was reestablished. Copra continues to be the most important export and its production is found throughout the archipelago. Sea products, especially fish, are second to copra in export value. Within the past few years, a seaweed (*agalagar*) native to Sulu reefs has been exported in great quantities to European and American manufacturing firms. Seashells and *trepang* are other important marine exports, but the postwar pearl industry has never reached its prewar peak. Some Suluanos have amassed quick postwar fortunes through the lucrative smuggling activities between Sulu and Sabah.

Airplanes and various watercraft connect Sulu to the rest of the Philippines. Daily flights tie Jolo to Zamboanga, and planes fly down the archipelago to Tawi-Tawi twice a week. Numerous interisland ships regularly move between Zamboanga and Jolo. Only three such ships make weekly trips down the entire archipelago with ports-of-call at Siasi, Bongao, and Sitangkai to pick up copra and marine products, and to deposit manufactured items which are transported by launches to the more remote islands.

Today, like much of the Philippines, Sulu is an interesting study in contrasts. Wealthy Jolo businessmen live in penthouse-like homes equipped with the luxuries and conveniences of the West, while at the wharf only a few hundred meters away, Sama Dilaut families live in the small houseboats they have occupied for unknown centuries. Airplanes fly up and down the archipelago above the colorful sails of native outrigger dugouts. Rock-and-roll dancing by the youthful elite in Jolo compete with the gongs and drums of traditional Muslim ceremonies. But as one moves away from Jolo and the main port towns, the guise of the West falls away. In the remote islands, life goes on much as it has for many years. A full moon at Sitangkai sets the scene for the graceful dances of the shamans who live there. An evening elsewhere evokes the plaintive song of an itinerant Sulu balladeer. Occasional pirates still rear their heads to make Manila headlines. Throughout the islands, the color of Islam has blended with native Sulu traditions to create spectacular ceremonies of marriage, healing, and prayer. Fishermen fish much as they have always fished, and farmers farm much as they have always farmed. And largely because of the different streams of history that have passed through its waters, Sulu exists as an archipelago apart from the rest of the Philippines. Thus, for a Filipino from the north, a visit to the Sulu Islands is a visit to a foreign land.

Ethnic Composition of Sulu

Although most Filipinos from the north still refer to all native peoples of Sulu as "Moros," a designation early bestowed on Filipino Muslims by the Spaniards, it has been recognized for some time that several ethnic groups reside in the Sulu archipelago (Saleeby, Landor, Arce, Stone), namely the Yakan, who live on Basilan island; the Tausug, who occupy the most fertile islands of Jolo and Siasi; and the Sama, who dominate the Tawi-Tawi and Sibutu islands but who also inhabit small islands throughout the archipelago. All are Muslims with the degree of acculturation to orthodox Islam varying among members of each group. The Yakan are less dispersed than the Tausug or Sama, and since their home island of Basilan is beyond the scope of this discussion, they are excluded from any generalizations about the people of Sulu. In addition to the Muslims of Sulu, important minorities of Christian Filipinos and Chinese are found in the port towns. Most Christians hold bureaucratic and military positions within the national government while the Chinese are primarily engaged in commerce.

Concentrated on Jolo and Siasi islands, the Tausug are clearly a distinct people; their language and other aspects of their culture distinguish them from the other people of Sulu. Historically, they have politically dominated the archipelago and they consider their Islam more orthodox than that of most Sama. Famous for their fierce pride, they were among the most formidable pirates of Malaysia in earlier centuries and were never completely subdued by the Spanish and American colonial forces. The 1960 Census of the Philippines lists their numbers at 238,386, and they continue to hold most major political positions in Sulu.

Scattered throughout the archipelago, but more concentrated in the south, the Sama are primarily fishermen and farmers with small copra plantations in the island interiors. According to the 1960 Census, the Sama population (including the Sama Dilaut, called "Bajau" in the Census which grouped them as a separate people) of Sulu is eighty-one thousand.[3] These people are more culturally diverse than the Tausug; members range from Sama Dilaut "sea gypsies," who spend nomadic lives in tiny houseboats, to university-educated Muslim *hadji* who have made the pilgrimage to Mecca. A Sama man from eastern Tawi-Tawi told me his people can be divided into three groups: (1) *Sama Dea*, those who live on land, such as the Sibutu people and some of the Sanga-Sanga people; (2) *Sama Bihing*, those who live on the shore line, such as the Simunul people and other eastern Tawi-Tawi people; and (3) *Sama Dilaut*, those who live on the sea in boats, such as the Tawi-Tawi Sama Dilaut, or over the sea in houses, such as the Sitangkai Sama Dilaut. The Sama population, however, is even more diverse and complex than this since almost every island—indeed, sometimes each village within an island—views itself as unique from other Sama groups and is known by a toponym. Earlier writers gleaned some notion of this complexity by singling out the Sama Dilaut as a separate people and calling them "Bajau," a name used for boat-dwelling people in eastern Indonesia and eastern Borneo.[4] This is, however, not the case. The Sama Dilaut speak dialects of the Sinama language, view themselves as Sama, and are identified as Sama by the other people of Sulu.[5] Perhaps their chief distinction from the other Sama is that some of them have not fully embraced the Islamic faith.[6] Nonetheless, some Muslim Sama view other Muslim Sama as different from them as the Sama Dilaut.

Although the Sama Dilaut are identified by a variety of local names, throughout the Sulu archipelago they are commonly called Sama Dilaut, their autonym. The Tausug sometimes call them *Luwa'an*, a Tausug word apparently derived from the word *luwa* which means, "to spit out," as something is spit out which is disagreeable to the taste. "Outcast" would probably be the best English translation of the word, but a more graphic explanation was offered by a Tausug informant who said the Tausug call the Sama Dilaut Luwa'an because each time they see a Sama Dilaut, they feel like vomiting. His explanation reflects the pariah position of most Sama Dilaut groups in the Sulu islands. Contrary to what Szanton says (1963, 468), this is not an autonym of the Sama Dilaut, but rather is the name most offensive to them, at least to those of the Tawi-Tawi and Sibutu areas. Another local name for the Sama Dilaut is *Pala'u*, the name for the house-like structure on some Sama Dilaut houseboats. Some Sama Dilaut find the name offensive, others think it simply silly, and still others are indifferent to it. "Bajau" is not widely used in Sulu, but is commonly used in eastern

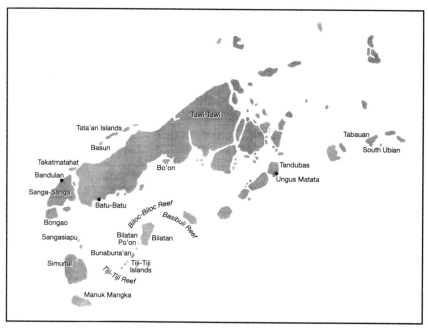

Fig. 2   The Tawi-Tawi islands

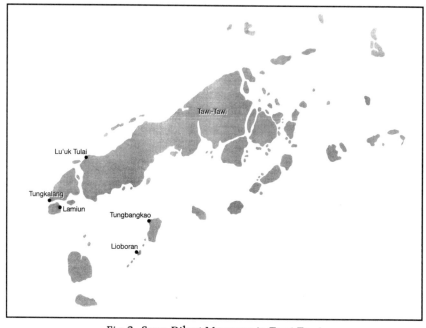

Fig. 3   Sama Dilaut Moorages in Tawi-Tawi

Borneo to identify the boat-dwelling Sama, as well as all other Sinama speakers, in that area (Sather 1997). "Sama Dilaut" will be used throughout this book to identify the boat-dwelling Sama population of Sulu, those who occasionally still use the boat as living quarters, and those who have recently abandoned the boat-dwelling habit.

Sama Dilaut have been reported as far north as Surigao, Davao, and Zamboanga on Mindanao island, in all the major island groups of Sulu, in eastern Borneo, and in eastern Indonesia. At least two major groups of Sama Dilaut are found in Sulu. The Sama Dilaut of Tawi-Tawi, Sibutu, and Semporna form one group connected by many and important kinship ties, and intermarriage among them is fairly common. Few and insignificant kin ties extend from these people to the northern Sama Dilaut. The southern Sama Dilaut view the Siasi, Jolo, Basilan, and Zamboanga Sama Dilaut as a different, albeit closely related, group of Sama. These northern Sama Dilaut probably subdivide their members further.

Several cultural features distinguish the southern Sama Dilaut from their northern kinsmen. Within the memory of living people, the three southern groups shared a common boat-type, the *djenging*; in fact, some of the Siasi Sama Dilaut still refer to the Tawi-Tawi Sama Dilaut as "Sama djenging." Today the djenging has been replaced by the outriggerless *lepa* (a boat-type from Borneo) among the Semporna and Sibutu people. Only in Tawi-Tawi is the djenging still found, and only occasionally. The fishing techniques of these people also distinguish them from other Sinama speakers of Sulu; their hand-woven fishing nets are not found elsewhere in Sulu. The art forms (songs, dances, grave markers and boat carvings) of the Tawi-Tawi, Sibutu, and Semporna Sama Dilaut also reveal close cultural relationships.[7]

Compared to the northern Sama Dilaut, the southern people are less nomadic as a group. They are predominantly reef dwellers and their movements are usually limited to nearby reefs, whereas some of the Sama Dilaut of Siasi, Jolo, Basilan, and Zamboanga journey seasonally to the waters of Palawan, Cagayan de Sulu, Borneo, or even distant Luzon in pursuit of fish. The southern Sama Dilaut normally travel and fish in nuclear family groups whereas the northern Sama Dilaut often fish in all-male groups while the wives and small children remain at home. A complex cult of shamanism, most highly developed at Sitangkai, also distinguishes the southern Sama Dilaut from their northern kinsmen.

At one time, the ancestors of the present boat-dwelling people of Tawi-Tawi, Sibutu and Semporna probably lived among the islands and reefs of the Sibutu Islands. These people still view themselves as a *bangsa*, or subculture, different from other Sama.[8] The Tawi-Tawi people are the most conservative of the three groups; over two-thirds of them still use boats as permanent living quarters, and some of their villages consist of flotillas with no houses. In Tawi-Tawi, some 1,600 Sama Dilaut are scattered among five different villages, namely Lu'uk Tulai, Tungkalang, Lamiun, Tungbangkao, and Lioboran (see fig. 2). In Sibutu, the Sama Dilaut villages at Sitangkai, Tungnehat, Tandowak, and Omapoi add approximately 3,500 to the Sama Dilaut population (see fig. 3). The Sibutu Sama Dilaut, as the Semporna Sama Dilaut, are predominantly house dwellers who use the boat as living quarters only during fishing trips. The two Semporna villages, Bangau-Bangau and Labuan Haji, have a combined population of approximately 660 (Sather 1997, 28). Thus a conservative population estimate of the entire bangsa is about 5,760. Intermarriage among the villages within each of the three areas is common, with intermarriage among the three population centers less so. Nonetheless, such intermarriages are still frequent between Semporna and Sibutu, and between Sibutu and Tawi-Tawi. I know of no recent marriages between Tawi-Tawi and Semporna, although the two areas have genealogical connections through Sibutu.

THE HISTORICAL REALM

Legendary Accounts

Long ago the ancestors of the Sama Dilaut lived at Johore, a place to the west of the Sulu Islands. One day they saw a typhoon approaching. To protect themselves from the storm, they stuck poles into the sea floor and tied their boats to them. Instead of sticking into the sea floor, however, the poles stuck into a giant stingray sleeping beneath the sea. As the Sama Dilaut slept that night, the stingray awakened and pulled their boats across the sea to Zamboanga. When they awakened they did not know the way back to Johore, so they began wandering the Sulu Sea. First, they went to Jolo where they settled for a while. Then they sailed to Siasi where they also stayed for awhile. Finally, they traveled to Tawi-Tawi where they decided to remain and where they have lived ever since. (Sama Dilaut legend)

Accepting legends as history is problematic for many historians, but they cannot be ignored in discussing a people's history. Where people think they came from is obviously important, and their legends frequently offer clues to their past. Such is the case with Sama Dilaut legends. The above legend is one of the stories the Sama Dilaut tell of their origins. Many variations of it are found, such as the following:

Long ago the ancestors of the Sama Dilaut lived at Johore, a place to the west near Mecca, in houseboats much like those they live in today in Tawi-Tawi. One day a strong wind began to blow. To secure his boat, the village headman stuck a pole into what he thought was the sea floor and tied his boat to it. The other villagers, also fearing the wind, tied their boats to that of the headman. It turned out, however, that instead of going into the sea floor, the pole of the headman was stuck in the nose of a giant stingray that lay sleeping beneath the flotilla. That night as the Sama Dilaut slept, the ray awakened and began to swim, pulling the boats behind it. When the Sama Dilaut awakened the next morning, they were adrift on the open sea and did not know the way back to Johore. For one week they drifted helplessly until finally the leader pleaded to *Tuhan* [God] for help. Within minutes, Tuhan sent down a *saitan* [spirit] which entered the leader, who thus became the first *djin* [shaman] among the Sama Dilaut. The saitan instructed the leader to sail for two days toward the east. The flotilla did as instructed and on the second day, land was spotted. Upon reaching shore, the headman again stuck a pole [called *samboang* in Sinama] into the sea floor and all the boats were tied to it. This was the first mooring place in the Philippines for the Sama Dilaut and was consequently called "Samboangan." Today it is still called this by the Sama Dilaut while the rest of the world knows it as "Zamboanga." Shortly after their arrival in Zamboanga, the Sama Dilaut became subjects of the powerful Sultan of Sulu. During the course of his many marriages throughout Sulu, the Sultan gave groups of Sama Dilaut as bride wealth; thus, the Sama Dilaut became scattered throughout the Sulu archipelago.

This story, the longest related to me, was collected in Sitangkai, but many versions of it are also found among the Tawi-Tawi Sama Dilaut. One version claims all the Sinama-speaking people were pulled from Johore to Sulu by the giant stingray; some of them continued to live in boats while others built houses on land and became farmers, thus the present diversity in Sulu's Sama population. Another version maintains that the ray pulled the Sama Dilaut from Zamboanga throughout the Sulu islands, with no mention of Johore or how they arrived at Zamboanga. Still another relates that only a single-family boat was pulled to the Sulu islands and its descendants became Sulu's Sama population. One of the present Sama Dilaut headmen at Sitangkai can trace his genealogy back seven generations to the time when his people lived at Johore.[1] Allowing a generous thirty years for the reign of each headman would date the Sama Dilaut departure from Johore some 240 years ago, a date much too recent since Magellan's crew saw boat dwellers in Zamboanga in 1521.[2]

Diverse though the individual accounts are, most share the common theme that the Sama Dilaut came from outside the Sulu archipelago, with Johore and Zamboanga as the most frequent homelands. The tradition of a homeland beyond the Sulu islands has suggested to some, such as Saleeby (1963) and Sopher (1977), that the Sama Dilaut have not been in the Philippines for a very long time, at least not long enough for the memory of a homeland to be lost from their traditions.

The Tausug tell another version of the origin of the Sama Dilaut. According to their story, long ago all the different people of the Sulu archipelago lived as a single people. One day a great tidal wave was seen approaching the islands. To escape the wave, half of the people built boats and the other half fled to the mountains. Those who built boats were washed to sea and became the boat-dwelling people of Sulu, whereas those who fled to the mountains became farmers, the present Tausug population. Significantly, this story does not mention other Sama groups, a typical Tausug view that all non-Tausug natives of the Sulu Islands are simply "Sama." Unless pressed to do so, most Tausug rarely subdivide the Sama population as Sinama speakers do.

Another Tausug story tells of an ancient time when the Sama Dilaut were devout Muslims. One Friday, as they were praying in their mosque built on piles over the sea, they saw a large school of fish pass below. Forgetting their prayers, they jumped into the sea to catch the fish. Allah became angry at them for interrupting their prayers and banished them from the mosque. Ever since, they have wandered'the sea as pagans.

An early mention of the Johore story occurs in the undated *Genealogy of Sulu*, the traditional history of the Tausug people of Jolo island. The following excerpt is the only mention of the Sama Dilaut in the *Genealogy*.

> After these [the Tausug people] came the Bajaw (Samals) [Sama Dilaut] from Juhur [Johore]. These were driven here by the tempest (monsoon) and were divided between both parties. Some of the Bajaw were driven by the tempest to Bruney and some to Mindanao. (Saleeby 1963, 33)

This brief mention of the arrival of the Sama was probably taken from the Sama Dilaut legendary accounts.

Anthropological Accounts

Two important studies have shed light on the prehistory of the Sama people, namely David Sopher's *The Sea Nomads* (1977) and A. Kemp Pallesen's *Culture Contact and Language Convergence* (1985).

Sopher collected the scattered published references to the sea nomads of Southeast Asia (including the Sama Dilaut of the Sulu islands) and pieced them together into a cultural-historical account of the nomadic boat peoples of Southeast Asia. He identified four major areas where sea nomads are found in Southeast Asia: (1) the west coast of Malaya and the Mergui archipelago; (2) the South China Sea, including the Riau-Lingga archipelago, the Tujuh islands, Bangka and Billiton islands and adjacent coasts; (3) north Borneo and the Sulu archipelago; and (4) eastern Indonesia, especially Sulawesi. After discussing the sea nomads as they occur in each of these areas, he proposes that they represent a single culture from a common place of origin.

He supports his proposal by listing the following characteristics which he claims are shared by all sea nomads of Southeast Asia: (1) the boat-dwelling habit, (2) sparse population, (3) Palaeomongoloid and Veddid physical features,

(4) a substratum of language different from surrounding populations, (5) great skill in handling and building boats, (6) simple fishing methods, (7) strand collecting for commercial and subsistence purposes, (8) a past history of piracy, (9) general poverty of material culture, (10) little or no agriculture, (11) domestic customs related to the forest primitives of Malaya, (12) social organization of small groups within set geographic limits under an elected leader, and (13) "Indonesian" animistic and shamanistic religion with Islamic influences.

Sopher believed the sea nomads were once Veddid hunters and gatherers on the coasts of the Riau-Lingga archipelago who later mixed with proto-Malays who moved from the north into Malaysia. As other cultures evolved, these hunters and gatherers persisted but became increasingly oriented to a life at sea. Various pressures such as overpopulation, unfriendly local populations, unmanageable winds and currents, and wanderlust then dispersed them throughout Southeast Asia.

Sopher identified four groups of closely related people in the Sulu area: (1) the nomadic Sama Dilaut, concentrated in the Sibutu islands and the Semporna region of Sabah; (2) the Lutangos, a little known sea people who reportedly once lived near Olutanga island in the Moro Gulf; (3) the sedentary Sama Dilaut (or Orang Sama) on the northwest coast of Borneo; and (4) the Samals (or Samales-Laut), a seafaring people found throughout the Sulu archipelago but more concentrated in the northern islands. Excepting the Lutangos, Sopher's categories describe the present Sinama-speaking population of Sulu. The Lutangos appear to be a group of boat dwellers who lived near Olutanga island during the latter half of the nineteenth century. Sopher's sources suggested to him that these sea nomads eventually intermarried with the forest people of Olutanga. The people are not found in the later literature. Most likely, they were boat dwellers who lived for a time in the Olutanga area and then moved on, a pattern still found among the Sama Dilaut of Tawi-Tawi. Sopher's "Nomadic Bajau" are the people I have described as the Sama Dilaut of Tawi-Tawi, Sibutu, and Semporna, whereas some of his "Samals" or "Samales-Laut" are the people I have called the "Sama Dilaut" of Siasi, Jolo, Basilan, and Zamboanga. These two groups are more closely related than Sopher was able to determine from the literature. Sopher's "sedentary Sama Dilauts" or "Orang Sama" are found not only on the eastern coasts of Borneo, but also throughout the Sulu islands. As earlier noted, they are usually called "Sama" by Tausug speakers, although they identify themselves by their specific island homes. In Borneo, as all Sinama speakers, they are more commonly called "Bajau." Their Islam is generally more orthodox than that of other Sinama-speaking people.

Sopher believed the present Sama Dilaut—indeed all Sinama speakers—are descendants of migrant boat dwellers from the Riau-Lingga archipelago who arrived in Sulu during the early part of the fourteenth century. His belief is based on the cultural, linguistic, and physical similarities shared by the Riau-Lingga and the Sulu people as well as on the Johore legend found among the Sulu Sama Dilaut. Sopher postulates that disrupting changes in the Johore region forced or frightened these boat dwellers to seek new homes in the east. He proposes two main dispersal routes: one along the northern and eastern Borneo coasts into the Sulu islands, and a second along the southern Borneo coasts. Some of these southern migrants went to Sulawesi where boat dwellers are still found, and a few of them may have gone to southern Mindanao and Zamboanga, and then northern Sulu.

The linguistic study by A. Kemp Pallesen (1985) suggests a different origin for the Sama Dilaut. His study describes the dispersal of Sama people throughout Sulu and their displacement by invading Tausug. Using the methods of historical linguistics, Pallesen attempts to arrive at dates for these movements. The results of his research are an important step to a greater understanding of the prehistory of Sulu, although as he cautions, additional linguistic and archeological research is needed before final conclusions can be drawn.

Linguistic evidence revealed to Pallesen that the present scattered communities of Sama-Bajaw speakers in the Sulu area were dispersed from the Sibuguey bay-Basilan strait area of the Zamboanga peninsula.[3] "Around 800 AD speakers of mutually intelligible PSB [Proto Sama-Bajaw] dialects lived in the area around the Basilan Strait and including what is now Zamboanga City" (1985, 117). From here, Sama groups moved southwestward into the Sulu islands, probably spurred by growing Arab and Chinese commercial interest in the area.[4] By 1100 AD, before the Tausug arrived in Sulu, Sama were scattered throughout Sulu.[5] When the Tausug arrived in Jolo some 700 years ago, parts of the island were inhabited by Sama who were ultimately displaced as the Tausug became a political power (p. 122).

Pallesen assigns the Tausug homeland to northwest Mindanao, specifically the area around the mouth of the Agusan River. Linguistic clues lead him to believe this was one of the trading stops and perhaps a stop for refurbishing boats and equipment for all-male crews of Sama fishermen and traders from Jolo, which was then a Sama settlement and already a significant trade center. Beginning about 700 years ago, this interaction between Sama and Tausug resulted in marriages between Sama men and Tausug women. Some of these women (and their male relatives) returned to Jolo with their husbands. More Tausug went to Jolo from northwest Mindanao, attracted to the growing economic activities in the area as trade with Brunei and with Arab and Chinese merchants increased in Sulu. Ultimately, the Tausug gained political sway over Jolo and either absorbed or drove out the Sama populations.

Pallesen's linguistic research revealed that the Sama-Bajaw language is one of the most widespread languages in Southeast Asia. Although noting the language is closely related to languages outside the Philippines, Pallesen believes it developed as a distinct language in the Zamboanga peninsula area and spread to its present locations. Its greatest concentration is in the Sulu archipelago, but the language is found in pockets throughout Indonesia, along the coasts of Borneo, and even on the eastern coasts of the Malay peninsula. The concentration of Sama-Bajaw speakers in eastern insular Southeast Asia suggests a homeland for the language in those waters, but only future research can provide more conclusive answers.

More recent linguistic research summarized by Clifford Sather (1997, 320–21) reveals that the sea nomads of Southeast Asia represent three different ethnolinguistic origins rather than only one as believed by Sopher, namely: (1) the Moken and Moklen of the Mergui archipelago of Burma and adjacent southern islands of Thailand; (2) the Orang Laut, a name for various boat-dwelling groups once found in the Riau-Lingga archipelago, Batam and the coastal waters of eastern Sumatra and southern Johore; and (3) the largest and most widely dispersed group, the Bajau Laut (Sama Dilaut) found throughout the Sulu archipelago, eastern Borneo, Sulawesi and the islands of eastern Indonesia. It appears that these three groups independently developed the boat-dwelling tradition in their similar environments.

Various factors were probably operative in dispersing the Sama throughout the southern Philippines, eastern Borneo and eastern Indonesia. Economic factors were doubtless prime motivators for the dispersal of some Sama from the Sulu area. As noted, Pallesen suggested that the penetration of Arab and Chinese traders into insular Southeast Asia during the Sung dynasty (960–1279 AD) and the markets they opened may have been the impetus for the Sama people to move southwestward into the Sulu islands to exploit the area's marine products (Pallesen 1977, 247). When Indians and Europeans arrived in search of trade, they, too, probably encouraged Sama fishermen to explore new regions and participate in newly created markets.

Some Sama were probably driven from their homes by invading people, not unlike the current displacement of Sama in Tawi-Tawi and Sitangkai by the Tausug (Nimmo 1986). It is difficult to generalize about a group as diverse as the Sinama-speaking people of Sulu, but most observers have noted that as a people they are less aggressive than the Tausug, notwithstanding the aggressive exploits of such groups as the Balingingi Sama. The boat-dwelling groups are notoriously nonaggressive and their history is punctuated with incidents that frightened them or drove them away. Historically, such incidents probably contributed to their dispersal.

The wanderlust of certain Sama groups was probably one reason why the population was dispersed. Although all Sama fishermen follow seasonal fishing cycles, the extent of the territory these cycles encompass varies from group to group. For example, the movements of the boat-dwelling Sama Dilaut of Tawi-Tawi are limited to the waters of the western Tawi-Tawi Islands. The Sama Dilaut of Sitangkai usually limit their fishing to the reefs between the Sibutu islands and Semporna. However, other Sama groups, such as some of the Siasi people and the Tabauan people of eastern Tawi-Tawi, travel great distances during annual fishing cycles. Some go as far north as Manila, to the eastern coasts of Mindanao, to Sulawesi and to the waters of eastern Borneo. A Sama fisherman from South Ubian told me of a fishing-trading trip he made that encompassed the entire island of Borneo. Although economic motivations are given as the reasons for such trips, wanderlust is surely a factor since most people of Sulu do not find it necessary to travel so far. For some Sama groups, such as the Tabauan people, all-male crews may be away from home for several weeks or even months on such trips. Among others, such as the Siasi and Zamboanga Sama, the fishing expeditions are flotillas of family houseboats. The various isolated communities of Sama-Bajaw speakers reported in such places as Sulawesi, Sumbawa, western Timor, and southern Moluccas are probably descendants of such fishing expeditions from the Sulu area who for various reasons decided to remain in their newly discovered fishing grounds. In some cases, they may have been all-male groups who married local women but retained their language; in other cases, they may have been family groups who settled in the new area and retained their separate linguistic identity.

The large Sama Dilaut population in the Sibutu islands suggests these reefs and islands were once the home of all the Sama Dilaut of southern Sulu. The fishing nets, which distinguish this group of Sama Dilaut from others, probably evolved in the reef environment of Sibutu. However, the large population is in no sense conclusive. Possibly the Sibutu waters were more conducive to the Sama Dilaut lifestyle and thereby led to a more rapid population growth.

Pallesen's linguistic study suggests the Sama Dilaut moved into Sibutu from the north. Sama Dilaut boat-types support this suggestion. The double-outriggered djenging, once found among all Sama Dilaut of southern Sulu, is more closely related to the outriggered watercraft of the northern Sulu islands and the rest of the Philippines than it is to the outriggerless boats, such as the *lepa*, more common to the eastern Borneo waters. Also, the narrow, deep-hulled djenging is not as well adapted to shallow reef waters as the broad-hulled lepa, the boat that has displaced the djenging. In addition, the central religious ceremony of the Sibutu people demands dry rice from the Tawi-Tawi islands; such rice from Borneo is considered improper unless no other is available.

Sitangkai is by far the largest Sama Dilaut community in the Sibutu islands, although it has become so only within fairly recent years (see fig. 4). Before the arrival of Chinese fish buyers in the early part of the twentieth century, the Sama Dilaut flotilla in that area was moored at the nearby tiny island of Bolong-Bolong, and Sitangkai island was used as a cemetery. At that time another Sama Dilaut moorage was located near the small island of Andulingan, west of Tumindao island. The moorage has since dispersed, but people coming from that place who now reside in Sitangkai can still be distinguished by the unique intonation of their speech. A third Sama Dilaut moorage was located at Omapoi, the northernmost island of the Tumindao group; a small Sama Dilaut community is still found at Omapoi, but its residents are now house dwellers. Like the Andulingan and Bolong-Bolong people, these Sama Dilaut buried their dead on Sitangkai island. The fourth and final Sama Dilaut community in Sibutu was located near Tandowak island at the southern end of Sibutu island. Unlike the other Sama Dilaut of Sibutu, the Tandowak people buried their dead at nearby Lu'uk Malebo on Sibutu island. A Sama Dilaut community of houses is still located at Tandowak, but it is much smaller than the earlier flotilla that moored there. Since World War II, the majority of the Tandowak people have moved to Tungnehat, a village of land-dwelling Sama north of Tandowak. Tungnehat has since become the Sama Dilaut population center of that area, and is second in

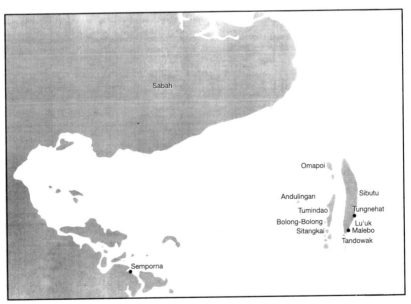

Fig. 4   The Sibutu islands

size only to Sitangkai. Like all Sibutu Sama Dilaut communities, it is now a village of houses with only a few transient boat dwellers.

The ancestors of the Tawi-Tawi Sama Dilaut were probably the first to move away from Sibutu. Their dialect (which the Sitangkai Sama Dilaut describe as "like birds singing") diverges more from the Sibutu Sama Dilaut than does the dialect of the Semporna Sama Dilaut; however, the Semporna people may have left the Sibutu region at an equally early time but retained their linguistic affinities with Sibutu because of the frequent and easy movement between the two areas. The swift Sibutu current still acts as an effective barrier to native watercraft between the Tawi-Tawi and Sibutu islands, and was even more effective before the advent of motor boats.

Sama Dilaut from Sibutu probably first began visiting the Tawi-Tawi reefs on fishing trips. The great reefs of the Bilatan islands of central Tawi-Tawi allowed them to use the same fishing techniques they knew from the Sibutu reefs, and eventually Bilatan became a permanent mooring place for Sama Dilaut boats. The two small islands in Bilatan that serve as the burial grounds for all the Tawi-Tawi Sama Dilaut further supports the belief that Bilatan was the first area of Tawi-Tawi visited by the Sama Dilaut. From Bilatan they spread to the Sanga-Sanga area. Old informants contend that Sama Dilaut houseboats were first moored at the small island of Takatmatahat (called Mandolan on most maps) located at the northern mouth of the channel between Tawi-Tawi and Sanga-Sanga islands. The reefs surrounding Takatmatahat, as well as the reefs of the nearby Basun islands, allowed these Bilatan migrants to use their familiar fishing nets. Lu'uk Tulai is a fairly recent Sama Dilaut moorage, and probably was formed by houseboats from Takatmatahat. Several old people at Bilatan told me that Sama Dilaut moorages did not exist in the Sanga-Sanga area during their youth; however, old people at Tungkalang near Sanga-Sanga told me they lived at that place when they were children. Sydney Cloman (1923, 4–5) reported "two tribes" of Sama Dilaut in Tawi-Tawi when he was stationed in Bongao in 1899; he may have been referring to the Bilatan and Sanga-Sanga groups. A longtime resident of Bongao claimed the only Sama Dilaut she recalled seeing at Bongao in the 1930s were occasional "wild-looking, long-haired, half-naked men" who sometimes peddled fish among the houses. Most likely Bongao's recent development as the commercial center of Tawi-Tawi has attracted some of the Bilatan people to that area.

In 1903, A. Henry Savage Landor traveled throughout the Sulu archipelago and later wrote a book (1904) about his experiences. Intrigued by Sulu's boat people, he described each of his encounters with them. However, the only Sama Dilaut he mentioned in Tawi-Tawi were a few he met in Bongao, even though he traveled along the northwest coasts of Sanga-Sanga and Tawi-Tawi islands where the present Sama Dilaut moorages of Tungkalang and Lu'uk Tulai are located. Similarly, Carl Taylor's writings on the Sitangkai Sama Dilaut do not mention the Tawi-Tawi moorages although he also traveled the coasts where they are now found. One traveling the same route today could not easily miss the moorages, and the failure of both writers to mention them suggests that the moorages were not there in 1903 and 1930, the time of their visits. In 1900, Phelps Whitmarsh described fleets of Sama Dilaut boats at Bongao; they may, however, have been transient fishermen from elsewhere. Such fishing fleets from Siasi and eastern Tawi-Tawi are still occasionally seen in Bongao. Probably the moorages at Sanga-Sanga were originally stopping places for Sama Dilaut fishermen from the Bilatan moorages, and eventually became permanent mooring places.

The Semporna Sama Dilaut are closely related to the Sibutu people; in fact, many of them consider themselves natives of Sibutu rather than Semporna (Richardson 1966, Sather 1997, 19). It is difficult to determine how long Semporna has been a permanent mooring place for Sama Dilaut, but they must have frequented the area for many years since Thomas Forrest described them when he visited eastern Borneo in the 1770s. Probably Sibutu Sama Dilaut frequented the Semporna waters even before they moved to Tawi-Tawi since many rich fishing reefs provide natural stepping-stones between Sibutu and Semporna whereas the swift Sibutu current between Sibutu and Bongao acts as a barrier to small craft movement during certain periods of the year. The small population of Sama Dilaut in Semporna suggests the Sama Dilaut moved into that area from elsewhere; however, as noted, the Sama Dilaut are extremely mobile, and their numbers may have been greater in Semporna in earlier years.

3

THE TAWI-TAWI REALM

Geography of Tawi-Tawi

The only full-time boat-dwelling Sama Dilaut in the Philippines live in the Tawi-Tawi islands of the Sulu archipelago (see fig. 2). This collection of some 300 islands takes its name from the long, narrow island of Tawi-Tawi that stretches some forty kilometers in a northeast-southwest direction. The verdant forests and rugged peaks of the island provide a mountainous backdrop for the dozens of small coral islands that flank its southern and eastern shores. For unknown centuries, its human inhabitants have lived in pile dwellings built along its miles of coast, and even today, except for a few settlements, the interior of the island is still sparsely populated.

To the north and west of the island are the deep waters of the open sea, dotted with rich fishing grounds well known to Tawi-Tawi's seafaring population. Compared to other seas of the world, these waters are gentle, but nonetheless during the monsoon seasons only the most hardy venture on them. To the east and especially to the south of the island, the seas are shallow and filled with myriad coral reefs and islands that make navigation by large ships virtually impossible. At high tide, the waters are as varicolored as only coral seas can be, but at low tide the great, sprawling reefs lie drab and exposed. It is among these southern reefs and islands that the Tawi-Tawi Sama Dilaut have carved their unique ecological niche; their small houseboats ply the waters as regularly and as persistently as the fishes themselves.

Fairly uniform climatic conditions prevail in Tawi-Tawi throughout the year, and no seasons of wind and rain prevent fishermen from going out to sea, although during certain months the sea is considerably rougher and the weather less predictable. The northeast monsoon is usually established by November and lasts until the latter part of March, but the winds never reach the force of gales in the south China Sea, and seldom cause more than occasional squalls. May ushers in the southwest monsoon that lasts until October.

For the most part, winds are gentle during this season, although heavy rain squalls and stormy weather characteristically occur in July and August. However, stretches of bad weather rarely last longer than two or three days during either of the monsoon seasons to prevent fishing or traveling.

Several ocean currents in Tawi-Tawi are fairly swift during the spring tides, but none is exceedingly dangerous to the experienced sailor. The most treacherous current, in the Sibutu passage between Simunul and Sibutu islands, has been known to drift unwary sailors well into the Celebes Sea. However, this current is well known to local seafarers, and they seldom venture into it during its greatest strength. Tawi-Tawi sailors utilize winds and currents whenever possible for their travels. Journeys may be delayed a day or so in order to catch a favorable wind, and similarly, travel is usually initiated during hours when tidal currents provide the most efficient transport.

Because of the many islands of Tawi-Tawi, it is impossible to travel in the area beyond the sight of land, and consequently islands and mountains are important navigational guides. Among the best-known landmarks are the fabled mountain peak of Bongao island, the Sibutu hill and the mountains of Tawi-Tawi island. During nocturnal hours, boats are guided by the stars, the moon, and the winds as well as by the mountains that are visible for some distance during full moon.

Important islands and settlements in Tawi-Tawi include Sanga-Sanga, home of the southernmost outpost of the Philippine Air Force and a landing strip for Philippine Air Lines; Bongao, the commercial and administrative center (fig. 5);

Fig. 5 Bongao island, 1965

33

and Batu-Batu, site of a small Philippine Navy base. Large Sama populations live on the islands of Tandubas, Tabauan, South Ubian, and Simunul. With the exceptions of Tawi-Tawi and Bongao, most islands are low coral islands planted to coconuts and cassava and perennially short of drinking water. Tawi-Tawi and Sanga-Sanga support the major agriculture of the area. Simunul island claims the oldest mosque in Tawi-Tawi, established in the 1300s. Certain islands are known for their specialization. For example, Simunul produces pottery, Sibutu is known for its launches, Ungus Matata is renowned for its fine mats, and Bo'on provides fresh water for central Tawi-Tawi residents.

The islands abound in lore that explains certain natural features of the landscape. Responsible for some of these features is Mbo' Hawis, legendary ancestor of the Sama people. The legend narrates that one day, while fishing the seas from a mountaintop, he hooked a giant fish. When he attempted to pull it in, the fish resisted and pulled Mbo' Hawis down the mountainside, clearing a path through the forest that is still visible today. Once when wading the channel between Sanga-Sanga and Tawi-Tawi, Mbo' Hawis caught his big toe in a giant clam. When he kicked in pain, half the clamshell flew to Mount Tumantangis on distant Jolo Island while the other half remained in the channel where it can still be seen. A boat-shaped stone near Batu-Batu is believed to be the petrified boat of pirates who long ago attempted to kidnap local women and children. Allah intervened and punished the pirates by turning their boat to stone. Recurring riptides in the channel between Sanga-Sanga and Tawi-Tawi are supposed to be evidence of the continual fighting between two daughters of a sultan who tied them together and tossed them into the channel when he could no longer tolerate their bickering. The ruins of an abandoned mosque on the eastern shores of Tawi-Tawi island are, it is said, the residence of a race of dwarfs who disappear when seen by humans. Other places are associated with Posong, the legendary popular trickster who managed to hoodwink sultans and seduce their beautiful daughters. Perhaps the best known site in Tawi-Tawi is atop Mount Bongao, two graves believed to belong to early Muslim missionaries. The graves are regularly visited by pilgrims and others instructed to do so by healers and mediums. A band of monkeys inhabits the site, and to avoid bad luck, visitors must offer them food before approaching the graves. Offerings must also be left along the mountain trail leading to the graves to appease a giant snake that will otherwise cause harm. Throughout the islands special trees, graves, islets, and unusual rock formations are associated with local spirits and early Muslim missionaries.

All trading routes in Tawi-Tawi lead to Bongao, the port-of-call for the interisland ships that travel weekly up and down the archipelago. Many motor launches also utilize Bongao's port for the goods and passengers they transport

Fig. 6 Sama Dilaut children

Fig. 7 Sama Dilaut boy

Fig. 8 Sama Dilaut teenage girl

Fig. 9 Mother and child

Fig. 10 Father and son

Fig. 11 Elderly man

Fig. 12 Elderly woman

throughout Tawi-Tawi. In addition, hundreds of locally made boats, still wind- and man-powered, daily visit the Bongao traders with their small wares of fish, handicrafts and garden produce. Bongao's population probably consists of some 5,000 people. This population, as in all of Tawi-Tawi, is predominantly Sama, with a growing Tausug community, which is mostly post-World War II. A few northern Christian Filipinos hold professional and government jobs, while the economy of the town is mostly in the hands of a few Chinese families. The market of Bongao, the so-called Chinese Pier, is built on piles over the sea and connected to land by boardwalks. Each morning, crowds from all over Tawi-Tawi throng the shops to obtain goods in exchange for their own wares. The colors of the clientele are only matched by the goods for sale. Here the buyer can purchase parrots in rattan cages, fish of every color of the rainbow, locally made mats and basketry, cigarettes from Borneo, dry goods from India, Javanese tea, petromax lanterns from the United States, Chinese medicines from Singapore, and Japanese transistor radios. The list is only suggestive of the variety of goods that enter and leave Bongao's shops.

Ethnic Composition of Tawi-Tawi

The 1960 Census does not provide a population breakdown by ethnicity for Tawi-Tawi, but probably 80 percent of the population is Sama, 15 percent Tausug, and the remaining 5 percent Chinese and Christian Filipino. The large number of Sama is somewhat misleading because it connotes a cultural uniformity in the area that is not entirely the case. Although a general "Sama culture" may be described for Tawi-Tawi, each island of Sama is nonetheless somewhat unique from the others. Dialectal differences, economic specialization, values, material culture, religious beliefs, and in some cases, physical differences tend to distin- guish the various groups. As a result, the Sama normally identify themselves by their island, sometimes even by their village, rather than by "Sama" which, because of its generic nature, has little value as an autonym.

Sama Dilaut By far the most unique group of Sama is the boat dwelling Sama Dilaut (figs. 6–12). In fact, their uniqueness led earlier observers to call them "Bajau" and to describe them as a people separate from the other Sama populations, but as noted, this is not the case and they are best regarded as a subculture of the general Sama culture. Their most obvious distinctions from the land-dwelling Sama are their boat-dwelling tradition, their religion, and certain physical features that directly relate to boat dwelling. All these traits mark them as a lowly pariah group in the eyes of the other Tawi-Tawi people.

The Sama Dilaut number approximately 1,600 and represent only about 4 percent of the total Tawi-Tawi population. Their moorages are all located in the western half of Tawi-Tawi, and except for occasional fishing trips, they rarely leave those waters. The Tawi-Tawi Sama Dilaut are the most conservative of all the Sulu Sama and probably reflect much of pre-Islamic Sama culture. Their seaborne homes, which effectively isolate them from the land-dwelling people, seem most responsible for this conservatism. Other Sama Dilaut groups in Sulu, such as the Sitangkai Sama Dilaut, who have abandoned boat dwelling to become house dwellers, have been or are quickly becoming amalgamated into Islamic Sama culture. Although greatly influenced by Sulu Islam, the Tawi-Tawi boat dwellers are still considered pagans by the surrounding Muslim people.

Most Sama Dilaut are physically distinct from the neighboring populations, but many of these distinctive features can be traced to their unique sea life and are not genetic. Because of frequent diving and exposure to the sun, Sama Dilaut are darker skinned than other Sulu people and their hair is often bleached to shades of red and sometimes even blond, especially among the children. A permanent squint, apparently from staring into the sun's reflection on the sea, is characteristic of many adults, and blindness is common in old age. The Sama Dilaut habit of chewing a mixture of betel nut, tobacco and lime (hereafter called "betel") causes blackened teeth and red-stained lips. Legs of adult Sama Dilaut are often underdeveloped due to the hours spent squatting with legs jack-knifed while paddling and living in the houseboats. Apparently as a result of this continual squatting, many older people are unable to lock their knees when standing upright. A deformation of the lower spine (also apparently due to the sitting position) causes the buttocks of some to protrude abnormally when they stand upright. These physical consequences of boat living make the Sama Dilaut gait distinctive and they are easily identified on this basis alone. On land, their walk appears clumsy and uncertain, but when moving on the boats, their movements are extremely agile. In contrast to the underdeveloped lower extremities, torsos and arms are often muscular and well developed among the men who spend much time paddling and handling the heavy boats.

Some Sama Dilaut, especially the youth and house dwellers, do not reveal these physical features and are not easily distinguished from the surrounding Sama populations. Nonetheless, after several months among the Tawi-Tawi Sama Dilaut, I was usually able to distinguish them from the land-dwelling people, as well as from the northern Sama Dilaut groups. Their physical distinction is no doubt partly due to a long history of endogamous marriage.

Sama Dilaut clothing is very simple. Children usually wear no clothes until about the age of ten. Men generally wear only short pants or the *hos*, a versatile sarong-like garment that can be worn as a skirt, a loincloth, a robe, or a turban. Sometimes men wear only a small cloth tied apron-like around their waists to cover their genitals, and frequently go nude when diving. Women usually wear only a sarong in the moorage, but always don blouses when they leave; teenaged girls always cover their breasts until they are married and have their first child. Both sexes wear loose, baggy trousers called *sahwal*, the legs of which the men sometimes pull up and tuck into the waist, thereby converting the garment into a loincloth. Shoes are never worn, and rubber sandals only rarely. Women prefer long hair, sometimes hanging loose to their shoulders, but more commonly tied into a knot at the backs of their necks. Formerly the men wore their hair long and loose, but now most have Western-style hair cuts, although some of the older men, especially shamans, still prefer their hair long.

Practically all Sama Dilaut interactions with non-Sama Dilaut are determined by economic need. Interaction for purely social reasons is rare. Even if the land dwellers cared to interact with the Sama Dilaut more frequently, their seaborne homes would create difficulties for easy daily interaction. In addition to the inaccessibility of the houseboats, the frequent movements of the Sama Dilaut discourage the formation of friendships with land dwellers.

Although some land dwellers live their entire lives near Sama Dilaut moorages, they are incredibly uninformed about them. A commonly held belief among land dwellers is that shortly after the birth of a Sama Dilaut baby, it is thrown overboard to initiate it into a life at sea. Another claims that if the Sama Dilaut remain on land for extended periods they become ill. Several land dwellers told me Sama Dilaut men could hold their breaths for five to ten minutes while diving. Others believe the Sama Dilaut deposit their dead in the sea. All these claims are false and reveal how uninformed most land dwellers are about their boat-dwelling neighbors.

The Sama Dilaut are considered untouchables by most land-dwelling Muslims. When Sama Dilaut visit the land villages, they are never invited into homes, are often derided, and in general are treated as inferiors. Not surprisingly, they avoid the land villages and visit them only when necessary to pursue economic ends.

Sama The Sama Dilaut interact most frequently with the Sama land dwellers that live in the villages neighboring their moorages. This interaction is mostly among men as they meet to trade fish for vegetable produce or when Sama Dilaut seek permission to cut trees from the nearby forest for boatbuilding. Sama Dilaut men often form ongoing trade relationships with land-dwelling Sama men. These relationships are based primarily on mutual economic need, but nonetheless genuine friendships sometimes develop between the men. For example, a Sama Dilaut may invite a Sama friend to attend the wedding celebration of his son or daughter, while a Sama man may invite his Sama Dilaut friend to the celebration of his son's circumcision. If a Sama Dilaut has a large catch of fish, he may give some to his Sama trading partner, while the partner might share a bumper crop of cassava with the Sama Dilaut. Such outright gifts are uncommon, however; more commonly the relationship involves a fair exchange of desired commodities and persists because it is economically advantageous to both parties. The Sama Dilaut knows where he can trade his fish for vegetables and the Sama knows where he can trade his agricultural produce for fish, where he can hire someone to repair his boat, or where he can find assistance in transporting his coconuts to Bongao.

The most important economic relationships between Sama Dilaut and Sama involve food exchanges. Frequently, this is simple barter. If a Sama Dilaut has a large catch of fish, he takes it to a nearby Sama village to barter for cassava or fruit. If he has a trading partner in the village, he will first approach him; if an exchange cannot be negotiated, he will go to another household. If a barter transaction cannot be arranged—or if he may prefer not to barter—he will try to negotiate a cash transaction. The relationship is not entirely symbiotic, since the Sama Dilaut are more dependent on the Sama. Most Sama Dilaut rely entirely on the land dwellers for vegetable produce and other forest products, whereas the land dwellers are never entirely dependent on Sama Dilaut for fish since many of them fish for their own needs, buy fish in the Bongao market, or occasionally purchase tinned fish. The Sama Dilaut supplies are often cheaper and more convenient, so they are usually preferred.

Although few formal land deeds exist in Tawi-Tawi, most land is nonetheless claimed. Individuals even claim some forests that are designated as public lands by the national government. A few Sama Dilaut claim ownership to small plots of land, but the overwhelming majority of land is owned by the land dwellers, both Sama and Tausug. Consequently, to use the land and the produce of the forests, the Sama Dilaut must obtain permission from owners. This is rarely a problem. Most land-dwelling families have traditions extending back several generations that allow Sama Dilaut to use forest plots for cutting trees for boatbuilding, collecting bark for caulking, or gathering firewood. Sama trading partners sometimes provide small plots of land for Sama Dilaut to cultivate cassava and other garden produce. For the use of the land, the Sama Dilaut may give the Sama a share of the produce, occasionally supply him with fish, or perform small jobs when assistance is needed.

I encountered only three cases of Sama Dilaut marriage with non-Sama Dilaut, and all were with land-dwelling Sama. Two ended in divorce, both were between Sama Dilaut women and Sama men, while the third, between a Sama Dilaut man and a Sama woman, was very unstable when I left Tawi-Tawi and probably has terminated by now. Neither group condones such marriages.

Tausug The Sama Dilaut consider the Sama natives of Tawi-Tawi, but such is not their view of the Tausug. The Tausug are outsiders. Their alien origin is reflected in the Sama Dilaut name for them, *a'a Suk*—"people of *Suk*," "*Suk*" being the Sama name for Jolo. To the Sama Dilaut they are fearful people who steal, cheat, murder, and humiliate, and are avoided whenever possible. Sama Dilaut do not live near their villages, nor do they approach them unless absolutely necessary. The Sama share much of this view of the Tausug; in fact, many of the stories of Tausug character come to the Sama Dilaut from the Sama who interact with them more frequently. The Tausug have probably been visiting the Tawi-Tawi waters ever since they arrived in Sulu. Their Jolo-based sultanates held sovereignty over Tawi-Tawi, but only in relatively recent years have significant numbers of them lived permanently in Tawi-Tawi. Some villages are composed entirely of Tausug, while many Sama villages have Tausug settlements at their peripheries. Some Tausug have purchased or leased land from Sama, while others have settled on unclaimed land.

Occasional friendships develop between Sama and Tausug and, in general, their social interaction is greater than between Sama Dilaut and Sama. They share the common bond of Islam that the Sama Dilaut lack and which sets them off as pagans in Muslim eyes. Nonetheless, the Sama Dilaut-Sama interaction is easier than that of Sama-Tausug. The Sama Dilaut-Sama relationship is one of slightly lopsided symbiosis in that they provide for each other's economic needs. Such is not the case with Sama-Tausug relations. In fact, the two groups compete for the same economic niches since both are mostly farmers and part-time fishermen. Although much Sama animosity toward the Tausug stems from the Tausug's historic roles as rulers and occasional plunderers, some of the present friction stems from competition for the same economic niches. This friction manifests itself most commonly in land feuds that occasionally result in killings. The relatively low population density of Tawi-Tawi initially attracted the Tausug from the more populated islands of Jolo and Siasi. As long as land was available in Tawi-Tawi, the Tausug were accommodated with little difficulty. But as population pressures are increasingly felt, friction has grown between the two groups.

A few Sama Dilaut have economic relations with the Tausug who live in Sama villages, but during my research I had no knowledge of Sama Dilaut who visited villages inhabited exclusively by Tausug. The Sama Dilaut economic interaction with the Tausug in the mixed villages is similar to Sama-Sama Dilaut interaction. The Sama Dilaut prefer to interact with the Sama, but if the Tausug are interested in their goods and if the Sama Dilaut feel secure in approaching them, trade interactions take place. I knew of no ongoing trade partnerships between Tausug and Sama Dilaut.

The Tausug are even more disdainful of the Sama Dilaut than are the Sama. The Tausug regard themselves as the superior people of Sulu; they regard the Sama as lowly, but at least they are Muslims (Stone 1962). But the Sama Dilaut are considered filthy pagans, unfit for any interaction beyond occasional economic transactions. To the Tausug, they are almost subhuman; in the Jolo area they held a caste-like, servile position in the past and still have a semi-servile relationship with some Tausug villages today (Kiefer 1972). However, in Tawi-Tawi, where the Tausug population is small, their attitudes toward the Sama Dilaut are somewhat more tolerant, reflecting the Sama view.

Some Tausug families who live in Sama villages interact with the Sama Dilaut as easily as the Sama. Even some Tausug within the all-Tausug communities have tried to cultivate friendships with the Sama Dilaut in order to induce the latter to bring their fish surplus to the villages. At one village, the Sama Dilaut found themselves in the unprecedented position of being sought by both the Tausug and Sama populations to form barter relationships, a further illustration of the competitive nature of Sama-Tausug relations.

Additional Sama Dilaut-Tausug interaction occurs in the Bongao market place. Some Tausug are fish dealers who occasionally buy the surplus catches of the Sama Dilaut. Others are vendors who give special prices to the Sama Dilaut so they will patronize their stalls. Again, in the market place, the Sama and Tausug compete for Sama Dilaut patronage.

Chinese Sama Dilaut interaction with the Chinese in Bongao is strictly economic, being limited to retail shopkeepers and fish buyers. Sama Dilaut frequent Chinese shops to purchase the few manufactured items they need for their everyday existence. Some Sama Dilaut sell dried fish from their surplus catches to Chinese fish dealers, but more often they sell to Sama or Tausug middlemen who then sell to the Chinese. The most important Sama Dilaut fishing interactions with Chinese involve agreements whereby the Chinese provide seine fishing nets to the Sama Dilaut who in turn must supply a certain amount of the catch at a prearranged price. For the most part, the Sama Dilaut are insignificant in the economic life of the Chinese and consequently receive few favors from them. They pay the prices the Chinese ask, often resenting them, but knowing they can do nothing since the goods cannot be obtained elsewhere.

The Sama Dilaut view the Chinese as exploitative but trustworthy in a business deal. Like most of the indigenous Tawi-Tawi people, the Sama Dilaut look on the Chinese as aliens necessary to the economic life of Tawi-Tawi. In turn, the Chinese share the general Tawi-Tawi view of the Sama Dilaut as lowly, dirty outcasts—harmless, but unsuitable to socialize with in any way.

The Chinese community in Bongao is small but powerful. In addition to controlling the major business concerns of the community, some Chinese families hold important political positions. Although the Sulu Chinese have intermarried with the local population more than Chinese elsewhere in the Philippines, they nonetheless remain apart from the local people. Children from mixed marriages are considered Chinese rather than Muslim. Chinese marriages with Muslims are rare today; rather the current mixed Chinese/Muslim population has become increasingly endogamous.

Christians The Sama Dilaut share the Sulu Muslims' view of Christians as outsiders who oppress and exploit the natives of Tawi-Tawi . This is largely because most Christians are either bureaucrats of the national government or members of law enforcement forces, such as the navy, the air force, or the Philippine Constabulary. The Sama Dilaut have little sense of belonging to the larger Philippine nation, and like most of Sulu's people, they regard its representatives as repressive outsiders with whom they seldom interact . The Sama Dilaut's minor role in the political and economic life of Tawi-Tawi precludes any need for interaction with the government bureaucracy, and their nonaggressive ways bring them into little contact with the militia. Still they share the Muslim view of Christians as arrogant and treacherous, and consequently they avoid them whenever possible.

Most Christians regard the Sama Dilaut more favorably than the Sama and the Tausug. Many look on the Sama Dilaut as innocent, childlike people who mind their own business and stay out of the smuggling, piracy, and occasional bloodshed that punctuate the Muslim communities. However, most concur with the Sama and Tausug that the Sama Dilaut are unsuitable for any sort of social interaction.

Exceptions to the Sama Dilaut and Muslim view of Christians are the Oblates of Mary Immaculate priests and the Medical Mission Sisters in Bongao. The Oblates have both Caucasian and Filipino priests while the Medical Mission Sisters are primarily Filipina nuns. Neither group does any active proselytizing. The Oblate priests operate schools in Bongao, Ungus Matata, Sibutu, and Tabauan while the Medical Mission Sisters provide medical services in Bongao previously unavailable to most local people. The helpfulness, honesty, and genuine kindness of these religious orders have won admiration and respect from most of the local people, although some militant Muslims resent their presence. Nonetheless, in the eyes of most local people, they are different from the other Christians in Tawi-Tawi. They are accepted probably because they pose little economic or political threat to the local population.

The Sama Dilaut share this view of the priests and nuns. Because of their poverty and outcast plight in Tawi-Tawi—and possibly because they are potential converts—the Sama Dilaut have received special favors from the priests and nuns. The priests built a small school in one of the Sama Dilaut moorages in an attempt to educate children who are afraid to attend public schools on land. The priests' efforts have been somewhat successful. The Medical Mission Sisters make special visits to the Sama Dilaut moorages to treat the sick and to encourage them to visit their Bongao clinic. The Sama Dilaut do not understand why these outsiders extend such kindnesses, but they willingly accept them.

Apparently throughout their history in Tawi-Tawi, the small numbers of Sama Dilaut never gave politicians serious concern. The Sama Dilaut were always at the periphery of the Sulu sultanate, and unlike at Jolo and Sitangkai, I learned of no tradition of allegiance to any of the Tawi-Tawi datus who administered the area for the sultan. The Spaniards had little influence on the Sama Dilaut. American administrators found the Sama Dilaut population small enough to ignore while they attended to the more pressing problems of the Muslims, and similarly, the government of the independent Philippine nation has had enough problems with Sulu's Muslim population without concerning itself with the affairs of a small population of boat dwellers.

Sama Dilaut Moorages in Tawi-Tawi

The total population of the Tawi-Tawi Sama Dilaut is no more than 1,600, an approximate 4 percent of the entire Tawi-Tawi population.* The Sama Dilaut moorages are concentrated in the western half of Tawi-Tawi, usually a few hundred meters from land-dwelling Sama villages. Individual Sama Dilaut houseboats and occasional clusters of houseboats can be seen at any time throughout the Tawi-Tawi waters. However, such small groupings generally consist of Sama Dilaut families on fishing trips or en route to some destination, and cannot be considered permanent Sama Dilaut settlements. Five sites are recognized as permanent boat villages by the Sama Dilaut; these are "villages" in that they are moorages where houseboats and sometimes houses are always found, the number of which depends on factors discussed below. These five moorages surround the seas most commonly exploited by the Sama Dilaut (see fig. 3).

The northernmost Tawi-Tawi Sama Dilaut moorage is Lu'uk Tulai, located about a half-kilometer seaward of the land village of the same name on the northwest tip of Tawi-Tawi island. The moorage has an average of twenty boats and six temporary houses, providing a total population of approximately 125 people. The boats are moored on a large reef, partly exposed at low tide, which extends seaward about one-and-a-half-kilometers.

Tungkalang is located on the southwest tip of Sanga-Sanga island, about twenty kilometers from Lu'uk Tulai (fig. 13). The name of the moorage is taken from the long, narrow, exposed reef that protects the community from the open

Fig. 13 Tungkalang, Sanga-Sanga island, 1965

sea, and means "coral-covered point." The moorage is also known among the Sama Dilaut as Landing, after the nearby air field; Tubig Salang, after the nearby land village; or simply Sanga-Sanga. At its southernmost point, the exposed reef is about a half-kilometer from Sanga-Sanga island and extends northward almost parallel to the island for about five kilometers until it joins the mainland. Thus, with Sanga-Sanga island, it forms a long, narrow, shallow bay, parts of which are exposed at low tide. The Sama Dilaut settlement is located at the mouth of this bay. Barren of vegetation, the southern extension of the exposed reef near the Sama Dilaut moorage is used for building and repairing boats, drying nets, children's play, and other moorage activities. The only structure on the reef is a Catholic school erected in 1962. When I first lived at the moorage in 1963, its population averaged about 400 over a six-month period; however, when I returned to the moorage in 1965, its population averaged only about 250 over an eighteen-month period. In addition to an average of forty boats, there were seventeen poorly constructed houses in January 1964; by April 1967, that number had grown to thirty.

Lamiun is a small Sama Dilaut settlement located near the northeast point of Bongao Island, near the town of Bongao. Lamiun has only nine houses and the number of boats varies greatly since Sama Dilaut visiting Bongao usually anchor their boats at this moorage. Located about 300 meters from Bongao Island, the Sama Dilaut houses and boats form a separate community, unconnected to the town of Bongao. For weddings and other ceremonies, the Lamiun people usually make the six-kilometer trip to Tungkalang. My count

44

of boats at Lamiun ranged from four to thirty, and because of the very transient nature of Lamiun's houseboat population, an average figure is not too meaningful. Nonetheless, the average I determined was nine which, added to the nine houses, provided a total population of ninety for the community for that period.

Located about forty-five kilometers east of Lamiun near the northwest point of Bilatan Island, Tungbangkao is the most prosperous Sama Dilaut community and the only one with non-Sama Dilaut residents (fig. 14). The rich fishing grounds nearby provide the chief income for the Sama Dilaut who reside there. The moorage is named after a nearby mangrove-covered islet, and is about five kilometers from Bilatan island. The moorage has forty houses, about half of which belong to Muslim Sama. In addition, about thirty house-boats normally moor at Tungbangkao, providing a total population of approximately 400. The Muslim Sama houses are fairly well dispersed among the Sama Dilaut houses, and considerable social intercourse occurs between the two groups; however, no intermarriage had occurred when I was doing fieldwork. The Muslim Sama have resided at Tungbangkao for about four years, many having come from nearby islands to buy the fish of the Sama Dilaut. The islands of Simunul, Sangasiapu, Bongao, Sanga-Sanga, Tawi-Tawi, Bilatan, and Tiji-Tiji surround the great Biloc-Biloc reef to provide a protective barrier from the open sea, thereby creating a lagoon-like calm in the Tawi-Tawi bay. The excellent fishing grounds within this bay attract Sama Dilaut from all over Tawi-Tawi.

Fig. 14 Tungbangkao. Tawi-Tawi island in background, 1965

Fig. 15 Lioboran, 1965

The fifth and final Sama Dilaut moorage in Tawi-Tawi is east of Lioboran, a tiny island in the Tiji-Tiji group, about fifteen kilometers south of Tungbangkao (fig15). This small moorage, also known as Lioboran, normally has about twenty-five boats and sometimes a couple of temporary houses with a total population of approximately 125. Like Tungbangkao, its population greatly increases at full moon when Sama Dilaut from the Sanga-Sanga area come to fish in the Biloc-Biloc reef. Like Tungbangkao, Lioboran has a perennial shortage of drinking water.

Two other islands important to the Tawi-Tawi Sama Dilaut are Bilatan Po'on, west of Bilatan island, and Bunabuna'an, between Bilatan and Lioboran. The traditional burial grounds of the Tawi-Tawi Sama Dilaut, these uninhabited, low islands distinguish the Tawi-Tawi Sama Dilaut from the other Sama Dilaut of the Sulu archipelago who have their own burial islands. On both islands the Sama Dilaut cemeteries are located near Muslim Sama graves, but the elaborate Sama Dilaut grave structures are quite distinct from the simple Muslim graves. The cemetery on Bunabuna'an is the largest, with about forty family graves, while Bilatan Po'on has only about ten graves. These islands are not particularly sacred to the Sama Dilaut, but are generally approached with some apprehension since it is believed the spirits of the deceased hover around the graves after death.

Although each of the Sama Dilaut moorages is in some respects unique, the five share several common features. All are located on a protected reef, partly exposed at low tide, which serves as a source of edible marine life. This reef may be very small as at Lamiun, or it may extend for several kilometers as at Tungbangkao. Part of this exposed reef, or the nearby beach, is used for boatbuilding and other work by the adults and as a playground by the children. Throughout the moorage, poles stuck into the reef are used for mooring the boats. Several shallow channels are found generally among the boats, as well as a deeper channel which serves as a main passage for boats entering and leaving the moorage at low tide. All waste is disposed of in the moorage waters, but the tidal currents sweep the waters clean twice a day. Because of the distance from land, flying insects such as mosquitoes, which plague the land villages, do not bother the sea villages. The Sama Dilaut are usually found only a few hundred meters from land villages, and relations between the two groups are normally symbiotic, with the sea people trading fish for the cassava and fruits of the land dwellers. With the exception of the Muslim Sama population at Tungbangkao, only Sama Dilaut people live in the moorages. Only Tungbangkao has a few small stores operated by the Muslim Sama fish buyers. No moorages have mosques, a feature that distinguishes the Sama Dilaut from other Sama communities of Tawi-Tawi. The number of houses at the moorages varies considerably throughout the year. Many families erect temporary houses when they repair their boats or take breaks from boat living. When their boats are repaired or when they are ready to fish elsewhere, they abandon the houses. In the course of my fieldwork, the number of houses at Lu'uk Tulai ranged from zero to fifteen. The houses at Tungkalang, Lamiun, and Tungbangkao were more permanent and generally better constructed.

Visitors to Tawi-Tawi would probably note other Sama Dilaut moorages. For example, a flotilla of five or six houseboats may moor for a week or so at an anchorage as they fish in the nearby waters; however, after exhausting the waters, they return to their home moorages or move on to other fishing grounds. During the northeast monsoons, some Sama Dilaut houseboats moor near land villages where they plant small plots of cassava on land leased from land-dwelling Sama, but after the planting they return to their home moorages, taking occasional trips back to tend the gardens until harvest time.

The five moorages described above have been Sama Dilaut moorages for some time, but should trouble occur, they could disappear overnight. About ten years ago, a Sama Dilaut flotilla regularly moored near the land village of Karundung on southeastern Sanga-Sanga island. Tausug outlaws from Jolo attacked the land village and killed seventeen people. Within a matter of hours after the conflict, the Sama Dilaut houseboats dispersed, some to Bongao to form the present moorage of Lamiun, and others to the Bilatan moorages. During my first visit to Tawi-Tawi in 1963, a sizeable Sama Dilaut flotilla was located south of Lu'uk Tulai at Bandulan. After I left, four Sama Dilaut men died mysteriously enough to convince the boat dwellers that evil spirits were plaguing the moorage and it was no longer a safe dwelling place. When I returned to the site in 1965, no Sama Dilaut houseboats were moored there. Disagreements with land-dwelling neighbors also sometimes cause the Sama Dilaut to move to other moorages.

The population of a Sama Dilaut moorage varies greatly at different times of the month and at different seasons of the year. For example, on a Monday in October 1965, a wedding attracted 120 houseboats to the moorage of Tungkalang; by Thursday of that week, only twenty-eight houseboats remained. During the season of the northeast monsoons, the winds sometimes build up swells in the open sea which break over the protective reefs of Lu'uk Tulai and Tungkalang, causing considerable agitation in the reef waters and occasional damage to houseboats. As a result, many Sama Dilaut choose to leave these moorages during this season to fish in the calm Bilatan waters or to moor near other land villages more protected from the destructive breakers where they sometimes plant gardens on leased land.

Fishing cycles also determine Sama Dilaut movements. During the spring tides of the full moon, seas spill over the normally exposed reefs of Bilatan to attract fish from deeper waters to the newly created feeding grounds. Awaiting their arrival are Sama Dilaut from all over Tawi-Tawi, including many from the Sanga-Sanga moorages, who travel monthly to Bilatan at full moon. During the neap tides, when fish are attracted to the Bilatan reefs in great schools for feeding, the Sama Dilaut practice intensive fishing in communal fish drives. During the neaps of some months, many Sanga-Sanga Sama Dilaut travel to Bilatan to join these drives. When the moon disappears completely, the Sama Dilaut engage in net fishing with pressure lanterns. This type of fishing is lucrative on many reefs throughout Tawi-Tawi and contributes to much Sama Dilaut movement; Bilatan Sama Dilaut regularly seek the fish on Sanga-Sanga reefs whereas the Sanga-Sanga people visit the Bilatan reefs. Other types of fishing are practiced during the month, but the above types result in the greatest movement of fishermen.

The deep seas to the west of the Sanga-Sanga moorages have fishing grounds that yield large fish to the hook-and-line fisherman, and some of these Sama Dilaut engage almost exclusively in this type of fishing and rarely travel to the Bilatan reefs. At one time, the reefs of the Basun islands attracted as many Sama Dilaut as the Bilatan reefs currently do; however, in recent years Tausug outlaws are rumored to frequent the reefs and Sama Dilaut fishermen consequently avoid them. More Sanga-Sanga Sama Dilaut travel to the Bilatan reefs for fishing than Bilatan Sama Dilaut travel to Sanga-Sanga; nonetheless, despite the rich fishing grounds in their home waters, many Bilatan Sama Dilaut regularly visit the deep-sea fishing grounds of the Sanga-Sanga moorages. Shark fishing attracts many of them to the seas off Sanga-Sanga during the southwest monsoons.

The Bilatan Sama Dilaut who wish to plant gardens during the growing season of the northeast monsoon must temporarily reside near Sanga-Sanga or Tawi-Tawi villages since the dry, rocky islands of Bilatan do not allow cultivation. Even the Sanga-Sanga Sama Dilaut sometimes go to other villages where land-dwelling friends provide land for their small gardens.

Post-marital residence patterns also contribute to movement. Although the Sama Dilaut profess an ideal of uxorilocal residence, in reality their residence tends to be ambilocal. If a couple are from two different moorages, they usually divide their time between the two places before eventually settling in one of them.

Ceremonies also contribute to much Sama Dilaut movement. Kinsmen are expected to attend ceremonies of marriage, healing, and superincision, which is not exactly the same as circumcision (see chapter 7). Since a Sama Dilaut's kinsmen are scattered among the five moorages, a ceremony at one of the moorages attracts visitors from the others. The ceremonial cycles complement the movements of the fishing cycles. The Bilatan moorages hold their ceremonies during full moon to take advantage of the many visiting fishermen already in the area, while in the Sanga-Sanga moorages, ceremonies are more often held during the moonless period, when the mooragers have returned from the full-moon fishing at Bilatan and many of the Bilatan people are in the area to sell their full-moon catches in Bongao.

The cemetery islands at Bunabuna'an and Bilatan Po'on also account for some Sama Dilaut movements. Since all Sama Dilaut are buried on these islands, a death in any of the moorages means that an entourage of mourners must travel to one of the cemetery islands for the burial. In addition, the nature of Sama Dilaut religious beliefs demands periodic visits to the graves of deceased relatives.

Because the Bilatan Islands produce no cassava and have no potable water, it is necessary for these Sama Dilaut to make periodic journeys to Tawi-Tawi or Sanga-Sanga to obtain these necessities. Moreover, the Bilatan islands have no trees suitable for boatbuilding. Consequently, if a Bilatan Sama Dilaut needs to construct or repair a boat, he moves to one of the Sanga-Sanga moorages located near forests with trees suitable for boatbuilding. Rather than tow the large logs back to his home moorage, he normally resides at the Sanga-Sanga moorage until his boat is completed.

The nomadic territory of the Tawi-Tawi Sama Dilaut is difficult to define since some Sama Dilaut have traveled the entire length of the Sulu archipelago while others have never been outside the Tawi-Tawi waters. Most Sama Dilaut travels are limited to the Tawi-Tawi vicinity with occasional fishing trips to Sitangkai. The area enclosed by the dotted lines on figure 2 is the territory most commonly frequented by the Tawi-Tawi Sama Dilaut. This territory must be considered approximate, however, since some Sama Dilaut seldom travel outside the Tawi-Tawi bay while others go far out to the open sea. Few Sama Dilaut travel more than sixty-five kilometers in any direction from their home moorages. Sama Dilaut men travel more extensively than women and young men travel most of all, sometimes pursuing long fishing trips of several months' duration. Although economic reasons are usually advanced for such trips, they are undertaken primarily to satisfy the young men's desires to explore their island world. Almost all Tawi-Tawi Sama Dilaut men have been to Sitangkai (a distance of 100 kilometers), whereas fewer have traveled to Siasi (190 kilometers) and Jolo (250 kilometers). Several Tawi-Tawi Sama Dilaut have traveled to Zamboanga (500 kilometers) and a considerable number have visited the Semporna region of Sabah (190 kilometers).

Much journalistic ink has been spilled on the reportedly aimless wanderings of these "sea gypsies" often depicted as simple wanderers drifting a carefree life over romantic seas. Such is certainly not the case. A touch of wanderlust accounts for some Sama Dilaut travels, but most are undertaken for practical, necessary reasons and are patterned as well as predictable.

THE MATERIAL REALM

If any single theme permeates all of Sama Dilaut culture, it is the sea. Born on the sea, a Sama Dilaut child spends his childhood following the cycles of the sea with his family, unconsciously learning its many moods and habits. When he is superincised at adolescence, he is bathed in the sea before his initiation into manhood; and later, in elaborately decorated boats, he is married on the same sea. And at his death when his boat is sometimes made into his coffin, his body is transported over the sea to the burial islands at Bilatan. Such a sea-oriented culture would be expected to excel in boatbuilding, and such is certainly the case with the Sama Dilaut. Boatbuilding is by far the most highly developed aspect of their material culture, and the Sama Dilaut are recognized as excellent builders throughout Tawi-Tawi.

Almost every Sama Dilaut man knows how to build some type of boat. A young boy early imitates his father's boatbuilding methods and competes with other boys in sailing his toy craft in the shallow waters of the moorage. Some of the toys are excellent replicas of the larger boats, while others are simply crudely shaped pieces of wood; but all are representative of the unconscious process by which some of the boys will become master boatbuilders. At the age of fourteen or fifteen, a youth usually makes his first full-sized dugout boat. Often he works through the heat of the midday sun or under the light of the full moon in order to hasten its completion. Throughout its construction he is given advice, although little actual supervision, by his older male relatives, and its completion is a source of great pride for him. Some of the boys themselves experiment or assist relatives in making the more elaborate water craft, and in a few years they are recognized as master boatbuilders themselves.

Boatbuilding

The moorages in western Tawi-Tawi, especially Tungkalang and Lu'uk Tulai, always have more boatbuilding activities than the other moorages. At

Fig. 16 Lepa houseboat

Tungkalang, I once saw eleven boats under construction and during a visit to Lu'uk Tulai, I observed thirteen boats being built. These numbers were exceptional, however; more typically three or four boats are under construction at any one time. Three factors are responsible for this specialization in these moorages: (1) the waters are less productive as fishing grounds and boatbuilding provides additional incomes; (2) the nearby islands have trees for boatbuilding; and (3) large logs suitable for boatbuilding, adrift from lumbering camps in Sabah, are often found in the nearby sea. Several boats are always under construction at these moorages whereas at the other three moorages, very little boatbuilding occurs.

Many men build boats only for their personal use whereas others are professional boatbuilders or at least depend on boatbuilding for a good share of their income. Such men sell their boats to Sama Dilaut who lack boatbuilding skills or to land-dwellers. Frequently a man supplies all the materials to the builder, assists him in what ways he can, and provides fish to him during the construction period. In addition, a cash sum is usually paid. This is especially true of newly married young men who are acquiring their first houseboat. Typically, the two men are kinsmen and the cash amount is considerably less than it would be for an unrelated person. For example, it is not unusual for a large lepa (fig. 16) to sell for 800 to 1,000 pesos to an outside buyer. But I knew several men who assisted relatives as they built lepa and paid them only 150 to 250 pesos. Sometimes valuables, such as jewelry, are given instead of cash.

Several factors determine how long it takes to build a boat. If the builder has all the necessary materials, does not need to interrupt his work to fish, and has someone to assist him, he may finish a large boat, such as a lepa, in two months. Typically, however, it takes longer. Usually not all the lumber is available, and after completing the hull, for instance, the builder must wait for another log to be found at sea or must search the forest for suitable timber. He often works alone and must take time off to fish to provide for his family. Under such conditions, the construction of a boat may stretch to six or eight months. The smaller boats, of course, take less time.

All boatbuilders I interviewed said they learned their craft by working with others, usually their fathers, when young. And expectedly, many of these men were assisted by their sons who would become boatbuilders themselves. Thus, it is very much a family skill passed through the generations. Men tend to specialize in one type of houseboat (always the one used by their kin group), but are usually able to construct several types of fishing boats. Among the Sama Dilaut men recognized as master boatbuilders in Tawi-Tawi during the 1960s were Hadjulani, Maisahani, Kaiyani, Suarani, Saraban, Amileludden, Lajahulan, and Salbaiyani. All had sons of varying ages who assisted them. During my stay, two of the sons made their first small dugouts and burst with pride as they paddled them through the moorage for the first time.

Logs are frequently found at sea by the Sama Dilaut while fishing.[1] These are great boons to the finders since they provide the best wood for boatbuilding, or if they are not interested in building themselves, they can sell the logs to boatbuilders. Such large logs are essential to building certain types of boats since trees of that size are difficult to find in the local forests, and if they are found, it is nearly impossible to drag them to the coast. Although rapidly being depleted, the forest is still an important source of materials for boatbuilding. A log found at sea never provides all the wood needed for a boat, and the forest supplies the additional requirements.

Most of the forested interiors of Sanga-Sanga and Tawi-Tawi islands are public land, but an individual may take trees from them if he obtains a permit from the Bureau of Forestry. Few Sama Dilaut bother to acquire such permits and consequently are sometimes fined when caught felling trees. When a Sama Dilaut needs a log from the interior, he always goes with one or two companions. Not only does he need assistance in the strenuous labor of felling and cutting the trees, but he also feels more secure with company in the forest, which to the Sama Dilaut is filled with outlaws and malevolent spirits. No special ceremonies are held prior to entering the forest or for any other stages of boatbuilding, but most men wear anting-anting, amulets believed to protect them from harm.

Finding a suitable tree for boatbuilding is no small job. The men must trek through the forest and cut through the underbrush until they find an appropriate tree. Often they must clear an area around the tree for space to start chopping. They then take turns chopping until the tree is felled.[2] Sometimes, before the smaller limbs can be cut from the felled tree, additional underbrush must be cleared away. Then after the trunk is cleared of branches, a deep V-shaped groove is cut down its length in order to split it. The trunk is rolled over (often a major job in itself) and another groove is cut opposite the first one. Wooden pegs made from branches of the tree are driven into the groove with a heavy mallet, also cut from one of the branches. As the log begins to split, limbs are placed in the fissure and the peg is moved forward to again drive into the log. Additional limbs are placed in the fissure until the log is split. Not infrequently, the center of the tree is rotten and unsuitable for the keel of the boat, although usually enough can be salvaged for planks. Once I was with two men who felled and split twelve trees before finding one that was not rotten. After the log or logs have been split into manageable lengths, they must be dragged to the beach. Frequently, a path must be cut through the dense vegetation. I once saw ten men drag a large log for one-and-a-half kilometers to the beach. The entire process, of course, takes several days and frequently the men get lost while trying to find their way out of the forest or trying to locate the log the following morning. Once the logs reach the water, they are tied to boats and taken to the home moorage where the boat will be constructed. Acquiring logs in this fashion is perhaps the most strenuous of all Sama Dilaut work.

If a man is fortunate enough to find a log floating in the sea, he is spared much of the labor described above. The owner carefully examines the log, and its size and quality determine what kind of boat he will make from it. If the log is exceptionally long and of good quality, most likely it will be used to construct a lepa (fig. 16). Before beginning work, the builder often erects a sun shelter consisting of upright poles that support a flimsy roof made of palm fronds spread over a lattice of smaller poles. Sometimes a sail stretched above the work area serves the same purpose. It is not uncommon for men to work during the full moon to take advantage of the cool night hours. After deciding which half of the log will be used for the keel, the builder splits the other half into rough planks that will be used for planking the sides of the boat. If the log is large, the owner may get as many as three planks—about twenty-five centimeters wide and five centimeters thick—from the top of the log and one from either side. The remainder of the log will be used for the keel. Any salvageable part of the log not needed for the boat is cut into boards of varying lengths and sold in the Bongao market. Practically all the work is done with the patuk, a general name applied to a variety of tools (fig. 17). The blade of this

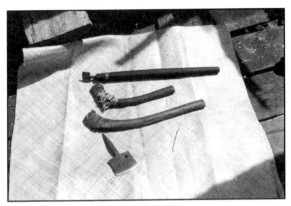

Fig. 17 Patuk and handles

tool may be attached to a long handle and used as an ax, attached to a shorter handle to become a hatchet, twisted in the same handle to become an adz, or stuck into the end of a handle to become a chisel. A man usually has several blades of different sizes. A large knife, or *bolo*, is useful for some stages of the work. Sanding is done either with the rough skin of a stingray attached to a block of wood or a piece of metal perforated with nail holes and attached to a block. A Western-style brace and bit is used for making the holes for the wooden dowels that attach the planks.

In making the planks, the end of the log is split. A wooden wedge, cut from any convenient piece of wood, is placed into the crack and pounded with a wooden mallet, also made from any handy wood, to expand the crack. As the split is lengthened, the wedge is moved forward until the entire plank has been split from the log. After being removed from the log, the plank is hewn into the desired width and thickness. It is then placed on a small pile of rocks, seesaw fashion, and large rocks are placed on both ends until they touch the ground. The plank is dampened periodically and allowed to remain in the sun several days until it is properly bowed to fit the keel. Bamboo poles for outrigger floats are bowed in similar fashion so the bow ends are elevated above the water line.

The keel is shaped with the patuk. After it has been scooped out, water is placed in it (or it is covered by palm fronds) when not being worked on to prevent cracking from the heat of the sun. After the keel is shaped, it may be submerged in the moorage waters for several hours, or perhaps overnight, in order to destroy insects that might damage the boat. Rocks are sometimes placed in the keel to expand its beam.

Wooden dowels, called *pasok*, are used to secure the parts of the boat together. Holes are drilled into the edges of abutting planks and dowels are placed in the holes to attach them. As the planks are forced together, the soft bark of the *gelum* tree, collected from nearby islands or purchased in the Bongao market, is placed between them to serve as caulking.[3] Dowels are also used to attach other parts of the boats. All bindings are done with rattan (*buai*) which is available in the island forests or the Bongao market place.

Two types of paddles are used by the Sama Dilaut, namely single-bladed paddles, or *busai*, and double-bladed paddles, or *keleh* (fig. 18). The single-bladed paddles are more common and vary in size from small ones made for children's boats to large ones that serve as steering paddles for the large boats. Other than size, the major variation in paddles is their handles. Four types of handles made by the Sama Dilaut are illustrated in figure 18. Type 3 is most common and type 1 the least common. Great variation is found in the width and length of the paddle blades. The double-bladed paddle is less common than the single-bladed and is generally used in propelling the small outriggerless dugouts.

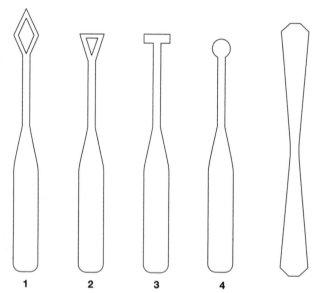

Fig. 18 Paddles: variations of the busai (1-4) and the keleh

The Tawi-Tawi Sama Dilaut build fifteen different types of boats.[4] These boats range from large houseboats that reach eighteen meters in length to miniature boats no more than sixty centimeters long that serve as gravemarkers. To my knowledge, the Sama Dilaut have no general term comparable to the English word "boat" that applies to all water craft. The most inclusive term I learned is *bangka*, which is applied rather indiscriminately to all non-houseboats, with or without outriggers. I have even heard houseboats referred to as bangka, but more typically they are called by their specific names. Although the Sama Dilaut have a term for each boat-type, they are often rather casual in their use of these terms. For example, two Sama Dilaut may use different names for the same boat, and similarly the names for the parts of the boats vary among individuals. This is probably partly because different types of boats have diffused to Tawi-Tawi from both the north and the south, sometimes bringing with them different names for similar boats and boat parts. Also, the presence of Tausug-speakers in Tawi-Tawi, as well as the various Sinama dialects, with their different names for boats and boat parts, have probably contributed to the variety of terms.[5] The result is a rather confusing array of terms to the outsider.

Houseboats

Of all the boats built by the Sama Dilaut, the houseboats are most central to their lives; these boats serve as their homes, their transportation and their fishing boats. Not surprisingly, the houseboats are the epitome of Sama Dilaut boatbuilding and display some of the finest carvings found in Tawi-Tawi, if not in all the Sulu Islands. Although houseboat interiors vary, certain general features apply to them all. The most spacious living space I measured was twelve meters long, one-and-seven-tenths meters wide and one-and-a-half meters high. The smallest I measured was only one-and-eight-tenths meters long, one-and-a-quarter meters wide and one meter high. The first was home for a family of six; the second was the dwelling of a young couple and their infant son who were living in the tiny boat as they saved money to acquire a more commodious one. Most living spaces fall between these extremes. Cooking is done on an earthenware hearth (lappohan) placed on boards or a sheet of metal on the open deck at the stern. Purchased from Simunul island potters, the hearth, about a half-meter long and a third-meter wide, is a shallow oval-shaped firebox with elevated prongs at one end to support cooking pots. A cache of firewood and a ceramic water jar of Chinese manufacture from Borneo are located nearby. A simple rack, sometimes decorated with carving, holds the few Sama Dilaut cooking utensils. Many boats have a sturdy tree branch in the cooking area with limbs that serve as hangers for pots and pans. The front open deck is usually kept clear. If a small child is in the household, a fence-like barrier may be placed at either end of the living space to prevent the child from entering the open deck areas where she may fall overboard. Mats of plaited coconut fronds are sometimes placed along the sides to fill the open space between the roof eaves and the gunwale as well as at either end of the shelter to provide privacy during the night and protection from inclement weather. The roof is not securely attached and is not watertight. Long fishing spears are placed atop the eaves and tied in place to help hold down the roof. Heavy rains eventually dampen most boat interiors and a strong wind sometimes removes several roofs in a moorage. The houseboat has no furniture. Mats used for sleeping at night are rolled up and stored along the sides during the day. Kapok-filled pillows provide comfort for sleeping and lounging. Unlike the Semporna Bajau Laut (Sather 1997, 133), the Tawi-Tawi Sama Dilaut have no taboo against sleeping lengthwise in the boat; in fact, some boat interiors make it impossible to do otherwise. Extra clothing is rolled into bundles and tied from the roof poles at either side. Articles that cannot be harmed by bilge water are stored in the hull under the deck. Coconut half-shells, or any convenient container, serve as bailers to periodically remove bilge water from the hull. Fishing nets are rolled up and placed along the sides while long fishing spears are tied to the roof beam or, as noted, tied outside at the eaves of the roof to hold it in place. These spears are sometimes erected atop the roof to provide a frame for drying fishing nets. Many houseboats have a *hainan*, an ornate, curvilinear carved bar hung to one side of the interior, about a meter-and-a-half long and painted in green, red, yellow, blue, and white. Associated with ancestral spirits, the hainan is the focus of certain religious ceremonies held in the boat. If an infant is in the household, a hammock-like cradle (*buahan*) is suspended from the central roof beam. A small kerosene lamp, usually a glass jar with a perforated lid for a wick placed in a section of bamboo with one side removed, is hung from the side of the boat to provide feeble light for nighttime. While in the moorage, a mooring pole (*samboang*) secures the bow of the boat while an anchor (*labuh*), usually a piece of heavy coral, is dropped from the stern to prevent the boat from drifting with the currents.

Several early writers (e.g., Orosa 1923, 62) have commented on the unsanitary conditions of Sama Dilaut houseboats. For the most part, these comments are ethnocentric and misleading. As among all people, families maintain their homes with different notions of cleanliness. Most houseboat interiors are kept clean although infestations of cockroaches and other undesirable insects sometimes occur. Even the occasional rat invades the large boats. Periodically the boat is dry docked. Using a dried palm frond as a torch, the keel is scorched to destroy algae and other parasites. The removable deck boards and the interior of the hull are scrubbed thoroughly with coconut-husk brushes. Most families do such a thorough cleaning about once a year, although more fastidious boat dwellers do it more often.

It is difficult to determine the longevity of a houseboat since worn parts are frequently replaced. Periodically the entire boat is taken apart. Worn planks and dowels are replaced and the boat is recaulked. Such a thorough overhauling occurs only when needed, but when done, the result is virtually a new boat. Consequently, a boat may be many years old, but its parts have been replaced several times.

The following descriptions apply to the *lepa, djenging, balutu* and *pilang*, the boats most commonly used as houseboats by the Tawi-Tawi Sama Dilaut. It must be remembered, however, that each boat is somewhat distinctive, reflecting the idiosyncrasies and tastes of the individual boatbuilder, and may not conform in detail to the following descriptions.

The Lepa The lepa (fig. 16) is the houseboat most commonly associated with the Sama Dilaut of Tawi-Tawi. The boat is also called *pidlas* by some Sama Dilaut, a name, however, more commonly used by the land-dwelling Sama.[6] Aesthetically, it is perhaps the most attractive of all the houseboats with its flowing lines that sweep into the prominent prow (*jung'ar*), the distinguishing feature of this boat. It is, however, the most recent boat-type to be adopted by the Sama Dilaut. Older Sama Dilaut claim it was not common among them prior to World War II and came into Tawi-Tawi from Borneo. Sitangkai Sama Dilaut informants support this view, also claiming it was introduced to them from Borneo some time before World War II.[7] According to the Tawi-Tawi Sama Dilaut, they first bought the lepa from Sitangkai boatbuilders, and then learned to build it themselves. Today it is one of the most popular houseboat types, with well over half the population using it as full-time living quarters. Its rapid spread throughout the Sitangkai and Tawi-Tawi waters seems largely due to its greater efficiency as a fishing, sailing and reef boat. The outriggerless lepa probably evolved in a shallow reef environment; it is the boat best adapted to the environment of the Tawi-Tawi Sama Dilaut. Its broad hull results in shallow displacement to allow easy movement through the shallow reef waters. Not surprisingly, it is found in greatest numbers among those Sama Dilaut whose home moorages are located on extensive reefs. The absence of outriggers makes it efficient as a fishing boat since most Tawi-Tawi Sama Dilaut are net fishermen and the outriggerless lepa allows greater ease in handling nets over the sides. Furthermore, the broad beam and great length of the boat provides a larger living space than is typically found in the other houseboats.

The lepa varies considerably in length, but in general it tends to be the longest of the Sama Dilaut houseboats. The longest lepa I measured was eighteen meters from bow to stern and one-and-eight-tenths meters wide at its beam; this was, however, an exceptionally long boat, and typically the length is about eleven meters. The keel (*tadas*), made from a single log and slanted outwardly from both the bow and stern, is built up with five planks attached by wooden dowels. Rib-like braces (*sunkol*) support the hull at about one-meter intervals. Cut from a single piece of wood, these ribs are added after the hull is completed and are secured under projections carved on the second plank. A deck of boards (*lantai*) that runs parallel to the planks of the hull is supported by cross braces, also called *sunkol*, that rest on the projections that support the ribs to provide a floor for the house area as well as open living spaces at either end. The beam of the deck is about one-and-a-half meters. The *nipa* mat roof (*sapao*), which also serves as a surface for drying fish and can easily be dismantled to convert the lepa into a sailing boat, is less than half the length of the boat and about one-and-a-third meters at its gable. The bow and stern, as well as wing-like braces (*sa'am*) that project from either side of the hull at both ends, are carved in curvilinear designs. Usually a panel of geometric painting adorns both sides of the hull.

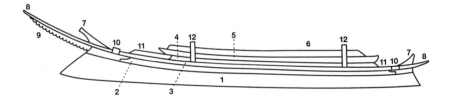

Fig. 19 Side view of lepa

1 *Tadas* — the keel

2 *Pangahapit* — the first plank of the hull

3 *Bingkol* — the second plank of the hull

4 *Kapi-kapi* — the third plank of the hull

5 *Durun-durun* (or *koyang-koyang*) — the fourth plank of the hull, usually with carving at either end

6 *Ding-ding* ("wall") — the final plank, or gunwale, of the hull, usually with carving at either end (also refers to the plaited palm frond panels sometimes hung from the eaves and the gables to enclose the living area)

7 *Tujah* — the main bow and stern pieces of the hull

8 *Jung'ar* — the long prow that extends beyond the tujah at the bow, and the small extension beyond the tujah at the stern

9 *Ling'ai'at* — the strip of carving sometimes found under the jung'ar

10 *Sikom* — the small brace at the bow and stern that holds the two tujah together

11 *Adjung-adjung* — the bow and stern extensions of the kapi-kapi, which usually have carving

12 *Sa'am* — the braces with carved wing-like projections, which extend beyond the hull at the bow and stern

Note: This and subsequent drawings are only approximately to scale and are intended to illustrate the different parts of the boats.

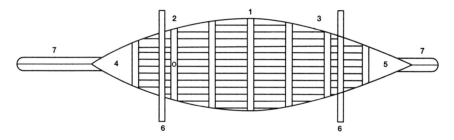

Fig. 20 Top view of lepa

1 *Sunkol* — the cross braces which support the deck boards; also the name for the rib-like braces in the hull (not shown)

2 *Patarukan* — the foremost cross brace with a hole for the mast (*taruk*) which rests in the *ponsot patarukan*, a depression in the bottom of the keel

3 *Lantai* — the deck boards (number and width vary)

4 *Panan-sahan* — the V-shaped deck board at the bow

5 *Sung'utan* — the V-shaped deck board at the stern (also sometimes used for the panan-sahan)

6 *Sa'am* — the braces with wing-like carved projections that extend beyond the hull at the bow and stern

7 *Jung'ar* — the long prow extension and the short stern extension

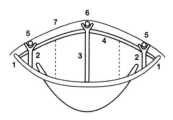

Fig. 21 Front view of lepa

1 *Sa'am* — the same as number 6 above

2 *Pang'ga* — the fork for supporting the roof poles (*dandang*) on either side

3 *Tubung-tubung* — the fork for supporting the center ridgepole of the roof (sometimes two of these are used as indicated by the dotted lines)

4 *Sungkelan* — the gable support (may be one or two pieces)

5 *Baihuan* — the pole that supports the roof eave

6 *Buhungan* — the ridgepole of the roof

7 *Sapao* — the nipa mat roof

Note: The parts of the front view of the lepa correspond to the numbers in figure 21. This drawing does not include the prow.

The Djenging According to many Sama Dilaut, the djenging (fig. 22) is the houseboat used by their forefathers and many remember when it was more widespread before the arrival of the lepa after World War II.[8] Some Sama from the Siasi area of Sulu still refer to the Tawi-Tawi Sama Dilaut as "Sama djenging," suggesting an old association between the Tawi-Tawi people and this type of houseboat.

Fig. 22 Djenging houseboat

The djenging is basically a planked log dugout with two to four double outriggers that support a deck that in turn supports a house. The djenging is typically shorter than the lepa, but it is not unusual for one to reach eleven meters. Some, however, are no more than four-and-a-half meters long. It has disappeared among the Sitangkai Sama Dilaut, but it is still found in Tawi-Tawi, although not in great numbers. I saw few djenging constructed during my field research whereas many lepa and pilang were built. It will probably soon disappear among the Sama Dilaut.

Distinctive features of the djenging include the intricate carving usually found at both the bow and stern which are almost equally elevated with the bow somewhat more prominent. The hull consists of a basic dugout keel (*baran balutu*), U-shaped in profile, with two planks (*tapid* and *lingkam*) attached by wooden dowels. Two to four outrigger booms (*batangan*) made of single pieces of wood pass through the first plank and are lashed to bamboo floats (*katig*). Shorter secondary booms (*sa'am*), also made of single pieces of wood, pass through the gunwale directly above the primary booms to which they are

Fig. 23 Side view of djenging

1 *Baran balutu* — the keel which usually has carving at either end
2 *Tapid* — the first plank of the hull
3 *Lingkam* — the second plank of the
   hull, or gunwale
4 *Dauk-gus* — the extension at either
   end of the lingkam (sometimes the

lingkam is long enough to negate the
need for these extensions)
5 *Tunggu* — the attachments to both
   ends of the tapid which create upward
   sweeps to the bow and stern (often
   absent in the simpler djenging)

Note: The parts of the side view of the djenging correspond to the numbers in figure 23.

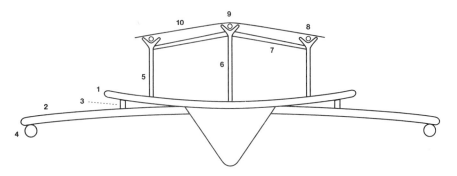

Fig. 24 Front view of djenging

1 *Sa'am* — the secondary boom that
   helps support the lower primary boom
2 *Batangan* — the primary boom
3 *Tuk'lug* — the rattan lashings between
   the primary and secondary booms;
   there may be one, two, or three of
   these on each side
4 *Katig* — the bamboo outrigger float
5 *Pang'ga* — the forked support for the
   roof eave pole

6 *Taruk* — the forked center support for
   the ridgepole (also used for the sailing
   mast)
7 *Sungkelan* — the gable supports; may
   be one or two pieces
8 *Dandang* — the pole to support the
   eaves of the roof
9 *Buhungan* — the ridgepole for the roof
10 *Sapao* — the nipa mat roof

Note: The parts of the front view of the djenging correspond to the numbers in figure 24.

attached by one, two or three rattan lashings (*tuk'lug*). The hull is decked with removable transverse planks (lantai). This deck is extended over the secondary outrigger booms by lantai, or less often by split bamboo, that run horizontally to the hull. The living space is the *pala'u*, a variation of the house structure on the lepa.[9] As on the lepa, this structure can be easily dismantled to convert the houseboat into a sailing or fishing boat.

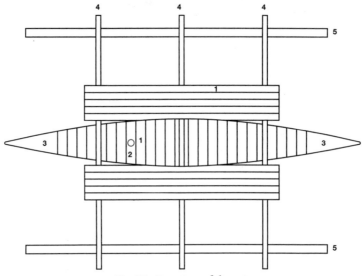

Fig. 25 Top view of djenging

1 *Lantai* — the deck boards, both horizontal and vertical

2 *Patarukan* — the cross brace with a hole for the mast (taruk) which rests in the *ponsot patarukan*, a depression in the bottom of the keel

3 *Panansa'am* — the V-shaped deck boards at bow and stern

4 *Batangan* — the primary boom

5 *Katig* — the bamboo outrigger float

Note: The parts of the front view of the djenging correspond to the numbers in figure 25.

The Balutu A type of large djenging, called balutu, *kubu*, or simply djenging by the Tawi-Tawi Sama Dilaut, has a large, permanently attached house (kubu) (fig. 26). I have chosen to call this houseboat balutu to distinguish it from the smaller djenging described above. Only about a half dozen of these boats remained during the period of my fieldwork in the 1960s and most of them were in various stages of disrepair and decay, probably the last of their kind. At one time, they were common dwellings for the Sitangkai Sama Dilaut

(Taylor 1931; Martenot 1981, 198–202), but they were no longer found at Sitangkai during the period of my research. The surviving pictures of these boats (Taylor 1931, 1936; Follett 1945, 130–31) reveal elaborate carvings much more extensive than those on existing Sama Dilaut boats. At one time large balutu apparently served as somewhat permanent living quarters at moorages while smaller boats were used for fishing and other travel. This seems to have been the situation in Sitangkai where, according to Taylor (1931, 483), "Crude houses ten feet wide and from twenty to thirty feet long are built upon these canoes. They never leave their anchorage and are used for residence purposes only; for the most part they are restricted to wealthy headmen." The ones I saw in Tawi-Tawi were not this large and no special status was associated with them; in fact, most were derelicts.

Fig. 26 Balutu houseboat

The basic hull of the balutu is identical to that of the djenging except that the former has bow and stern attachments not found on the latter. Upward-sweeping winglike projections (tunggu) above the carved bow and stern create gaping mouths which the Sama Dilaut call *buaia*, "crocodile" (fig. 27), acknowledging the open mouth of the crocodile as the inspiration (or perhaps after-the-fact explanation) of the feature. Extensions (*salagunting*) of the gunwales on both sides and at both ends are attached to the upper part of the prow and extend about one-and-a-half meters above and beyond the bow and stern. The ends of these extensions are secured together by caps (*tunpang*) decorated with carving. As in the djenging, the bow and stern of this boat are almost indistinguishable.

Fig. 27 Balutu prow

The house, or kubu, is permanently attached and built of upright planks secured to a framework attached to the boat. Carved latticework provides cross ventilation at one or both ends of the house. The sides of the house were originally painted in geometric designs of bright colors, but all I saw were almost completely faded. The house has an open door at either end with plaited

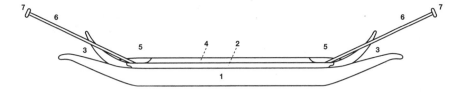

Fig. 28 Side view of balutu

1 *Baran balutu* — the keel, which usually has carving at either end

2 *Tapid* — the first plank of the hull

3 *Tunggu* — the attachments to both ends of the tapid, which form upward sweeps to the bow and stern

4 *Lingkam* — the second plank, or gunwale

5 *Dauk-gus* — the extension at either end of the lingkam (sometimes the

lingkam is long enough to negate the need for these extensions)

6 *Salagunting* — the planks attached to the dauk-gus at either end, which extend above and beyond the bow and stern

7 *Tunpang* — the cap, at either end, often carved, which holds together the ends of the salagunting

Note: The parts of the side view of the balutu correspond to the numbers in figure 28. Names for the outrigger parts of the balutu are identical to those of the djenging.

66

palm frond covers used at night or during inclement weather. The house is spacious compared to most Sama Dilaut houseboats. Although not as long as some lepa houses, it is wider (sometimes over two meters) and sometimes high enough to allow an adult to stand upright at the gable. The larger living space allows more storage for items above deck and sometimes provides residence for two or even three families. As with the lepa, the kitchen area is on the open deck at the stern. These large djenging are difficult to sail (perhaps impossible; I never saw one under sail) and awkward as fishing boats. These limitations were pointed out to me as reasons why they are unpopular as houseboats.

The Pilang The pilang (figs. 29 and 30), like the lepa, appears to have originated outside Tawi-Tawi, in this case from the northern Sulu islands. This double outriggered boat is related to boats of that area, especially the so-called *vinta*, and the Tawi-Tawi Sama Dilaut who use it as a houseboat trace many of their kin ties to the Siasi and Jolo areas.[10] Nonetheless, it is firmly established in Tawi-Tawi as a houseboat. Taylor (1931) claims the Sitangkai Sama Dilaut built the vinta (pilang) at the time he visited them. I question his claim, however, since during the course of my fieldwork in Sitangkai, I learned of no tradition of building pilang. Nor apparently did Martenot (1981), since he does not mention it in his article on the boats of the Sitangkai Sama Dilaut. It is possible that pilang were in Sitangkai at the time of Taylor's visit and he assumed that Sitangkai Sama Dilaut owned and built them rather than Tausug and other Sama. Tausug and other Sama people resided in Sitangkai at the time of my fieldwork in the 1960s, and very likely similar populations were there when Taylor visited the area. It is also possible Taylor confused the pilang with the standard djenging which was in Sitangkai at the time of his visit but which he does not mention.

Fig. 29 Pilang   Fig. 30 Pilang prow

The pilang has a U-shaped keel (baran) with five added planks to form a deep and rather narrow hull. The length of this boat, from bow to stern, ranges from four-and-a-half meters to ten meters. The longer boats have as many as four booms (batangan) to support the bamboo floats (katig). The outstanding feature of most pilang is the elaborately carved prow, gaping like an crocodile's open mouth. Some of these prows are among the finest carvings in the Sulu Archipelago. The stern is a simpler and smaller uncarved version of the prow. Some of the finer boats have two rows of intricate curvilinear carvings or intricately painted bands of geometric patterns along either side of the hull. As with the djenging, the hull is decked with removable transverse planks (lantai). This deck is extended over the secondary outrigger booms (sa'am) by planks (lantai), or less often by split bamboo, that run horizontally to the hull. The house (pala'u) erected over the deck is like that described for the djenging and can be easily taken down to convert the houseboat into a sailing boat. Smaller than the lepa or the balutu, the living space on the pilang is similar to the djenging.

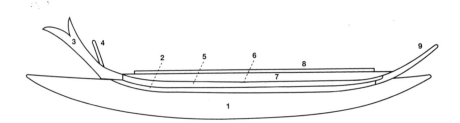

Fig. 31 Side view of pilang

1 *Baran* — the keel; carving is usually found at the bow

2 *Tapid* — the first plank added to the keel

3 *Palansar* — the upper part of the prow, often elaborately carved

4 *Sap'lun* — the washboard at the prow, often carved

5 *Dudung* — the second plank; usually has carving or painted design its entire length

6 *Dudung* — the narrow strip of carving on the second plank

7 *Dudung* — the third plank

8 *Tihim sa'am* — the fourth plank, or gunwale

9 *Sangpad-sangpad* — the upper extension of the stern

Note: The parts of the side view of the pilang correspond to the numbers in figure 31. The names for the outrigger and house structure are identical to those for the djenging.

Boat Art

Art (*okil*), as carving or painting, is reserved for the houseboats, although some of the elaborate *tonda'an*, small pilang used primarily for fishing, are sometimes decorated with art; even these, however, frequently serve as part-time living quarters. Since the houseboats are the most important boats to the Sama Dilaut, it is not surprising they are decorated with some of their finest art. The carvings on some boat prows are surpassed only by some of the Sama Dilaut grave markers, which are among the finest art in all of Sulu.

Carvings on Sama Dilaut boats can be reduced to a very limited number of motifs; the combination and execution of these motifs by the artist results in the intricately carved prows found on the houseboats. *Dau'an-dau'an* (leaves) is one of the most common motifs. In combination with the *kalo'on* (curlicues or curved lines), it is used to decorate the spectacular buaia prow of the pilang (fig. 30). The dau'an-dau'an and kalo'on motifs are used in combination with the fishlike *agta-agta* motif on the bow and stern of the djenging (figs. 27, 32 and 33).[11] Dau'an-dau'an is also commonly used with the kalo'on motif for the prow (fig. 34) and sa'am (fig. 35) of the lepa.

Fig. 32 Djenging prow

Fig. 33 Djenging stern

Fig. 34 Lepa prow

Fig. 35 Lepa sa'am

Fig. 36 Pilang hull with bahan-bahan
type carvings

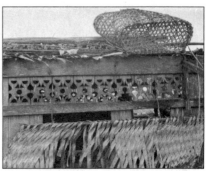

Fig. 37 Balutu kubu panel with lauwa-
lauwa type carving

Fig. 38 Lepa hull with pinis gunting
and sambili patterns

Fig. 39 Lepa hull with sabit and pis
sabit patterns

The hull of the pilang is frequently carved with one, two, or three lines of curvilinear carvings called *bahan-bahan*, which means "bending or curving." Figure 36 reveals variations of this pattern; the upper line has a floral motif; the middle line is reminiscent of both the kalo'on and agta-agta motifs; while the lower line is a variation suggesting small waves. Sometimes these lines are painted in great detail in the traditional Sama Dilaut colors of red, blue, green, yellow, and white. Typically, they are painted when the boat is new, but as the paint fades it is not repainted.

The few remaining balutu reveal a carving style not found on other Sama Dilaut boats. Frequently, an upper panel on either side at the bow or stern of the house is carved to allow air circulation (fig. 37). This type of carving is called *lauwa-lauwa*, which means "web," as in spider's web.

In addition to carvings, the Sama Dilaut decorate their boats with bands of geometric paintings. The few remaining balutu have faded remnants of such paintings on the sides of their houses, and they are frequently found on the sides of the lepa, seemingly having been transferred to this boat which superseded the balutu. Several motifs are used in these paintings. In figure 38, *pinis gunting* is the upper wide band that consists of squares of two different types of triangles separated by white bands. The lower line, a bahan-bahan carving that has been painted, was identified as *sambili.* Figure 39 reveals two more patterns. The upper band of triangles with center circles is called *sabit,* or "many-colored." The lower band is called *pis sabit,* meaning "the many colors of the *pis,*" pis being the colorful hand-woven textile traditionally worn by Tausug men as turbans. These bands are also painted on pilang, as shown in figure 40. The upper band is called *dudung,* also the name of the plank on which the painting appears. The second line is called *gipis.*

Fig. 40   Pilang hull with dudung and gipis patterns

The quantity and quality of the carving and painting on boats vary considerably. It is likely that most boats had more painting when they were new. I never saw anyone repainting an old boat and I frequently saw boats, especially lepa, with bands of painting almost faded away. Virtually all lepa have carvings at the prow, stern, and sa'am, but the quality of it varies considerably. Although most djenging have carving on both the bow and stern, some have it only on the bow and some have none at all. The pilang usually has carving at the prow and at least one line of carving the length of the hull on both sides. Some, however, lack the band of carving on the hull and some have no carving at all.

Carving is a talent limited to a few men. I knew no women carvers. Not all boatbuilders can execute the carvings and must hire someone else, usually a relative, to do the work. When I was in Tawi-Tawi during the 1960s, Salbaiyani was one of the most respected carvers and boatbuilders in the area. The pilang was his specialty and figures 29 and 30 illustrate his skill as a boatbuilder and carver. Suluhani was another highly respected carver. Although he was not among the finest boatbuilders, he was often hired to execute carvings on boats built by men who could not carve. He excelled in lepa carvings. A Sama Dilaut cultural ideal dictates that a carver must always be paid for his services, even if he is carving the boat of a close kinsman. I also encountered this cultural dictate in the realm of religion. Certain chants important in healing are effective only if the chanter is paid, and if not paid, the ceremony is ineffective. Similarly, if the carver is not paid, misfortunes will befall those involved. In reality, carvers often do not accept payment from close kinsmen, or if they do, it is a very small amount, since they know the reciprocal nature of Sama Dilaut kin relationships will compensate them for their service. However, more distant kinsmen and especially non-kinsmen are expected to pay for the talents of these gifted men.

The fine carvings are highly regarded by the Sama Dilaut and they sometimes pass through several boats if they can be detached from old boats and incorporated into new ones. Several men told me the carvings on their boats were their gifts to their children. Sama Dilaut tradition dictates that the prow of a man's boat be left on his grave at his death. Rarely, however, is the prow of a boat that still serves as a houseboat taken, but it is common to leave unusable boat carvings on graves.

Fishing Boats

"Fishing boats" are used primarily for fishing, but they also serve for moving among the houseboats at the moorages. Each houseboat has at least one such boat and frequently two. These boats are sometimes used as temporary houseboats on fishing trips or when the larger houseboat is being repaired. Newlyweds sometimes live in a fishing boat until they acquire a suitable houseboat. Five such boats are recognized by the Tawi-Tawi Sama Dilaut, namely the *boggo'*, the *birau*, the *junkun*, the *bitok* and the *tonda'an*. Sometimes when the keel of a lepa, djenging or pilang has been replaced, the old keel, with perhaps an added plank, is kept as a fishing boat.

The Boggo' One of the simplest Sama Dilaut boats, the boggo' is made from a single log (fig. 41). This simple dugout has a rounded bottom that comes to a point at the bow and stern. The sides do not slope inward until about seven centimeters down, thereby giving the appearance of an added plank or gunwale. Both the bow and stern are capped by rectangular knobs, are slightly elevated, and drop perpendicularly or slope outwardly. The bow and stern are indistinguishable. The interior of the hull may have several projections opposite one another at the gunwale to hold boards for seating. A plank is occasionally added to give the hull greater depth, but more commonly the boggo' is unplanked. Sometimes outriggers are added by attaching two booms to the gunwale with rattan, or by passing the booms through holes drilled through the gunwale and attaching them with rattan. Boggo' range from one-and-a-half to four-and-a-half meters in length.

Fig. 41 Boggo'

The Birau The birau (fig. 42) is almost identical to the boggo'. There are only two differences between them: the bow and stern of the birau slope inwardly whereas those of the boggo' drop perpendicularly or outwardly; and the birau does not have the "false" gunwale. Its length is similar to that of the boggo'. It, too, may have outriggers added like the boggo'.

Fig. 42 Birau

The Bitok This simple dugout is almost identical to the birau except that it lacks the knobs at the bow and stern and is generally smaller. It has a wider beam and the hull is usually shallower than either the boggo' or birau. It rarely has outriggers or added planks.

The Junkun The junkun typically consists of a simple dugout hull, although a plank is sometimes added to either side (fig. 43). Lengths range from two-and-a-half to eight meters. The longer boats often have several half-circle braces, or ribs, made of single pieces of wood and secured under projections carved in the hull at the gunwale. Above these projections, boards are placed for sitting, or they may hold cross-braces that support deck planks on some of the larger boats. Like the boggo', the bow and stern are capped by a rectangular knob and are of the same height, indistinguishable from one another. Unlike the boggo', however, both bow and stern sweep up considerably from the water line. Outriggers are sometimes added to the junkun. As with the boggo', the booms are simply passed over the gunwale and tied with rattan, or passed through holes drilled in the gunwale and secured with rattan. Two junkun served as full-time houseboats during my stay, but both owners claimed they were living in them only because they could not yet afford a proper houseboat. More typically the junkun are used for fishing or short distance travel.

Fig. 43 Junkun

The Tonda'an This fishing boat is a smaller version of the pilang. It is shorter, has fewer planks and usually lacks the elaborate carving of the pilang. The outrigger attachment is much simpler. Usually only two primary booms are secured to the gunwale with rattan or passed through holes drilled in the gunwale. It is frequently used for extended fishing trips when a temporary house (pala'u) may be erected on it. Sometimes it is used as a houseboat while its occupants await a more commodious boat.

Miniature Boats

Six miniature boats are made by the Sama Dilaut, namely the *palungan*, the *ontang*, the *pamatulakan*, the *pamatulakan ta'u ta'u*, the *bangka anak-anak* and toy boats. The palungan, pamatulakan, pamatulakan ta'u ta'u and bangka anak-anak are patterned after the boggo' or birau. The ontang is a small raft.

The Palungan These small boats, usually no more than a meter long and patterned after the boggo', birau, or bitok, are hung from either side of the larger houseboats at the stern near the cooking area. Filled with soil, they serve as planters for herbs and medicinal plants. I once saw a palungan planted with colorful flowers, but typically the plants are more utilitarian. Although not all houseboats have palungan, they are fairly common.

The Ontang The ontang is a small raft used in fishing. It consists of two bamboo floats, about a meter long, connected by two bow-shaped booms that support a small platform. Sometimes the ontang serves as a small raft to hold a lantern used in certain types of nighttime fishing. At other times, it is pulled behind a houseboat. Lines with hooks are attached to the towrope, and periodically the rope is pulled in to collect the hooked fish and rebait the hooks.

The Pamatulakan This small boat, used in a special religious ceremony to rid the moorage of evil spirits, is usually a crude version of the boggo' or birau. During times of misfortune or illness, the moorage shamans sometimes construct a pamatulakan. Different families of the moorage make the different parts and contribute such items as food, betel, cigarettes and perfume to place in the hull. Sometimes carved anthropomorphic images, called ta'u ta'u, are also placed in the boat. When finished and filled with its cargo, several shamans pull it through the moorage waters to attract the disease-causing spirits. After canvassing the moorage, the shamans take the pamatulakan with its evil spirits to the open sea and set it adrift on currents that take it away from the moorage. Sometimes a small, abandoned boggo' or birau is used for the ceremony.

The Pamatulakan Ta'u-Ta'u These small boats, rarely more than a meter long and decorated with traditional Sama Dilaut carving, are used as male grave markers. A male human figure, called ta'u ta'u, is placed in the boat (sometimes it is carved as a single piece with the boat) and left atop the grave. The marker is frequently called simply ta'u ta'u.

The Bangka Anak-Anak Fathers frequently make small boats for their children called bangka anak-anak (children's boats). The boats are used for transportation within the moorage, or sometimes for playing in the surf at the moorage's edge. They are very simple dugouts and usually patterned after the boggo' or birau, with miniature paddles fashioned after the larger paddles. For very small children, such boats may be no more than one-and-a-half meters long. Children learn to handle boats at a very early age and not uncommonly a child of three or four paddles his or her own dugout among the moorage boats.

Toy Boats Fathers often make toy boats for their sons, or boys may make their own. The most sophisticated of these are small lepa, perhaps a meter long, carved from a single piece of wood while the simpler ones are crudely made little dugouts or outrigger boats. Boys often make sails for their toy boats and hold races in the moorage waters.

Sailing

The maritime territory traveled by the Tawi-Tawi Sama Dilaut is usually no more than forty kilometers in any direction from the home moorage and dotted with hundreds of islands. Thus they seldom travel long distances and their travel is within sight of numerous islands, their most important navigational guides. They rarely travel long distances at night, but when they do, the moon, stars, winds, and currents serve as guides if islands are not visible. Although the Sama Dilaut identify many stars and constellations, my impression is that their knowledge of them is no greater than that of other people who live intimately with nature. Sama Dilaut do not like to travel in rough seas and frequently postpone trips until waters are calm. They avoid the swift currents of the area, and have a folklore (no doubt based on actual events) of unwary boats that ventured into them and were swept to Sulawesi.

Although all Sama Dilaut families have sails, or lamak, and most houseboats can be easily converted to sailing boats, Sama Dilaut do not utilize sails on their houseboats unless they are in a hurry to get from one place to another, which is not usual. If a Sama Dilaut family visits another moorage or travels to a fishing area, it is usually a slow journey with stops along the way for water, purchasing cassava, or fishing. The boat is normally poled or paddled in the shoals of nearby islands, taking advantage of tidal currents that dictate times of travel more than do winds. If they need to cross a wide channel between islands, the family may put up a sail to take advantage of a wind or perhaps wait several hours for a wind to come up. Once shoals are reached again, unless the family is in a hurry, the sail is dismantled and the boat poled through the shallow waters with an eye for possible fish. Thus, a trip that would take only a matter of hours by sail with a good wind may take a couple of days. Poling the heavy boats, especially the lepa, is not as formidable as it may seem. The prows of the larger lepa provide about a two-meter walkway for the poler. He thrusts his pole into the reef floor, walks forward and leans backward on the pole as the weight of his body moves the boat forward. His wife or perhaps an older child sits at the stern with a steering paddle.

Sails are utilized on fishing boats more frequently than on houseboats. If the fishing grounds are distant from the moorage and winds are favorable, sails are used to get to and from the grounds. Fishing boats are generally smaller than the houseboats, and sails for such boats are correspondingly smaller. One man can handle a small boat and sail, although typically one man handles the sail while another mans the steering paddle.

Sama Dilaut sails are made of whatever materials are available. A few are made of canvas, but more typically they have been patched many times with rice bags or any other available materials. Most resemble patchwork quilts more than anything else. I was told that in earlier years the sails were mats of plaited *pandan* leaves and displayed a variety of colorful designs. Now the availability of materials determines both color and design. Sails vary in size; the larger sails used on houseboats may be three-and-a-half meters square or larger whereas the ones used on the smaller fishing boats may be no more than two meters square.

The Sama Dilaut recognize four different types of sails. *Kapis* is a small rectangular lug sail, two parallel spars hung from the mast. The *banog pindang*, a sprit-type sail, is attached to the mast with ties and has a spar on its outer side (fig. 44). The *bukai*, a large rectangular lug sail often used on the lepa and other large boats, has two parallel spars with the upper spar attached at the center to the mast (fig. 45). The *banog binabagan* is a bukai-type sail with a single spar across the top and the lower end pulled to a mouth; it, too, is frequently used on the lepa.

Fig. 44 Banog pindang sail

Fig. 45 Bukai sail

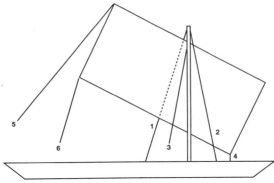

Fig. 46 Sail ropes

Six different ropes are used on the sail, as illustrated in figure 46:

1 *talih-talih* — secures the mast (taruk) aft
2 *tunbilan,* sometimes called *pintal* — secures the mast fore
3 *hambauwan* — raises and lowers the sail on the mast
4 *ingkot boah* — ties the bottom spar to the gunwale
5 *kelat diata* — used for steering
6 *kelat dea* — used for steering

For such a small population, the Tawi-Tawi Sama Dilaut have a great variety of boats. Some of these boats are found among other peoples of Sulu, but not in such great variety.[12] For example, the Sama Dilaut of Sitangkai have only the lepa and the boggo'. The variety of boats among the Tawi-Tawi Sama Dilaut may be partly due to their conservatism as well as their geographic location. They are among the most traditional people in Sulu and have retained features of their culture, including boats, which others have lost. Their location between northern Sulu and Borneo also explains the many boat-types among them. Although most genealogies of the Tawi-Tawi Sama Dilaut reveal kin connections to the Sitangkai Sama Dilaut, some families trace kin ties to Siasi and even Jolo; it is significant that these are the families who make and use the pilang, a boat found among the Sama Dilaut of Siasi and Jolo. Further research among these peoples may reveal that the junkun and birau, boats not found in Sitangkai, are also part of the watercraft traditions of northern Sulu. As noted, the lepa has entered Tawi-Tawi from Borneo via Sitangkai within the memories of some living Sama Dilaut.

Houses

Within the past few years, the Tawi-Tawi Sama Dilaut have built permanent houses in three of their moorages, namely Tungkalang, Lamiun, and Tungbangkao. Although generally inferior in materials and construction, the houses are patterned after those of the land people. They differ mainly in being entirely over the water with no connection to land, whereas most Muslim houses, although built on the beach and surrounded by water at high tide, are connected to land by walkways. The houses at Tungbangkao are generally better constructed than the ones at Tungkalang and Lamiun. Most Bajau do not intend to live in their houses permanently and consequently do not invest a lot of time or money in their construction.

Sama Dilaut houses are built on piles which extend about six feet above the reef floor. The builders work these piles, sharpened on one end, into holes in the reef floor by pushing and pulling them back and forth, until they stand upright. The number of piles for each house ranges from twelve to twenty-five, depending on the size of the house as well as the size of the piles. Atop the piles is attached a framework of handcut boards or poles, roughly the size of two-by-four each, on which the planks or poles that form the floor are secured. Sometimes the walls of the house enclose the entire floor, but more often the dwelling is built on only part of the floor, leaving an uncovered deck area (*pantan*) in front of the house. Sometimes the deck is constructed after the house is built. Many houses are very small, occupying only a corner of the deck. Sizes of houses vary greatly. The largest one at Tungkalang has a floor area of about six by eight meters and a height of about four meters at the gable, while the smallest is only about three-by-four meters and only about one-and-a-half meters at the gable. Such small houses, called kubu-kubu (also the name for the house on the houseboats) are usually temporary structures occupied while the house-boat is being repaired. The framework of the walls and roof is made of either roughly hewn two-by-fours or poles gathered from the forest. The better-con-structed houses have plank walls, although most walls are made of plaited coconut fronds; some have a combination of the two materials, with boards added as they are afforded. Each wall has one or two windows. Two doors may lead to the deck on the larger houses, but only one is found on the smaller ones. The better houses have wooden shutters, whereas the poorer ones have only old rags or mats to pull over the windows at night and during inclement weather. Most roofs are made of palm fronds, but some of the better houses at Tungbangkao have galvanized tin roofs. Some houses have a separate covered cooking area (*kusina*) on the deck, whereas the poorer ones have a cooking area inside the house. At very high tide, the house is only a few centimeters above sea level, but at low tide, two meters may separate the house floor from the water. A ladder (*haronan*), or a pole with notched steps, extends from the deck to the reef floor for entering and leaving the house.

All members of the family utilize the deck. The men use it for drying and repairing fishing nets, cleaning and drying fish, and carpentry work. The women clean and grind cassava, chop firewood, cook, and prepare materials for mat making on the deck, and the children play there during high tide when they cannot go ashore. Some houses of closely related families are connected by planks or boardwalks; however, at none of the three Tawi-Tawi Sama Dilaut moorages are all the houses connected by a maze of boardwalks as in parts of Jolo, Siasi, and Sitangkai.

The interior of the house is usually a single room, but it is sometimes partitioned into two or, more rarely, three rooms. A few of the houses have benches, but most have no furniture. Planks are sometimes placed on the rafters for storage, while fishing nets, tools, and other such items are hung on the walls. The inhabitants sleep directly on the floor, lying on mats only occasionally.

Only six of the seventeen houses at Tungkalang were occupied full-time during my first stay in Tawi-Tawi. The others were abandoned for various reasons. Frequently, after a few months of steady house living, the Sama Dilaut become restless and return to their houseboats. It is not uncommon to see a Sama Dilaut family living in a houseboat tied to their vacated house. In the event of illness or other misfortune, the Sama Dilaut frequently abandon their houses and return to the security of their houseboats. If an adult or an older child of the household dies, the house is abandoned, torn down, or allowed to fall away into the sea; however, some of the materials from the old house are often used for constructing a new one. The Lamiun and Tungbangkao people are more confirmed house dwellers.

It is difficult to determine how long a house lasts since most of them are recent. The temporary houses are not intended to last long and are usually allowed to fall away after they are abandoned within a year. The better-constructed houses probably last many years, with occasional replacement of parts.

5

THE ECONOMIC REALM

At Bongao, fleets of Bajaus [Sama Dilaut] who live wholly in their boats may be seen . . . they live almost entirely upon fish, and are as nearly amphibious as human beings can be. (Phelps Whitmarsh 1901)

Whitmarsh's observation about Sama Dilaut eating habits was as apropos in the 1960s as it was in 1901. Other than cassava and occasional rice and fruits, virtually all their diet comes from the sea. The Sama Dilaut near Semporna reportedly consume more than 200 varieties of fish (*daing*) and over forty varieties of shellfish (Sather 1997, 95). I made no inventory of the fish and shellfish eaten by the Tawi-Tawi Sama Dilaut, but they probably eat comparable quantities. The Sama Dilaut fish the seas for food and they sell their surplus catches for their other needs. All men and many women fish, some almost every day and some only occasionally. The sea and the life within it dictate their technology, shape their social organization, and flavor their worldview.

Earlier writers (Sopher 1977, 218; Taylor 1931, 483) have commented on the allegedly poor fishing techniques of the Sama Dilaut, depicting them as people who spend their lives on the sea, but who, ironically, are poor fishermen. I found no evidence to support this view. Although they cannot compete with the Visayan commercial fishermen in Tawi-Tawi, they nonetheless compare very favorably with the Sama and Tausug fishermen who often told me the Sama Dilaut are the best fishermen in Tawi-Tawi. The following discussion illustrates the versatility of their fishing methods as well as the variety of their catches.

Fishing Cycles

The Sama Dilaut fish the coastal areas (*tebba*), the reefs (*hallo*), and the open sea (*sellang*). Depending on the time of year, the moorage location, and the stages of the moon, these zones are exploited in different ways. In general the Sama Dilaut collect and spearfish along the coasts, net-fish on the reefs, and hook-and line-fish on the open sea.

Most Sama Dilaut engage in several types of fishing as they follow the monthly lunar calendar and the accompanying tides and currents that determine what kinds of fishing are profitable at different places. For example, during the full moon (*bulan allum*), many Sama Dilaut travel to the eastern moorages for the fish attracted to the Biloc-Biloc, Tiji-Tiji, and Basibuli reefs, an area the Sama Dilaut identify as "Bilatan" after the largest island located there.[1] The moorages at Tungbangkao and Lioboran sometimes expand to five or six times their normal population as boats gather for net fishing during this time of month. Ceremonies in these moorages are always scheduled during this period to take advantage of the many visitors. Not every month results in a large movement to the area, but if conditions are optimal for fishing and an important ceremony is scheduled at one of the moorages, many boats congregate. As the moon wanes and the night darkens, other types of fishing become profitable in the Sanga-Sanga moorages, and some Sama Dilaut move to those waters. The moorages in Sanga-Sanga hold their ceremonies during the period of the dark moon (*bulan matai*), when the largest gatherings of boats are found in their waters. Some have come from the Bilatan moorages to sell their full-moon catches in Bongao while others have come to participate in fishing activities. Some fishermen remain in the Sanga-Sanga moorages throughout the year to fish with hook and line in the open sea to the west of Sanga-Sanga island. Basuk and Simalak reefs, surrounding the Tata'an islands, and Takut Mataha reef at the northern entrance to the channel between Tawi-Tawi and Sanga-Sanga islands attract boats for seine net fishing during the time of the new moon (*bulan anak*).[2] In general, more boats travel to the Bilatan waters for fishing than to the Sanga-Sanga waters.

The monsoon seasons contribute to Sama Dilaut fishing cycles also. During the winter monsoons, the calmer waters of the Bilatan reefs attract Sanga-Sanga fishermen when the seas near their home moorages become too turbulent for fishing and sometimes destructive to their houses and houseboats. And during the summer monsoons, many Sama Dilaut from throughout Tawi-Tawi visit the open waters west of Sanga-Sanga for several weeks of shark fishing.

In addition to monthly and seasonal movements to the east and west, most Sama Dilaut families periodically take extended fishing trips to accumulate cash reserves. For the Sama Dilaut from the Sanga-Sanga moorages, these trips consist of two or three months of fishing in the Bilatan waters. The trips of the Bilatan Sama Dilaut are of shorter duration since they live closer to the rich fishing reefs. Families sometimes travel alone for the duration of the trip, but more often they form groups of two, three, or four related families. Following monthly fishing cycles to best exploit fishing grounds, they move throughout the Bilatan waters in their houseboats with fishing boats in tow. Typically, they moor together at night and fish separately during the day except for certain types of fishing when they fish together and divide the catch. Friends and relatives are encountered along the way who sometimes join the family groups for a few days and then go their separate ways. The families occasionally stop at moorages to rest from fishing, visit relatives, and participate in ceremonies.

Fishing is very much a family affair during these trips. The houseboat becomes a fishing boat and all family members participate in fishing. The husband plans and directs the activities, but the wife and children are equally important participants. Many women are very adept at spearing, handling nets, and navigating boats, and children early learn fishing and boating skills. Individual family fishing excursions, especially netting, often demand the participation of all household members. If two or three family boats are traveling together, the men sometimes form fishing crews, but even on these occasions, women and children frequently participate. Cleaning, salting, and drying the catch also involve the entire family—men split and gut the fish, women salt them, and children find drying surfaces for them. At the end of the trip, each family sells its salted fish (*daing toho*) to fish dealers in Tungbangkao or more often in Bongao, where the prices are higher. These extended fishing trips provide the chief cash income for most Sama Dilaut.

The frequency of these trips varies among families. Some who practice agriculture and boatbuilding in the Sanga-Sanga moorages rarely undertake the trips, others may make two a year, and still others may spend a good portion of the year in such travels. Usually at the end of the trip when the family returns to its home moorage, an intensive period of boat maintenance follows. Houseboats are dismantled, cleaned, and repaired. Old nets are mended and new ones woven. Much time is also spent visiting friends and relatives not seen for several months.

Throughout the rest of the year, fishing is primarily for subsistence, especially in the Sanga-Sanga moorages. Most Sama Dilaut fish daily to keep the family in food. During very inclement weather when fishing is impossible, women and children search the nearby reefs for shells and sea slugs if they have no dried fish in reserve. Sama Dilaut rarely buy fish since most are reluctant to spend their cash, which is needed for ceremonies of superincision, marriage, and curing. The nature of Sama Dilaut kin relations insures that if someone has surplus fish, it will be shared with relatives who have none.

Other factors contribute to Sama Dilaut movements and are incorporated into the fishing cycles. Uxorilocal residence is a Sama Dilaut cultural ideal, but in reality residence more often takes the form of ambilocality whereby the family spends time in both the husband's and wife's home moorages, if they are different from one another. Movements from one to the other are usually dictated by fishing cycles and are sometimes monthly as the family moves back and forth between two moorages, locating at each when fishing is best at that site. For those families in the Sanga-Sanga moorages who cultivate gardens, movements are determined by the crop cycle. They remain in the area for planting and initial care of the gardens and then take short fishing trips until the crops are ready to harvest after which they may take an extended fishing trip of several months' duration before returning to prepare their plots for the next crop.

Periodically, Bongao fish dealers recruit Sama Dilaut for fishing trips to Palawan that sometimes last up to three months. These are predominantly male crews, although sometimes women and children accompany them. The men tend to be young and the adventure of the trip is as enticing as the possible financial remuneration. The Sama Dilaut travel to Palawan on the fish dealer's launch with their fishing boats in tow. On arrival, they fish in small groups and sleep and eat on the launch. Sometimes they are paid a prenegotiated price for the fish they catch and at other times, the fish are equally divided among the participants with the launch owner receiving a larger share.

Fishing Magic

Fishing magic is not important to most Sama Dilaut fishermen. Many Sama Dilaut carry anting-anting while fishing, but they are usually carried for general protection and not specifically for success in fishing. Some fishermen, however, believe the amulets bring them luck. One fisherman told me his anting-anting lured fish to his hook and caused sharks to leap into his boat to be slaughtered. In addition, it protected him from outlaws and spirits while he was at sea. However, if someone slept in his boat, the anting-anting was ineffective.

Discontented spirits are sometimes believed responsible for misfortune in fishing. Once, during a long stretch of unsuccessful fishing at the moorage of Tungkalang, several djin (shamans) decided that saitan (spirits) were responsible for the shortage of fish and they held a ceremony to appease them. On another occasion, the death of a man killed while dynamiting fish was attributed to a saitan believed to reside in a large fish known to frequent the waters where the accident occurred.

If Sama Dilaut fish near beaches or islets believed inhabited by saitan, they sometimes leave small offerings of betel nut, cigarettes, rice, cassava, or small flags to placate the spirits who might otherwise be offended by their presence. Some men believe the songs sung during shark fishing are essential to attract the sharks.

Most Sama Dilaut know, however, that success in fishing depends on time-tested procedures which must be followed. Even men who utilize magical or ritual aids know they are useless without the practical application of their fishing knowledge.

Fishing Nets

Two types of fishing nets are used by the Sama Dilaut, namely cotton twine, handwoven drift nets called *linggi* and *salibut*, and commercially-made nylon seine nets called *sinsoro*.[3] The cotton twine nets are the traditional nets of the Sama Dilaut while the sinsoro are recent introductions.

An old fisherman told me the following story about the origin of the handwoven nets. Long ago when the Sama Dilaut lived at Johore (a homeland that appears frequently in Sama Dilaut origin stories), they made sennit twine from the fibrous bark of certain trees. One night a man accidentally dropped a wadded bunch of twine overboard. When he awakened the next morning, he discovered a school of *bakit* (a favorite fish of the Sama Dilaut) entangled in the discarded twine. He saw the usefulness of the wadded twine and the Sama Dilaut have made nets for fishing ever since.

The Sama Dilaut presently use cotton twine for weaving the driftnets, but many old people remember when sennit was used for making the nets. The men gathered the bark from forest trees, the women made it into sennit and the men wove it into nets. Within Sulu, handwoven driftnets are associated with the Sama Dilaut of Tawi-Tawi (especially the Bilatan moorages), Sitangkai, and Semporna, all of whom are related by kin ties and live near extensive reefs, the environment the fishermen most successfully exploit with driftnets. To my knowledge, other people of the Sulu archipelago do not make driftnets.

The men weave the nets from cotton twine purchased in Bongao.[4] Using their toes to hold the completed section of the net, they sit as they weave, measuring the mesh with the thickness of their fingers and tying each individually (fig. 47). The size of the mesh varies; the salibut net is designed for small fish and has smaller mesh than the linggi, which is intended for large fish. The width of nets ranges from one to two meters to accommodate different depths while the length may be as long as fifteen meters. Ropes at either end of the nets are used to tie them together if greater length is needed. The net is attached to rope headlines and footlines. Pieces of tree limbs, about five centimeters in diameter and about two-and-a-half centimeters long, are attached with rattan through holes drilled in their centers to the headline at about ten-centimeter intervals to serve as floats. Seashells, usually cowries, are perforated and attached to the footline at similar intervals to serve as weights. Generally, a man has three or four such nets of various mesh sizes, widths, and lengths. Like all

Fig. 47 Repairing salibut   Fig. 48 Aneba to'oging fishing
         fishing nets

fishing gear, the nets are owned by individual fishermen. Keeping the nets in proper repair is a constant job when they are used frequently. A man may fish all morning, dry his nets when he returns home, and spend the rest of the afternoon and evening mending them. Frequently, when a man awakens at night, he works an hour or so mending his nets by the feeble kerosene lamp before returning to sleep. If repairs are extensive, the new section is always boiled in seawater—as are new nets—before the net is used. The Sama Dilaut claim the boiling water strengthens the twine and prevents it from rotting. The floats are replaced periodically as old ones lose buoyancy. Nets are always dried after use, rolled into bundles and stored along the sides of the houseboat interior. House dwellers usually store their nets on ceiling rafters. At the end of my fieldwork in the 1960s, commercially made nylon gill nets were beginning to appear in Tawi-Tawi. Because of their expense, few Sama Dilaut owned them. They were, however, considered superior to the traditional cotton twine nets because they are more durable and need not be dried after each use. They will probably eventually replace the handwoven cotton twine nets.

The other net used by Sama Dilaut fishermen is the sinsoro, a commercially made seine net introduced to Tawi-Tawi in relatively recent years. Made of closely woven nylon mesh resembling screen wire and usually dark green in color, the sinsoro are about a meter wide and often reach lengths of twenty-five meters. Sometimes two lengths are sewn together to increase their widths. The wooden floats and shell weights used on the cotton twine nets are also used on the sinsoro, although sometimes lead pieces serve as weights. Like the nylon gill nets, the sinsoro demand much less maintenance than the cotton twine nets. The sinsoro nets are used primarily for catching *pinatai*, an anchovy-like fish used in the popular fish paste found throughout the Philippines. The sinsoro is considerably more expensive than the cotton twine nets. A large sinsoro may cost as much as 150 pesos, while the twine needed to weave a cotton twine net can be purchased for about twenty pesos. Consequently, probably no more than a quarter of the Sama Dilaut who use sinsoro own them; most use nets provided by fish dealers in Bongao or Tungbangkao. For use of the nets, the Sama Dilaut agree to sell a portion of their catch to the fish buyers at a predetermined price, always below market prices. After they have fulfilled the terms of their agreement, they are sometimes allowed to keep the nets, which, however, are frequently quite worn by then. Most Sama Dilaut avoid these contracts, which they feel are exploitative, and either buy their own nets or do not engage in sinsoro fishing.

Types of Fishing

Aneba Fishing The largest group-fishing activity of the Tawi-Tawi Sama Dilaut is a type of driftnet fishing called *aneba to'oging*.[5] This sometimes attracts as many as seventy-five boats to the reefs surrounding Tungbangkao (fig. 48).[6] Aneba to'oging fishing is practiced in the daytime during the receding neap tides at half-moon and three-quarters moon, a time called *tahi a'dikit* ("little sea water"), when a fish called to'oging feeds on the reefs in large schools. Only a few days of the month are suitable for aneba to'oging fishing. Some say this fishing is best done when a light wind ripples the surface to allow the fishermen to see the to'oging as they swim near the surface of the sea. Since certain conditions are necessary for a successful aneba, such as wind, no rain, and sufficient men to participate, several months may pass before all conditions are met and an aneba is organized. When conditions are favorable, a leader, or *nakura*, spreads word that an aneba is being formed. The boats gather at the edge of the moorage where the nakura discusses with other fishermen the best route to follow. As in all net fishing, the lepa and other outriggerless boats are preferred since the nets can be more easily handled over their sides. Generally the route pursued is circular around the moorage of Tungbangkao. An aneba I joined began to the west of Tungbangkao and moved south and counter-clockwise around the moorage and returned to the spot from which we departed. The fishing demands at least two people in a boat, usually adult men, but occasionally women and children participate. The boats travel single file from reef to reef led by the nakura. When a school of fish is spotted, they move into a horseshoe-like formation to enclose the fish as the fishermen shout, beat the sides of their boats with oars, and splash the water with poles to drive the fish into the horseshoe. At the appropriate time, as signaled by the nakura, the boats form a complete circle and move closer together. Then the nakura signals them to drop their nets into the water to entrap the fish. A man jumps from each boat to handle the nets as a second unravels more nets into the water while a third (often a woman or child) steers the boat. If the boat has only a two-man crew, the man in the boat assumes the third position. As the fish attempt to escape they become entangled in the nets, which the fishermen pull in to harvest. Sometimes the nets are tossed back for a second catch. When the area is depleted of fish, the flotilla moves on to the next reef. The longest trip I participated in lasted seven hours and we lowered our nets eleven times. If weather and tidal conditions are favorable and the catches good, the boats sometimes stay out two or three days visiting reefs some distance from the moorage, such as those around Manuk Mangka.[7] After the final catch, the boats gather at the edge of the moorage where the nakura and his assistants supervise the equal division of the fish among all the fishermen. Children who participated are given half-shares.[8] A good deal of joking and mock quarreling takes place during the division, but serious disagreements seldom occur. Catches vary greatly, of course, depending on conditions, but during the above-mentioned drive with eleven stops, we caught about 2,500 fish. Although the fishermen were pleased with the catch, many said they had participated in more successful aneba.

When the boats return to Tungbangkao, they are greeted by the resident fish dealers who offer to buy the fish. Most Sama Dilaut, however, prefer to sell their fish in Bongao where they bring higher prices. Fish are dried either with or without salt. If prepared for sale they are always salted, but if prepared for home consumption, salt is usually not used. Fish are gutted and if not large they are simply sliced at the belly to the backbone and flattened. Larger fish are split lengthwise into three sections, salt is rubbed into their flesh, and they are dried in the sun. Less commonly, fish are soaked in salty brine before drying. The roof of the houseboat, decks of houses, and any other available surfaces serve as drying racks.

The Tawi-Tawi Sama Dilaut more commonly practice another type of aneba fishing involving only three or four boats. This type of fishing is frequently practiced during the extended fishing trips of families. When fish are spotted on the reef, nets are dropped to form a large half-circle around them. Rattan vines are attached to the nets at either end of the half-circle. Men, women, and children beat the sides of their boats, splash the water, and shout to frighten the fish toward the nets. As the nets are pulled to encircle the fish, the fishermen spear them and sometimes jump into the water to harvest them from the nets. When the area is depleted, the boats move to other parts of the reef to repeat the procedure. At the end of the day, the fish are equally divided among participants.

The Sama Dilaut sometimes use the poisonous root of a plant called *tua* with driftnet fishing.[9] The root is collected from the island interiors of Tawi-Tawi and Sanga-Sanga or purchased from vendors in Bongao. Occasionally land dwellers provide the root to the Sama Dilaut in exchange for a portion of their catches. When fish are spotted among the coral heads, the fishermen encircle them with driftnets. They then beat the tua to a pulp, spread it among the coral heads and wait for it to act. Within minutes, the poison stupefies the fish and as they drift to the surface or dart into the nets, the fishermen collect them. I once saw fishermen catch a school of over 200 medium-sized fish using tua. The poison is not fatal to the fish and does not render them inedible; if fish remain in the water, they eventually recover.

Occasionally, very impromptu netting occurs in the moorage. Several times during my fieldwork, someone in the moorage spotted a school of fish in nearby waters. Word spread among the mooragers, and men, women, and children quickly threw nets into fishing boats and rushed to the spot. They poled their boats to encircle the fish and tossed their nets into the water to entrap them. The catch was divided equally among the participants. Such impromptu nettings are usually less rewarding than the organized ones, but once I saw a dozen men net about 100 fish during impromptu netting.

Anoha Fishing Anoha fishing, using sinsoro nets, is typically done with two or three boats, usually with two people in a boat who are often members of the same household, such as a man and his teenage son, a man and his wife, or a man and his elderly father. "Anoha" means "to pole," as boats are poled through the shallow reef waters by men standing at the prows. During the full moon as well as the dark moon, anoha fishermen leave the moorage for fishing on the receding tide. As in aneba fishing, boats without outriggers are preferred so the nets can be easily raised and lowered from the sides. One man stands at the prow to pole the boat through the shallow sandy-bottomed waters while another, frequently a woman or an elderly man, sits at the back with a steering

Fig. 49 Anoha fishing with sinsoro nets

89

paddle as they move from reef to reef in search of pinatai (anchovies). When a school is spotted, the net is lowered over the sides as the paddler at the stern handles the boat. The other boats lower their nets to form a horseshoe-like enclosure, perhaps eighteen meters in diameter. Two men enter the water to hold the nets at the mouth of the enclosure. Other men wade in the water to position the nets and to untangle them from coral on the reef floor. As the two men at the opening pull the nets to diminish the enclosure, the other men splash the water with poles to frighten the fish toward the closed end of the horseshoe. The two men at the opening continue to pull until only a small circle of net encloses the entrapped fish. A third man pulls the undersides of the net together to further entrap the fish (fig. 49). The net is then lifted and the netted fish are dumped into one of the boats where they are packed in five-gallon tins with a small amount of seawater and salt. The nets are then pulled from the water and positioned in the boat so they can be easily lowered again. The fishermen move on to the next reef and the procedure is repeated. On a good day, fishermen may get as many as fifty five-gallon tins of pinatai; one man told me he was once with a group that caught 200 tins of pinatai. This type of fishing is also practiced at night during the period of dark moon with lanterns.

Magsaut Fishing A few Tawi-Tawi Sama Dilaut practice a type of liftnet fishing on the Bilatan reefs called magsaut. It is much more commonly practiced on the Sibutu reefs, and I was told the Sitangkai Sama Dilaut introduced it to Tawi-Tawi. Such may be the case since the man who organized the two magsaut I witnessed was originally from Sitangkai.[10] Liftnet fishing is widespread in the Philippines, especially in the central islands where it is called *basnig* (Spoehr 1980, 75).

Like aneba fishing, magsaut requires the coordinated efforts of several boats, but unlike aneba fishing, it is practiced at night. I was told magsaut is most successful during the dark hours of the nights between the twentieth and the eighth moons, when the sea is calm with no wind or wave action. In Sitangkai, I once saw fifty boats participate in this type of fishing, but in Tawi-Tawi, twenty was the largest number I ever saw.

The owner of the magsaut net plans the fishing expedition and acts as nakura, or leader. Anyone who wishes to join may do so. The boats planning to participate gather at the edge of the moorage in the late afternoon and sail together to the fishing grounds. As in all Sama Dilaut fishing, the crews are kinsmen, frequently husband and wife or other combinations of household members so the catches need not be divided. When the tide is appropriately high and the night dark, usually around midnight, the fishing equipment is readied. The equipment consists of the magsaut net, small rafts (*ontang*) and pressurized lanterns. Prior to the introduction of pressurized kerosene lanterns, torches made from tightly woven coconut fronds and other wood were used for night fishing. The net is made of several strips of sinsoro net sewn together to form approximately nine square meters. Poles, also about nine meters long, are attached to the top and bottom of the square and, when not in use, the net is rolled around them for storage. The raft consists of two bamboo floats about a meter long connected by two bow-shaped booms that support a small platform about half a square meter. The nakura decides when it is time to begin fishing and lights several pressurized lanterns to provide illumination. Two lepa are secured together by two poles, about nine meters long, attached to their prows and sterns. The magsaut net is then unrolled and stretched between the two lepa. Smaller boats attach poles, also about nine meters long, to the unsupported sides of the net so that all four sides of the magsaut net are supported. Anchors (usually coral weights) are secured to each corner of the net, after which it is submerged. Attached to a raft, a pressurized lantern is shaded to reflect light into the water to attract fish. With a long pole, the raft is directed over the center of the submerged net between the two lepa. When fish are attracted to the lantern, the net is lifted and the entrapped fish are harvested. Meanwhile, other boats have taken other illuminated rafts into the surrounding waters to find fish. The net is submerged again and throughout the night, fishermen bring schools of fish attracted to their lanterns over the net to be harvested. The boat that brings in the fish keeps most of the catch, but must pay the nakura a sum agreed upon (one peso and ten centavos per basket of fish was the price during both times I observed magsaut fishing). In addition, the nakura takes a share of the catch. The fishing continues until the waters are depleted or it becomes light.

Catches vary, but are frequently considerable. During the first magsaut I accompanied, each time the net was lifted it contained about two bushels of fish. The net was raised ten times for a total of twenty bushels of fish. During the second night, however, we only harvested about six bushels. In the early morning the boats return to Tungbangkao, the fish are sold to fish dealers (or salted to sell in Bongao), and the fishermen pay the nakura from their earnings. In addition to the money he receives from other fishermen, the nakura makes money from his share of the catch. His initial cash outlay for the magsaut net is significant, but once his investment is paid off, his income can be considerable. In Sitangkai, Chinese fish dealers sometimes supply the nets, but in Tawi-Tawi Sama Dilaut fishermen owned them. Magsaut fishing is very important in the Sitangkai economy (where it is frequently practiced with explosives), but it is less so in Tawi-Tawi. The rapid depletion of the Tawi-Tawi reefs will probably prevent it from ever becoming too firmly established there.

Spear Fishing Spear fishing (*ahiah*) at night with pressurized lanterns is practiced during the periods of dark moon at both high and low tides along the coastal areas and on the reefs. It is less commonly practiced during the daytime. High tide attracts fish for feeding on normally exposed reefs, whereas low tide makes reefs normally covered with deep water more accessible. For good spear fishing, the sea must be calm with little wind; otherwise, ripples on the water's surface prevent the spearer from easily seeing his prey. The spear used in this type of fishing is about two-and-a-half meters long, with a detachable barbed trident called *salubang*. A fisherman usually has several salubang of different sizes suitable for different kinds of fish that he changes during the course of the night. Standard-sized salubang are purchased in the Bongao marketplace, but if a fisherman wants a special size, he carves a model in wood for a blacksmith to copy.

At least two people participate in spear fishing—the fisherman and a paddler/steersman. The fisherman needs assistance with the boat as well as companionship during the dark hours that are believed by many to be dangerous because of potential encounters with outlaws and malevolent spirits. Frequently, a man fishes with his wife or young son, a preferred arrangement since then he need not divide the catch. Not uncommonly, small children accompany their parents and sleep under makeshift shelters during most of the outing. Often an elderly man, or less commonly an elderly woman, acts as steersman. Teenage boys sometimes fish together, especially if they think teenage girls may be fishing nearby.

When the fishing grounds are reached, a pressurized lantern is lighted and secured to the prow of the boat where the fisherman stands, using his spear to pole the boat through the shallow reef waters as he calls directions to the paddler in the stern. Sometimes they trade positions during the night. The lantern illuminates the reef floor and as fish appear, the fisherman spears them. If conditions are good, a popular fishing spot may be visited by dozens of boats. Friends and relatives fish together and converse as they search the reef waters for fish. Paddlers often sing to help pass the time and periodically, the fishermen rest to smoke cigarettes or eat snacks. During a good night, a fisherman may spear two- to three-dozen fish, but on a less successful night, he may return home with only enough small fish for the children's morning meal.

Amissi Fishing The deep waters of the open sea to the west of Sanga-Sanga island are a favorite fishing ground for hook-and-line (*amissi*) fishermen. This type of fishing is practiced almost exclusively by Sama Dilaut from Tungkalang, Lu'uk Tulai and Lamiun who do not use the driftnets typical of the reef-based moorages of Tungbangkao and Lioboran. I have seen as many as eighteen boats engaged in this type of fishing in the waters west of Tungkalang. Amissi fishing is usually done by two men in a boat, each with his own line, with other men fishing nearby. The only gear used is a nylon line with a hook or sometimes several hooks placed at intervals on the line that is unwound from a spool into the water. Squid and small fish are used as bait, although sometimes no bait is used. Most amissi fishing takes place in the daytime, when currents and sea conditions are favorable. Late afternoon and early evening are favorite times, although nighttime fishing with lanterns is also undertaken. During occasional long waiting periods, the men often sing to pass the time. Some fishermen sell their catches to fish dealers in Bongao who sometimes supply their hooks, lines, and even bait. Although not as spectacular as some of the catches from nets, amissi fishing provides many fishermen with decent incomes. The fish caught are often large—ten kilograms is not unusual—and a fisherman may catch several such fish in a day. If the fisherman has no commitments to fish dealers, he peddles his surplus fish in a nearby land village or salts them for future sale to fish dealers in Bongao. Amissi fishermen are among the most sedentary members of the moorage and frequently cultivate gardens on nearby Sanga-Sanga Island.

Pana Fishing Some fishermen use a spear gun, or *pana*, for underwater fishing (fig. 50). All men I knew who used this method were from the Sanga-Sanga moorages and traced their ancestry to Siasi and Jolo, where the spear gun is commonly used. Those Sama Dilaut who practice net fishing on the Bilatan reefs use the pana less often.

Fig. 50 Pana fisherman

The spear gun is carved like a rifle stock with a top groove for a metal spear. Sturdy rubber bands (made from inner tubes of tires) originating from the gun point are stretched backward and locked into the notches in the shaft.

Barbed steel spears, sometimes as long as one and a half meters, are placed in the barrel and cocked into firing position by stretching the rubber band over the spear butt. A trigger releases the spear. Goggles, called *tipara*, are usually worn when diving with the pana. The frames are carved from wood, any available glass is used for lenses, and a string tied around the head secures them in place.

Individual fishermen sometimes pana-fish alone, but more typically two men fish together and take turns paddling and diving. Sometimes a wife, a young son, or an elderly father accompanies the fisherman to serve as paddler. Pana fishing is practiced during high tide in water no more than two to three meters deep. The paddler sits at the stern as the fisherman at the prow scans the sea floor for suitable prey. Like many fishermen who dive, he often removes his clothes so he can swim more freely. Before entering the water, he wets his face and secures his goggles in place. After inhaling and exhaling deeply several times, he fills his lungs with air and places his head under water as he directs the paddler with his arms. When he sees suitable fish, he slips overboard with his cocked pana. When he is within firing range, the fisherman fires and if successful, spears the fish. The spear is attached to the gun by a long cord so it can be easily retrieved. Pana fishing is sometimes practiced at night with a pressurized lantern secured to the prow of the boat to illuminate the sea floor.

A fisherman told me that in a good day of pana fishing, he could catch as many as twenty-five fish. The men I accompanied, however, usually caught eight or ten fish. But since fish acquired in this fashion are often quite large, this is a good day's catch. It is obviously a successful method of fishing since some men rely on it almost exclusively for their fish needs.

Shark Fishing Shark fishing (*anangkalia*) is the most dangerous of all Sama Dilaut fishing (fig. 51). I knew several men who lost fingers, hands, and even arms during encounters with sharks. Occasionally, some are killed. Sama Dilaut claim the best time for shark fishing is during the southeast monsoon, when high tide currents are strong and swells are high. The deep waters west of Tungkalang and Lu'uk Tulai are popular shark-fishing spots and attract Sama Dilaut from throughout Tawi-Tawi. The equipment needed for shark fishing is a shark hook, a shark rattle, and a wooden club. The shark hook is a large steel hook about twenty-five centimeters long purchased from local blacksmiths. The shark rattle, *bohehtna*, has a bamboo pole handle about one-and-a-half meters long. The base of the pole is split to a length of about half a meter. Rattan is tied around the pole to prevent the split from extending further. A stick, about half a meter long, is passed through the centers of six coconut half-shells and secured between the split ends of the pole, forming a triangular base. The base of the pole is submerged in the water and shaken up and down to simulate the presence of fish. The wooden club is a crudely made wooden bat used for killing the shark once it is hooked.

Shark fishing is typically done by one man, perhaps assisted by his son or an older male relative. Wives occasionally accompany their husbands. If fishing by himself in his own boat, the fisherman is always with others, usually relatives, fishing nearby. Not only do the others provide company, but they also offer assistance if needed. En route to the shark waters, the fisherman obtains fresh bait by spearing in the shallow reef waters. Even if he is unable to hook

Fig. 51 Shark fishermen

a shark, he usually catches enough fish for the evening meal. Upon reaching the fishing grounds, often by sail, the fisherman scans the waters for sharks. He baits his hook and secures it to a rope about three meters long that is fastened to the boat and cast into the sea. Such a hook and line is sometimes cast at either end of the boat. When the hook is overboard, the fisherman shakes the rattle in the water as he sings dirge-like shark songs (*kalangan kalitan*) to attract the sharks. Many men claim the songs have no magical qualities and are used only because it is traditional to do so; nonetheless, few Sama Dilaut fish for sharks without singing the songs. It is significant that musical, magical fishing aids of this sort are used only in shark fishing, the most dangerous of all Sama Dilaut fishing.

Before long a shark usually appears, revealing itself by its fin. When it takes the bait, the fisherman pulls it to the boat, spears it, and clubs it to death, and then loads it into the boat. The activity sometimes attracts other sharks, and the fisherman must hurry to retrieve the carcass before they attack it.

If successful in catching a shark, a fisherman can make a substantial profit from his efforts. A good eating shark, two meters long, may sell for as much as twenty pesos to Bongao vendors. A less desirable shark, however, may bring no more than five pesos. If the fisherman butchers the shark and sells its parts in a nearby village, he can make more money. Tawi-Tawi people consider the liver a delicacy and the fins always have a ready market with the Chinese population in Bongao. Some men shark-fish each day when conditions allow, and earn good incomes during the season. Others are less motivated and fish only during breaks from the activities that normally dominate their days. The excitement of the beginning season usually attracts many fishermen to the Sanga-Sanga waters, but as the season progresses and success wanes, fewer men participate.

Pahi Hunting The giant stingray (*Dasyatis centroura*), or *pahi*, is occasionally sought by Sama Dilaut fishermen. The waters around Sanga Siapu island and Bilatan are favorite spots for hunting pahi. The pahi tends to skim the surface of the sea and consequently, periods of calm seas and weak currents are best for spotting it. Two or three boats with at least two men in each typically participate in pahi hunts. After reaching waters frequented by pahi, the boats separate as the men scan the waters for movements that reveal the fish's presence. When one is sighted, a call is sounded and all the boats rush to the site. The man who reaches the pahi first throws a harpoon, a pole about two meters long shoved into the socket of a barbed, detachable gig called *nihiak pahi*, about twenty-five centimeters long. The gig is attached to a rope tied to the boat. If successful, the gig is embedded in the pahi which, as it tries to escape often pulls the boat with it, and sometimes attempts to dive and capsizes the boat. The fishermen are careful to avoid the pahi's barbed tail for it can inflict considerable pain as it thrashes in the water. When it tires, the boats close in and the men complete the kill with additional spears. The catch is butchered and divided equally among participants. What cannot be consumed or sold immediately is salted and later sold to fish dealers in Bongao. Pahi are not sought as intensively as sharks, but at times they significantly dominate Sama Dilaut fishing activities. The hunts are often spontaneous. Someone in the moorage may spot a pahi in nearby waters and quickly organize a group to pursue it. Pahi hunting, however, is frequently unrewarding. Several times I accompanied Sama Dilaut on hunts of six- and eight-hours duration, during which we spotted several pahi but were unable to catch a single one.

Explosives Although much more widely used by land-dwelling fishermen, explosives (*timbak*) are used by some Sama Dilaut fishermen. This method is extremely dangerous and most Sama Dilaut are afraid to use it. During my fieldwork, explosives killed two Sama Dilaut fishermen and I knew several others who lost fingers, hands, and arms from timbak accidents. Although illegal for fishing, explosives are widely used in Tawi-Tawi and are readily available despite the futile (and usually feeble) efforts of local law-enforcement officers to enforce the ban.

The explosive is placed in a beer or soft drink bottle with waterproof paper packed around an extended fuse. When a school of fish is spotted, the fisherman lights the fuse and throws the bottle into the school. The fish killed by the explosion are then speared and collected by divers. The sound usually attracts other fishermen to the area to share the catch, although the man who tossed the explosive always takes the choice fish. Acquiring fish by explosives is often quite rewarding. Once I was fishing with Sama Dilaut friends when we heard a blast from a nearby Tausug fishing crew. We rushed to participate in the catch, and the share we were allowed to keep amounted to forty-eight good-sized tuna. The men who exploded the charge, of course, claimed even more. Besides the risk of personal injury or death, explosives are extremely destructive to the reef since they destroy practically all life where they are used. Even in the mid-1960s, certain fishing grounds had become sterile because of extensive use of explosives. The reef destruction has grown considerably in more recent years.

Kamun Trapping One of the most delicious of Sulu's seafoods is a reef-dwelling crustacean called kamun *(Squilla sp.)*. Light pink in color, it is about twenty centimeters long, with large front claws and smaller legs the length of its body. Certain reefs are known as the habitat of the kamun, and Sama Dilaut fishermen in the Bilatan moorages, especially boys, periodically visit these reefs at low tide to catch the animal. The kamun lives in the natural holes of the reef floor, and a male and female are usually found together. Fishermen prepare a special baited noose attached to a pole that is stuck into the kamun hole. When the bait is taken, the pole moves to spring the noose and catch the kamun's head and claws. The fisherman then pulls it out of the hole. The male is always caught first and usually the female is reluctant to take the proffered bait after her mate has disappeared. While waiting for the kamun to take the bait, the fishermen sing kamun songs (*kalangan kamun*).

Dolphin Fishing Although not important in their diets, the Sama Dilaut occasionally harpoon dolphins (*ebbung* or *sapid dilaut*, "cow of the sea"). I never heard of expeditions organized to seek dolphins, but if they are near Sama Dilaut fishing grounds or approach boats, they are sometimes harpooned with the same spear used for pahi. Only twice during my fieldwork did Sama Dilaut fishermen catch dolphins. They were butchered and sold to other Sama Dilaut and eaten as a special treat. The Muslim people of Sulu do not eat dolphins.

Lauwani-Lauwani Some Sama Dilaut practice lauwani-lauwani, a fishing technique utilizing an ontang, the same raft used in magsaut fishing. The raft is towed behind a houseboat or fishing boat on a rope about eight meters long. Lines with baited or unbaited hooks are secured along the towrope. Periodically, someone paddles the length of the towrope in a small boat to collect the catch and, if necessary, rebait the hooks. I knew no Sama Dilaut who undertook excursions in order to practice this type of fishing. Rather, all such fishing I observed was incidental to some other journey.

Fish Traps The Sama Dilaut use two types of fish traps made of loosely woven rattan. One is rectangular in shape, called *togong* or *bobu*, and varies in size from about a half-meter deep by about a half-meter wide, with lengths ranging from one to two meters (fig. 37). The second type, *panggal*, is circular in shape. The size of this trap varies also, but it is typically one-and-a-half meters in diameter and half a meter deep. Both traps have funnel-like openings that allow easy entry for the fish, but make escape difficult. The traps are placed in shallow water and secured in position. The fisherman periodically pulls them up to check for fish and then replaces them. Sometimes schools of fish are driven into the traps. Not all Sama Dilaut use traps, but they are fairly widespread.

Economics of Fishing

The income a fisherman derives from fishing depends on his initiative, his skill, the location of his moorage, the amount of time he spends fishing, and weather conditions. No Sama Dilaut are truly subsistence fishermen since all of them periodically sell fish for cash. Incomes from fishing, however, vary greatly. Some men fish only enough to meet basic needs whereas others fish to accumulate capital to advance their wealth. Some men are very skilled fishermen with a sophisticated understanding of marine environments whereas others are less knowledgeable. In general, the Bilatan moorages enjoy greater catches than the Sanga-Sanga moorages and, consequently, those Sama Dilaut who live full time in Bilatan tend to profit more from fishing. But whatever the skill of the fisherman and wherever he lives, weather conditions are obviously critical to success. A month of bad weather results in poor catches for even the most motivated, skilled fisherman living on the rich reefs of Bilatan.

Large catches are sold fresh or salted to fish dealers in Tungbangkao or Bongao. Most Sama Dilaut prefer to sell in Bongao, where prices are higher. Prices vary with supply. In late January 1966, Tungbangkao fish buyers paid twenty-five centavos per kilo for fresh, cleaned fish and fifty centavos per kilo for dried, salted fish. Bongao buyers were paying thirty-five centavos per kilo for fresh fish and sixty centavos per kilo for dried, salted fish.

It is difficult to generalize about monthly earnings from fishing since they vary so greatly depending on the factors discussed above. The monthly earnings of sixteen different men from November 1965 to March 1966 ranged from twenty pesos to 200 pesos, with a median earning of seventy pesos. At this time, a pubic schoolteacher in Tawi-Tawi made about 200 pesos a month; the exchange rate was about four pesos to one US dollar.

Anoha fishing is sometimes very profitable and if a man has a good night of fishing, he can increase his monthly income considerably. On an exceptionally good night, a fishing crew can catch up to 200 five-gallon cans of pinatai. More typically, however, a good night results in about twenty cans. The price per can varies by the season. During my stay, prices ranged from one-and-a-half pesos to three-and-a-half pesos per can, with an average of about three pesos. However if a fisherman uses the nets, salt, and cans of a fish dealer, he may receive no more than one peso per can under the terms of the contract. Or if he sells his catch to dealers in Tungbangkao, he will receive less than if he sells it in Bongao. The independent fisherman must buy his own nets, which will cost him about 200 pesos, and he must also buy his own salt. In addition, he must make some arrangement for acquiring the cans for packing the fish. Nonetheless, in the long run, the independent fisherman is better off. Since he has the greater investment in anoha fishing, he tends to practice it more frequently than fishermen who have contracts with fish dealers. Several Bilatan Sama Dilaut who regularly practice anoha are quite affluent by Tawi-Tawi standards.

Wives generally handle the family finances, although both husband and wife discuss expenditures before they are made. Gold jewelry is sometimes purchased with surplus cash and serves as family savings to be sold when funds are needed.

Collecting

Collecting from the exposed reefs is an important supplement to the Sama Dilaut diet and income. Collecting is most important in the Bilatan moorages where the largest reefs are located. While men are fishing, women and children search the reefs especially during the low tides of the full moon for edible crustaceans, shells, and seaweed. If the seas are too turbulent for fishing, or if the husband is ill and cannot fish, or if he is busy with some nonfishing activity such as boatbuilding, the collecting activities of the women and children may provide the only protein for the family meals. The edible crustaceans, shells, and sea slugs are less desirable food for most Sama Dilaut, but they provide important emergency food. At Bilatan, during days when the low tide fills most of the daylight hours, men and especially boys sometimes go to the reefs in small boats on the receding tide and spend the low tide searching tidal pools for fish and other marine life. In addition to supplementing the family diet, some collecting activities add to the family income. Shells, *beche de mer*, and certain seaweed are cleaned, dried, and sold to local buyers.

Periodically, groups of closely related women spend several hours walking the beaches and nearby coastal areas in search of firewood. And when men go to the island interiors in search of trees for boatbuilding or to tend gardens, they usually return with a load of firewood on their backs.

Certain plants that grow wild in the forests are collected for medicinal and culinary uses. Men collect bark from the gelum tree for caulking boats, while tua is collected for fish poisoning. The eggs of the *tambun* bird, buried in loose soil in the forest, are sometimes dug up and eaten by the Sama Dilaut. Turtle eggs are also collected to eat or sell when nests are found on beaches.

Gardening

Some Sama Dilaut families cultivate small plots of land leased to them by land-dwelling Sama on Sanga-Sanga Island and Tawi-Tawi Island.[11] The lease sometimes continues through several generations. Occasionally the Sama Dilaut are allowed to use uncleared land without payment if they clear it, with the understanding that it will revert to the owner at a specified date. More often, they are required to give a portion of their crops to the owner or to provide him fish at a price lower than they would normally receive. Sometimes they are permitted to use the land only if they plant some of it to coconuts, which then become the property of the landowner. Occasionally an unscrupulous landowner will renege on his promise and cheat the Sama Dilaut of their agricultural labors, but generally the agreement is fulfilled on both sides. I knew only two Sama Dilaut men who claimed ownership to the land they cultivated; however, neither had a deed to the land. Sama Dilaut land is almost always marginal farming land but suitable for cassava, which is the most common crop they grow.

The dry, rocky islands of the Bilatan area are unsuitable for any agriculture except copra production; consequently, if these Sama Dilaut want to cultivate crops they must go to the more fertile islands of Sanga-Sanga and Tawi-Tawi. Some Bilatan families spend several months of the year in the Sanga-Sanga area where they cultivate gardens during the southwest monsoon. However, most Bilatan Sama Dilaut do not cultivate gardens; they obtain their fruits and vegetables from Tawi-Tawi farmers, usually by bartering fish.

The Sama Dilaut in the Sanga-Sanga moorages of Tungkalang and Lu'uk Tulai are the most confirmed gardeners. Although some of these families garden throughout the year, they are nonetheless primarily fishermen. Many of them garden a few months, spend a few months fishing at Bilatan, and then return to Sanga-Sanga to replant their gardens. No Sama Dilaut subsist on gardening alone, although several boatbuilders at Tungkalang engage in almost no fishing and live on the income of boatbuilding and the produce of their gardens.

Sama Dilaut gardens are small, generally about an eighth of an acre, and within easy walking distance of the moorages. After selecting a garden site, the Sama Dilaut family first cuts away the growth, allows it to dry, burns it off—if no fruit trees will be harmed by the fire—and then clears away the charred remains. Only enough ground is broken to plant the seeds and/or seedlings. Most gardens are planted almost entirely to cassava, although sugar cane and bananas are sometimes grown. A few families occasionally plant dry rice, papayas, squash, maize, onions, peppers and other spices. Almost all gardening is at subsistence level, but surplus crops are sometimes sold to other Sama Dilaut or less often to the Bongao market. Some gardens have small rest houses that provide respite from the sun and rain when it is necessary to spend the entire day in the garden; these are very simple structures consisting of only a thatched roof supported by poles. Some land-dwelling farmers construct fences around their gardens to keep out wild pigs, but the Sama Dilaut seldom take this precaution. Some gardens are separated from one another by underbrush and trees but are connected by the many trails that wind through the forest.

Fig. 52 Preparing cassava

Most crops require little attention after they are planted, with cassava (*pang'gih kayu*) being perhaps the easiest to grow. When a cassava plant is harvested, a piece of stem is placed in the loosened ground and within a few months it is ready to harvest. As a result, a garden always has cassava in various stages of maturity and it is harvested the year round. The bitter white variety of cassava (*Manihot esculenta*) is most commonly grown by the Sama Dilaut and is their carbohydrate staple. After the mature tubers are harvested, they are taken to the moorage where they are peeled, dried in the sun, ground to a fine pulp, and placed in a burlap bag or old cloth (fig. 52). The bitter juices are then squeezed out of the pulp, after which it must sit overnight before being cooked. If not eaten immediately, it can be stored for several days wrapped in banana leaves or in a covered container. The yellow variety of cassava (*Manihot dulcis*) grows less easily, does not have to be ground and leached, but does not store as well. It is less commonly eaten by the Sama Dilaut.

The majority of Sama Dilaut gardens are cultivated by individual nuclear families, with most work done by women and children while the men are fishing. However, some men who dislike fishing, or older men who no longer fish, work in the gardens as frequently as some women. Men always do the heavy work of initially clearing the land.

Eating

Eating is no great occasion among the Sama Dilaut; rather it is a necessity taken care of as quickly and conveniently as possible. Fish is eaten directly from the cooking pot with the fingers, and cassava is eaten the same way from the wok. The number of meals eaten a day depends largely on the amount of food available, although most families ideally eat morning, noon, and evening. However, if food is not available for some reason, such as bad weather that does not allow fishing, a family may eat only once a day and sometimes goes several days with only a daily meal of cassava with perhaps some sea slugs collected from the nearby reef. On the other hand, I have seen families eat five times a day when food was abundant; often a family will finish eating only to eat again an hour later after receiving a gift of fish. Many times after several days of eating only cassava, I was awakened in the middle of the night to eat fish brought home by returning fishermen. If food is unavailable for all members of the family, adults forego eating so children can be fed.

The Sama Dilaut are extremely conservative in their eating habits. Many do not eat the common fruits and vegetables of Tawi-Tawi. Nor do they eat chicken, beef, and goat, the choice meats of Sulu's land dwelling people. White cassava is their carbohydrate staple, and rice is eaten only on ceremonial and other special occasions. Other than cassava and occasional fruits (especially bananas), their entire diet comes from the sea. Fish is definitely their preferred food, but they also eat certain shells and crustaceans when it is difficult to obtain fish. Canned fish, especially sardines, are considered a special treat but are eaten only rarely. The Sama Dilaut eat few sea plants even though a variety of edible types are found in Sulu. Other than sweet coffee sometimes served at ceremonies, water is the only beverage of the Sama Dilaut, except occasional coconut water.

Women do most of the cooking, but all men know how to cook and frequently do so. Fresh fish is almost always boiled, usually with no condiments, and dried fish is roasted over an open fire. Cassava is prepared in several ways. The yellow variety is simply peeled, boiled, and eaten, but it is seldom used by the Sama Dilaut since it is more difficult to grow, more expensive to buy, and preserves less easily than the white variety. As noted, the white variety involves much more preparation. It is cooked in three different ways. Most commonly the ground cassava is simply placed in a wok, heated, and stirred until cooked. Cassava is also cooked as big pancakes that the men take on fishing trips. A more elaborate but less common preparation steams the ground cassava, sometimes with grated coconut, as cakes in a double-decked pan similar to a Dutch oven.

THE SOCIAL REALM

The Sama Dilaut day begins before dawn.

Families leaving the moorage for travel quietly pole their boats past the sleeping households into the open waters to catch a favorable wind or current. Children dart back and forth in small dugouts to borrow fire for cooking the morning meals.

Women prepare breakfasts of fish and cassava as their husbands ready for a day of fishing or boatbuilding. After breakfast, small children meet playmates on the nearby beach while their older siblings assist in household chores. Men go to the beach to work on boats, or they may fish the reef or open sea. Most women remain in the moorage to attend to household duties, but some leave after breakfast with children to work in the gardens before the sun becomes too intense. Others paddle to shore to fill water containers at a nearby well, but for some mooragers, it may be a half-day's journey to obtain water from a neighboring island.

By mid-morning, the moorage has settled down to a steady hum of activities. If it happens to be low tide, some couples prop up their houseboats to dry the hulls so they can burn off the accumulated parasites with dried coconut frond torches. Groups of women and children wade among the exposed reefs in search of edible fauna, while others scavenge the beaches for firewood. Women visit back and forth among the houseboats as they assist one another with household chores.

At mid-day, women and children begin returning from the gardens laden with cassava, bananas, and other produce. Whether or not the family eats at noon depends on the availability of food. Leftovers from breakfast are often the noon meal, but if food is plentiful a fresh meal is prepared. Morning activities blend into the afternoon as children and adults return to the houseboats for mid-afternoon naps. In late afternoon, fishermen return home, calling out their day's catches to friends and family as they pole their boats through the moorage waters.

At dusk, women prepare the evening meal as the men gather in small groups on the beach to discuss the day's fishing. Children continue their play nearby and teenagers congregate to flirt and show off.

Eventually the beach is cleared as people return to their households to eat. Darkness descends, cooking fires brighten households, and the moorage dwellings become silhouettes with an occasional face illuminated by the flames. After dinner, small children fall asleep, while others in the household gossip, weave mats, or repair fishing nets. A mother's lullaby or the songs of a group of teenagers add to the evening sounds.

If the moon is in the proper phase and the weather agreeable, boats with lanterns attached to their prows leave the moorage for nighttime fishing. Soon the surrounding waters are dotted with lights. Fishermen encounter one another at sea and stop to chat as the songs of others drift over the waters. They stay out most of the night if fishing is good, but more frequently they return home after a couple of hours. If a fisherman is successful and the evening meal was without fish, his wife cooks the catch upon his return. Children are generally not awakened to eat unless the household has been without fish for some time. After eating, the husband and wife retire, often taking advantage of the sleeping children to engage in sexual intercourse.

Silence is rare in the moorage during the night. If the moon is full, boatbuilders use the bright, cool hours to work on boats on the nearby beach. A crying child may awaken a mother who, after singing it back to sleep, decides to weave a mat rather than return to sleep. Songs are heard throughout the night, and periodically wakes and healing ceremonies greet early risers as they prepare for another day.

Thus the sounds of the night become the sounds that began the day.

The Household

Household Composition The independent nuclear family of a man, his wife and their children is the basic unit of Sama Dilaut society.[1] The strongest, most enduring, and important kin relationships are fostered within this unit which the Sama Dilaut call *mataan*. The nuclear family, which typically has five members, is the only face-to-face group that endures an extensive period of time, and even its span is limited by the life of its members and the marriage of its offspring. Although regularly associated with a larger group of kinsmen, the nuclear family is extremely self-sufficient. Much of its time is spent traveling or fishing away from the larger Sama Dilaut community, and even when in a moorage, the isolation provided each houseboat by the water separating it from others gives a great deal of privacy to its occupants.

A survey of Sama Dilaut households, both houses and houseboats, reveals two basic features: (1) the household consists of a single nuclear family and any variation of this is either temporary or an adjustment to a fragmented nuclear family, and (2) each fragmented nuclear family adds persons to approximate the structure of the nuclear household. Reasons for this are practical. First, the size of a Sama Dilaut houseboat limits the size of the household, since the average living space of a houseboat is only about ten feet long, five feet wide, and four feet high; consequently, few houseboats are large enough to accommodate more than one nuclear family. The living spaces of most houses are larger, but even they do not easily accommodate several families. Secondly, the Sama Dilaut household has a fairly well-defined division of labor between husband and wife; typically, the husband fishes, the wife tends the household, and both look after the children. Although it is not impossible for a widow or widower to live alone, it is difficult and often taxes the resources of their immediate kinsmen who must frequently fill the vacant role. As a result, widows and widowers remarry as soon as possible or form alliances with kinsmen left in similar circumstances.

Although the most common household composition among both the boat-dwelling and house-dwelling Sama Dilaut is the nuclear family, Tables 1 and 2 reveal considerable variation within this structure.[2] A biological rather than structural variant of the nuclear family occurs when a couple adopts children. A childless couple sometime raise an orphaned child or a child of a sibling who has more children than he or she can manage. Sometimes the adopted children are the only ones in the household or they may have adoptive siblings, but in either case, they are treated as biological offspring. Adoption is probably more common than I was able to determine since such children are referred to by the same term for biological children and their adopted status is insignificant in the family structure and sentiment. Consequently, unless pressed to do so, a Sama Dilaut rarely says that a child is adopted.[3]

Tables 1 and 2 reveal the household compositions of boat dwellers and house dwellers respectively. Note the greater number of extended families among the house dwellers and the tendency toward uxorilocality. These extended family households are often temporary arrangements. When boat dwellers arrive at a moorage, they often stay with house-dwelling kinsmen as they repair their boats or cultivate nearby gardens. After completing their tasks, they return to their boats for fishing trips or travel to another moorage.

Frequently an aged widow or widower is part of a nuclear household. Most commonly, this is a parent of either the husband or wife. Occasionally an aged couple joins a nuclear family household, but usually as long as both are able, they live alone. If an aged person has several children, she normally moves among their several households instead of staying with one child permanently. Occasionally, however, an aged adult chooses to live permanently with one married child because no space is available elsewhere, the household has greater need for her small services, or she has closer emotional ties to that particular child. Sometimes the aged live alone, but I encountered only three such elderly people among the Tawi-Tawi Sama Dilaut. One was an eccentric old widow who was believed to have such great supernatural powers that even her own children were afraid of her. Another widow had two married sons, but both had several children and consequently full houseboats. As a result, she moored her houseboat next to one of the sons, and although she was not

Table 1. Household Composition of Boat Dwelling Sama Dilaut

1.	Nuclear family	103	(78%)
2.	Nuclear family plus additional members	11	(8%)
	Nuclear family and widowed father of husband	1	
	Nuclear family and widowed mother of wife	6	
	Nuclear family, widowed mother of wife, divorced sister of wife	1	
	Nuclear family and wife's widowed mother and widowed sister	1	
	Nuclear family and unmarried adult nephew of husband	1	
	Nuclear family and unmarried male patrilateral cousin of husband	1	
	Total	11	
3.	Extended families	10	(8%)
	Nuclear family and married son and family	4	
	Nuclear family and two married sons and families	1	
	Nuclear family and married daughter and husband	2	
	Nuclear family and mother and father of husband and wife	2	
	Widow and children and her nephew and his wife	1	
	Total	10	
4.	Fragmented families	8	(6%)
	Widower and children	1	
	Widow and children	2	
	Widow, her two sons, her two teenaged brothers, and her widowed father	1	
	Widow	1	
	Widower and his grandson	1	
	Widow and her children and her widowed mother	1	
	Two widows (second cousins) and children of one	1	
	Total	8	
	Total	132	(100%)

Table 2. Household Composition of House-Dwelling Sama Dilaut

1. Nuclear family 48 (55%)
2. Nuclear family plus additional members 9 (10%)
    Nuclear family plus widowed mother of wife 2
    Nuclear family plus widowed mother of husband 1
    Nuclear family plus widowed father of wife 1
    Nuclear family plus widowed daughter and child 1
    Nuclear family plus nephew of husband 1
    Nuclear family plus divorced brother of husband 1
    Nuclear family plus mother and grandfather of wife 1
    Nuclear family plus widower of wife's sister 1
    Total 9
3. Extended families 25 (29%)
    Nuclear family and married daughter and family 12
    Nuclear family and married son and family 6
    Nuclear family and wife's brother and his wife 1
    Nuclear family and married nephew of husband 1
    Nuclear family, wife's married niece and family,
        and wife's widowed sister 1
    Nuclear family, husband's married sister and
        family, and husband's widowed mother 1
    Nuclear family and wife's married sister and family 3
    Total 25
4. Fragmented families 5 (6%)
    Divorced man and his widowed mother 1
    Two widowed second cousins and children 1
    Widow and unmarried son 2
    Widow and her divorced daughter and children 1
    Total 5
    Total 87 (100%)

an actual resident of his household, she was intimately involved in its activities. The third person was an old widower so quarrelsome he could not get along with any of his children; they provided him sustenance, but he refused to live with any of them.

Other variants of the Sama Dilaut household include the extended family. This normally consists of a newly married couple who are temporarily staying with parents or perhaps an older married sibling until they obtain their own houseboat. Frequently, such newlyweds move among the several houseboats of their parents and married siblings for a week or so at a time, becoming better acquainted with their in-laws as they work toward their own houseboat. Another variation of the extended family, noted above, is an aged couple living with a married child.

Two fragmented families of closely related adults left without spouses sometimes form a household for their mutual benefit. In one case a widow and her two small children lived with her aged, widowed father and her two unmarried teenaged brothers. The benefits of such an arrangement are mutual. Alone the widow and her sons would always be in need of fish and other goods normally supplied by a man, while, similarly, the old man and his two sons would find it troublesome to live without a woman to perform the female duties of the household. By joining together, the two fragmented families complete the economic structure of the household and all members benefit from the arrangement. I encountered a second household of this type which included a widow and her widowed brother and his three children. Although the two adults maintained their separate houseboats, they acted as a single household unit and normally ate together. In another case, a newly married couple, both from large households, lived with the groom's widowed aunt (mother's sister) and her children, because both parental households were crowded and the widow needed an adult male in her household.

Orphaned, unmarried siblings of either the husband or wife usually join nuclear family units. Normally they are the youngest members of their families and stay with siblings until they marry and form their own households.

Residence Patterns   Much diversity is revealed as to where each household, whether a nuclear family or a variant form of it, moors its houseboat. By far the most common Sama Dilaut residence pattern is ambilocality, a general term which covers a number of residence variations. For the few truly nomadic families it describes their lifelong movements among the Sama Dilaut moorages and fishing grounds of Tawi-Tawi. For couples who otherwise permanently reside at a moorage, it refers to their monthly movements away from the moorage in search of fish. For some couples it is a conscious decision to spend half the year in the husband's home moorage and the other half in the wife's home moorage. And for still other couples, it complements their seasonal residence near certain islands where they practice agriculture.

Because of the frequent movements of Sama Dilaut houseboats, the residence patterns in a Sama Dilaut moorage on any particular day is different, and sometimes dramatically different, from the patterns found on other days. Tables 3 and 4 reveal that the residence patterns of boat-dwelling and house-dwelling Sama Dilaut are not significantly different.

Table 3. Residence of Boat-Dwelling Sama Dilaut

1. Uxorilocal moorage 23 (22%)
2. Virilocal moorage 13 (12%)
3. Natolocal moorage 34 (32%)
4. Neolocal moorage 30 (28%)
5. Virilocal moorage and virilocal household 4 (4%)
6. Uxorilocal moorage and virilocal household 1 (1%)
7. Uxorilocal moorage and uxorilocal household 1 (1%)
   Total 106 (100%)

Table 4. Residence of House-Dwelling Sama Dilaut

1. Uxorilocal moorage 21 (18%)
2. Virilocal moorage 14 (12%)
3. Natolocal moorage 15 (13%)
4. Neolocal moorage 37 (32%)
5. Ambilocal 1 (1%)
6. Uxorilocal moorage and uxorilocal household 9 (8%)
7. Virilocal moorage and virilocal household 6 (5%)
8. Virilocal moorage and uxorilocal household 1 (1%)
9. Natolocal moorage and uxorilocal household 4 (4%)
10. Natolocal moorage and virilocal household 3 (3%)
11. Neolocal moorage and uxorilocal household 2 (2%)
12. Neolocal moorage and virilocal household 1 (1%)
    Total 114 (100%)

Most Sama Dilaut claim that after marriage a couple should move between the moorages or households of their parents the first few months and then settle in the moorage of the wife. In other words, an initial ambilocality becomes uxorilocal. However, like many social ideals, this custom does not always reflect reality, and more practical considerations determine actual residence patterns.

An initial ambilocality is typical of most marriages. Since newlyweds are frequently from different moorages, the ambilocal practice allows them to become acquainted with their new in-laws while relieving the strain from a single household of supporting and finding space for them. Sometimes the couple forego the initial ambilocality and live in the houseboat of a kinsman who needs a male or female to complete the household unit. In one case, noted earlier, the groom's widowed aunt needed an adult male in her household and had space for the couple. In another case, a widower needed his daughter-in-law to assume the female responsibilities of his household. Sometimes, if one set of parents has a crowded household, the couple may spend their first months with the other parents who have more space for them. But whatever the case, the couple expect, and are expected, to have their own household within a year or so after marriage and most usually do.

Residence becomes even more varied when the couple acquire their own home. Some Sama Dilaut seldom leave their home moorage whereas others spend their lives moving among the five moorages in Tawi-Tawi; most fall somewhere between these extremes. Those couples who rarely travel beyond their home moorage are normally both from that moorage. Often they are less dependent on fishing as a livelihood and practice boatbuilding or gardening. Their fishing is limited to the nearby waters and except for occasional fishing trips to other parts of Tawi-Tawi or visits to the cemetery islands, they seldom leave the moorage. They consequently represent the stable element of the moorage population.

Other considerations influence a couple's decision to spend most of their time at one moorage. If one of them has few and insignificant kinsmen, they normally moor where the most numerous and important kinsmen live. Or if the couple are on unfriendly terms with one set of kinsmen, they live at a moorage where they have friendly kinsmen.

A virilocality found among some couples is related to ecological factors. Sama Dilaut men living in the Sanga-Sanga moorages most commonly practice hook-and-line fishing in the nearby fishing grounds and seldom practice net fishing on the small reefs of the area. The reverse situation is found in the Bilatan moorages where extensive reefs allow profitable net fishing, but little hook-and-line fishing. As a result, men grow up in the two areas learning the fishing techniques that most profitably exploit the environments. And since successful fishing is obviously important in Sama Dilaut society, men prefer to fish those waters where they can use familiar fishing methods and harvest greater catches. Consequently, if men marry outside their home waters, most commonly the wife goes to live in the husband's moorage since he can more profitably fish those waters. Women's work is less specialized and allows greater freedom of movement.

Marriage Patterns The Sama Dilaut believe it is best to marry relatives, and most do. Indeed, if the web of kinship ties among the Sama Dilaut could be unraveled, it would probably reveal that all Tawi-Tawi Sama Dilaut couples are related in some manner. Sama Dilaut are free to marry all relatives, except grandparents, siblings of parents and grandparents, and members of the nuclear family. Such marriages are considered incestuous (*sumbang*). First-cousin marriage is permissible, except between patrilateral parallel cousins who, before their marriage is sanctioned, must perform a ritual which involves throwing valuables into the sea. Also, any couple who nursed from the same woman or were reared together intimately are considered improper marriage partners. Tables 5 and 6 reveal the variations found in Sama Dilaut marriage patterns among both boat-dwelling and house-dwelling couples. Again, little difference occurs between the two groups.

Table 5. Marriages of Boat-Dwelling Sama Dilaut

Type of marriage relationship Number

1.	Patrilateral parallel first cousins	8 (5%)
2.	Matrilateral parallel first cousins	9 (6%)
3.	Cross cousins	14 (9%)
4.	Second cousins	46 (29.5%)
5.	Third cousins	11 (7%)
6.	Second *kamanakan**	14 (9%)
7.	Distant relationship (exact relationship unknown)	20 (13%)
8.	Uncertain as to whether or not relationship exists	7 (4.5%)
9.	No relationship	26 (17%)
	Total	155 (100%)

*The category second kamanakan is a relationship of persons separated by one generation in the second degree of collaterality.

Table 6. Marriages of House-Dwelling Sama Dilaut

Type of marriage relationship Number

1.	Patrilateral parallel first cousins	3 (3%)
2.	Matrilateral parallel first cousins	6 (6%)
3.	Cross cousins	9 (8%)
4.	Second cousins	33 (30%)
5.	Third cousins	3 (3%)
6.	Fourth cousins	1 (1%)
7.	Second kamanakan	13 (12%)
8.	Distant relationship (exact relationship unknown)	12 (11%)
9.	Uncertain whether relationship exists	7 (6%)
10.	No relationship	22 (20%)
	Total	109 (100%)

The second- and third-cousin categories should not be interpreted too literally. Rather than strictly defining a degree of collaterality, the terms are often
used to indicate closeness of relationship relative to first cousins; thus someone
identified as a second cousin may in reality be distantly related, but in terms
of sentiment is considered more closely related. Few Sama Dilaut are able to
actually trace collaterality to third cousins while a few more can identify second
cousins.

Although romantic love is no prerequisite to marriage, many young couples
are in love at the time of their marriage. These couples express to their parents
their desire to marry, or elope rather than await the formalities and possible
opposition to their marriage. Since Sama Dilaut youth are rarely forced into a
distasteful match, attraction between the couple characterizes most marriages.
After the romantic love diminishes, it is frequently replaced by a genuine deep,
mutual affection. If not, the marriage may end in divorce, or if a child is on the
way, the couple learns to tolerate one another.

Generally, the longer the marriage, the stronger the ties between husband
and wife. On several occasions, I accompanied Sama Dilaut men on three- or
four-day fishing trips who complained of homesickness for their wives and
children. One man planned to fish for several weeks with his brother while his
wife remained at home, but after two days, he became so lonely for his wife
that he returned home to join her. They had been married almost ten years. A
widow who had been married for about twelve years refused to remarry because
she said she could never find a man she loved as much as her husband, despite
the fact that her unmarried state created hardships for her and placed burdens
on her siblings who supported her. On several occasions I saw widows cry when
they recalled husbands who had been dead several years. This strong tie between husband and wife is fostered by the intimacy of living together in the
small houseboat. The Sama Dilaut husband is rarely away from his household
overnight, and frequently he is with his wife and children twenty-four hours a
day. And since the houseboat is often at sea separated from the larger Sama
Dilaut community, it is not surprising that extremely intimate and close ties
characterize the nuclear family.

The husband is head of the household, although household matters are
discussed with his wife before decisions are made. Most commonly the wife
handles the family finances. The husband fishes, maintains the boat, and weaves
and repairs fishing nets; the wife cooks, prepares cassava, weaves mats, gathers
firewood, collects from the reef, and frequently assists in fishing. Both are actively
involved in child rearing, although the wife almost exclusively tends infants. If
the family has a garden, the wife and older children do most of the work,
although the husband helps in the heavy tasks.

If the husband or wife dies, the surviving spouse expresses real as well as conventional grief at the death. When the husband dies, his sons inherit his property, especially his fishing equipment, but the house or houseboat continues as the wife's home. Sometimes the houseboat is destroyed at a man's death, but only in cases of extreme grief or if the living do not need the boat. More commonly a house is destroyed or abandoned after an adult dies. A woman's property normally passes to her daughters, or to her sisters if she has no daughters. An aged couple usually have few belongings by the time one or both die since they have either given them away to children or worn them out. Certain personal items of the deceased, such as clothing, betel boxes and jewelry, are left in the grave with the corpse.

Divorce If the married couple find their marriage distasteful and decide that even their children are not reason enough to maintain an unhappy marriage, divorce (*magbutas*) is the way out. Relatives always try to reconcile a separated couple, but if unsuccessful they seek the counsel of the headman and moorage elders. When all attempts at reconciliation fail, the headman grants the couple a divorce. Barrenness, irresponsibility, incompatible personalities, and interfering relatives are the most common causes of divorce. If divorce occurs shortly after marriage, the bridewealth, or a portion of it, is returned to the husband's family. Money and goods acquired by the couple, and sometimes even the children, are divided between them. Tables 7 and 8 summarize divorce patterns among boat dwellers and house dwellers. Once again, the differences between the two groups are insignificant.

Table 7. Divorces of Boat-Dwelling Sama Dilaut

Number of marriages Males

1	126	(76%)
2	34	(21%)
3	5	(3%)
Total	165	(100%)

Number of marriages Females

1	122	(79%)
2	25	(16%)
3	6	(4%)
4	1	(1%)
Total	154	(100%)

Table 8. Divorces of House-Dwelling Sama Dilaut

Number of marriages Males

1	90	(79%)
2	21	(18%)
3	3	(3%)
Total	114	(100%)

Number of marriages Females

1	86	(76%)
2	22	(19%)
3	6	(5%)
Total	114	(100%)

Family Relations The intimacy that fosters close ties between husband and wife fosters similar ties between parents and children. Children are desired for emotional as well as practical reasons. Indeed, barrenness is just cause for divorce, and those barren couples who do not want to divorce sometimes acquire children from more fortunate siblings. The few children a Sama Dilaut family has are cherished even more because of the high infant mortality rate. Girls and boys are equally desired, and most parents prefer children of each gender so both will have assistance in their work.

Children are inseparable from their parents and learn to swim almost as soon as they learn to walk. When in the moorage, they join playmates on the reef or beach during the day, but when the family is away from the moorage, they are always with their parents. At a very early age mothers take nursing infants with them in small boats under sunshades as they collect from the nearby reefs. If the husband needs his wife's assistance in fishing away from the houseboat, they construct a shelter on the fishing boat to protect the infant from the sun or the night mists.

Although permissiveness characterizes most aspects of Sama Dilaut child rearing, and children are allowed, within reason, almost anything they want, they participate in household work at an early age and assist wherever needed. Girls work more closely with their mothers while boys work with their fathers, but the smallness of the household fosters sharing that crosses gender lines. Sama Dilaut sleeping habits illustrate the closeness of the family. Frequently, a Sama Dilaut couple and their small children sleep together within a single *sarong*. Family members prefer to sleep near one another, often entwined together, partly because of affection and partly because it is warmer.[4]

115

Parents frequently become involved in their children's quarrels. In fact, one of the most common causes of adult dissent within the moorage is parental involvement in children's disagreements. Similarly, children are staunch defenders of their parents' actions.

Sibling relationships are characteristically intimate and protective. If the family is away from the moorage, the only playmates available for the children are siblings. When the family houseboat is at a moorage, siblings spend the day playing together with other children on the nearby beach. If a child acquires food, he invariably shares it with his siblings but feels no obligation to share it with nonsiblings who may be watching hungrily as he gorges himself. In serious quarrels between two children, the siblings of each usually become involved also. Older girls assume maternal responsibilities for younger siblings if the mother's time is occupied with an infant. This intimacy between siblings continues after marriage when they prefer to moor their houseboats together and work as a sibling group.

As noted, the Sama Dilaut household sometimes includes aged adults, parents of either the husband or wife. So long as the aged are physically active and mentally alert, they are respected members of the household. But when they become senile or physically incapacitated, the rest of the household usually disregards them. They are, however, never mistreated because of the responsibility children feel toward elderly parents and the belief that old people can curse others with illness and misfortune. Often the aged Sama Dilaut retain their prestige because of their knowledge of ritual and curing, and some old women enjoy renown as midwives. The aged Sama Dilaut do whatever jobs they can as long as they are able and then depend on their children for sustenance.

Two men of approximately the same age, but in different conditions of health and senility, illustrate the different statuses of the Sama Dilaut aged. The differences are due partly to the personalities of the two men, but they also reveal physical and mental factors that determine the status of Sama Dilaut old people.

Laja'udden, about sixty years old, is still physically active and mentally alert. A respected *djin*, headman, fisherman, and boatbuilder, he enjoys considerable renown among the Tawi-Tawi Sama Dilaut. Thrice married, Laja'udden is still the head of his household and has a great deal of influence over his five married sons and four married daughters who often seek his advice. His grandchildren heed his commands more than they heed their own parents. He organizes most family activities in his houseboat, which is the center of family activities. Because of his many marriages, children, and stepchildren, his kinship ties extend to practically every Sama Dilaut kin group in Tawi-Tawi.

116

Bulahani is about the same age as Laja'udden. Bulahani is senile, almost blind, probably has tuberculosis, and his legs are so weak that most of the time he squats. At one time he was an outstanding fisherman, but now he spends most of his days sleeping or sullenly watching the moorage activities from his houseboat where he lives alone. His only wife died five years ago, but his five daughters and four sons are still living. The two youngest sons, unmarried teenagers, live with their oldest sister, and like the rest of the family, seldom go to Bulahani's houseboat. His children mostly ignore him; they joke about his senility, but always provide him with food.

Similar differences occur among old women, but they generally contribute more to the household since their work requires less physical effort than that of men.

Unmarried adult siblings of either the husband or wife who live in the household are expected to assist in duties appropriate to their gender. Their position in the household is regarded as temporary and they usually leave upon getting married.

Additional couples in the household are also regarded as temporary members and they, too, assist in duties appropriate to their gender. The crowded houseboat resulting from extended family households discourages their formation, and they last only until the visiting family acquires its own boat.

The Family Alliance Unit

Although extremely independent, the Sama Dilaut nuclear family is not an isolated unit, but rather periodically attaches itself to a larger group, especially when at a moorage. When a family arrives at a moorage, it anchors near the houses or houseboats of kinsmen living there. Usually these kinsmen are siblings of either the wife or husband, and are the chief reason the family has chosen to stop at the moorage. This group of married siblings who moor together and assist one another in work and ceremonies is the second most important social unit in Sama Dilaut society, second only to the nuclear family (figs. 53 and 54). Although the Sama Dilaut call such a group *pagmundah*, a group of boats traveling or mooring together, I shall refer to it by the more descriptive term "family alliance unit."

Structure of the Family Alliance Unit Family alliance units follow no single structural type, but they are rarely more than two generations and seldom extend collaterally beyond siblings. The unit consists of a married man and his several married sons, a married man and his several married daughters or a married man and his several married sons and daughters. Or its members may be siblings, such as several married brothers, several married sisters, or several married brothers and sisters. However, not all married siblings at a moorage are necessarily members of the same alliance unit. Family quarrels, social prestige, or economic factors may cause married siblings to align themselves with their spouses' siblings rather than their own.

Fig. 53 Family alliance unit in moorage

Of the twenty-five alliance units I knew, one was composed of two nuclear families, one had six nuclear families, six had three nuclear families each, ten had four nuclear families each, and seven had five nuclear families each. Six had married siblings: one had married brothers, and five had married brothers

Fig. 54 Family alliance unit at sea

and sisters. Seventeen had two generations: eleven had a married man and his married children, and six had married siblings and their married child or children. Two had three generations: in both cases, they were a couple, their married children and their married grandchildren. Thus the most common family alliance unit among the Sama Dilaut has twenty members representing four nuclear families of two generations.

Within the family alliance units, work groups form for certain activities. Sometimes these work groups, such as certain fishing groups, consist of all the adult men of the unit whereas at other times only two or three members comprise a group. In general, the family alliance unit provides a group of closely related reliable persons from which work alliances are formed.

The composition of work groups, as well as family alliance units, is determined by occupational preferences and age, as well as compatibility. Obviously, only persons who get along well can work well together. Also, if members of an alliance unit have different occupational interests, they rarely work together in a work group. And since some fishing techniques require the efforts of several able-bodied men, a family alliance unit must have several men of this age group among its members. If siblings satisfy these requirements, the work group consists of siblings or their affinal counterparts. Otherwise, less closely related persons are sought for alliances. I found no alliances between nonkinsmen, either in work groups or family alliance units, partly because if forced to do so, a Sama Dilaut can trace a kin connection to almost every Sama Dilaut in Tawi-Tawi. The Sama Dilaut ideally align with siblings, and most family alliance units and work groups realize this ideal.

Because of the frequent movements of nuclear families, the composition of a family alliance unit is constantly changing. While at his home moorage, a man normally forms an alliance with his own siblings who live there, but when in his wife's moorage, he joins a unit composed primarily of her siblings. When at moorages different from his own or his wife's, he forms alliances with his siblings or his wife's siblings, or with less closely related persons.

Sama Dilaut households leave traditional alliances as younger members of the household marry and form their own households. When a man has married children, he tends to dissolve alliances with his siblings in favor of alliances with his children. Eventually this alliance replaces his earlier ones and he never again participates in a unit with his former partners. Most commonly he acts as leader of the newly formed unit, but as he becomes older he relinquishes his leadership to a younger member.

The sedentary households of the moorage provide stability to the otherwise fluid family alliance units because it is around them that the nomadic households cluster. These sedentary households, as noted earlier, are families who rarely travel beyond the waters of the home moorage. Both spouses are often from that moorage and if they fish, they fish the nearby waters. Frequently, they are boatbuilders or farmers who have no need to follow the fishing cycles. Because they are almost always at the home moorage, their less sedentary siblings form alliances with them when they arrive at the moorage. However, not all family alliance units have these sedentary members.

Generally one man acts as leader, or nakura, of the alliance unit. If a unit is composed of a man and his married children, he invariably acts as its leader as long as he is physically and mentally able. When he becomes too old to handle the leadership responsibilities, his position passes to the next most capable adult male, usually one of his sons or sons-in-law.

Leaders are not chosen through any formal decision, but rather emerge through innate personal qualities. Frequently, but not always, they are among the sedentary members of the alliance and have some respected skill, such as boatbuilding or fishing, as well as charismatic personalities that distinguish them from their peers. Leadership, however, is as subject to change as the composition of the unit itself and different leaders emerge for different activities. For example, ceremonies are led by a person familiar with the proper ritual; fishing activities are organized by an expert fisherman; medicines are administered by a woman knowledgeable about herbs; boatbuilding activities are in the hands of a master boatbuilder; and children are delivered by the most experienced midwife. To add further complexity, all positions are subject to change as the composition of the alliance unit changes.

The history of one man's alliances during the course of a year illustrates the fluid nature of Sama Dilaut alliance units. Masarani, his wife, and their five children live as a nuclear family in their houseboat. From October through December, Masarani lived at Tungkalang, his wife's home moorage, while he made major repairs on his houseboat. During this period he was a member of an alliance unit composed primarily of his wife's siblings and led by his wife's oldest brother. In January he left Tungkalang with his wife's married sister and her two married brothers for an extended fishing trip in the Bilatan waters. Masarani is a respected fisherman and during this trip he acted as the unit's leader even though his wife's brother was the unit's leader when they were at Tungkalang. After the two-month fishing trip, Masarani's wife's siblings returned to Tungkalang while he and his family went to Tungbangkao, his home moorage. During his stay there, Masarani participated in an alliance with his two married brothers. He again acted as fishing leader for the group while one of his brothers officiated at the unit's ceremonies. After about two months at Tungbangkao, Masarani went to Lu'uk Tulai to assist his wife's sister's husband in building a boat. During this period he was a member of an alliance unit that included him, his wife's married brother and sister, and his wife's first cousin. His wife's sister's husband, who regularly moored at Lu'uk Tulai, acted as leader. During this period, Masarani worked almost exclusively at boatbuilding while the other members divided their time between fishing and woodworking in the forest. Five months later, after completing his boat, Masarani and one of his wife's brothers from Lu'uk Tulai and two of her married sisters from Tungkalang went to Bilatan on a fishing trip, during which time Masarani again acted as leader. When I left Sulu, Masarani had again returned to Tungkalang for boatbuilding and gardening on Sanga-Sanga island. The pattern is even more complex because within each of these sibling alliance units, Masarani frequently changed his work group affiliation. Masarani's movements are not excessive; in fact, they are considerably less than some of the truly nomadic Sama Dilaut families.

Economic Activities The family alliance unit is not a corporate group. Even when intimately involved with a unit for a long time, the nuclear family remains economically independent of the larger unit. A great deal of borrowing of food, water, firewood, betel, and cigarettes occurs among members of an alliance unit, but it is always reciprocal. Anyone who borrows from fellow members too frequently without reciprocating will eventually find himself without an alliance unit.

When traveling together on fishing trips as an alliance unit, each nuclear family normally fishes independently unless the husband has no one in the family to help him, either because his children are too young or his wife has demanding household duties. In such cases, he may form a work group with another man or two of the unit. But if at all possible, each man fishes with his nuclear family since then he need not divide the catch. During these trips, the boats of the alliance unit anchor at a central place and members fish in smaller boats in nuclear family groups. Elderly family members remain in the houseboats to tend small children. If a family does not catch enough fish for immediate consumption, others of the alliance unit give them fish, but surplus catches are the property of each nuclear family. Certain types of fishing are more profitable with the participation of several boats and for these types of fishing, work groups are formed. At night, if tides and winds are favorable, Sama Dilaut practice spear fishing with kerosene lanterns. For such fishing, nuclear families accompany one another, but each is in its own boat with its own lantern and claims its own catch. The combined lanterns illuminate more fish for the benefit of all and the additional people provide companionship and security.

During the day when the men are fishing away from the houseboats, women who have not accompanied their husbands scavenge the reefs at low tide. They always collect together, but whatever each finds is claimed individually and no division occurs unless someone finds nothing. The women individually collect firewood in similar groups.

When at a moorage, nuclear families continue to act economically independent. During these stays, men sometimes seek additional income and diversion from fishing by making boards from trees cut in the forests. They go to the forest in groups, but once there, each works individually and claims the boards he cuts. The group provides companionship and occasional assistance, and allays fears of traveling alone in the forest.

Boatbuilding is normally an individual project, but occasionally a man needs assistance to help him over a difficult stage of construction or to provide skills he may not have, such as carving. At such times, he calls upon members of his family alliance unit to form a work group. Unless their assistance is needed for a long time, these members expect no payment beyond reciprocal favors. A man with little talent for boatbuilding, or a young inexperienced man, depends on members of his alliance unit to construct his entire boat. He furnishes the materials for the boat and does whatever work he can under the direction of the boatbuilder. He is sometimes expected to provide fish for the builder during the construction. If the men are close relatives, the boatbuilder might demand no payment but he expects reciprocation in kind. On rare occasions, two or three men of an alliance unit build a boat to sell and divide the profits equally.

Ceremonial Activities Unlike economic activities, Sama Dilaut ceremonies often demand the participation of the entire alliance unit and sometimes even more distantly related kinsmen.

Individuals or nuclear families perform the simplest Sama Dilaut ceremonies. If a family happens to be in the vicinity of a cemetery island, some members may visit graves to leave small offerings for a recently deceased relative. Sometimes the offering is left to the deceased as a remembrance, but more commonly it is given to insure that the deceased's spirit will not visit the living with illness or bad luck. A similar ceremony occurs when a Sama Dilaut inadvertently passes too close to a place where saitan (spirits) dwell. To placate the saitan for having possibly aroused its displeasure, the trespassers leave small offerings.

The majority of Sama Dilaut ceremonies involve the attendance and participation of the entire family alliance unit. Participation frequently extends beyond the alliance unit, but the unit is most actively involved in the planning and execution of the affair. Certain healing ceremonies, attended only by alliance unit members, are held in response to serious or prolonged illnesses. Members of the unit congregate in the household of the patient while a *djin* asks the spirits responsible for the illness to desist. Each unit normally has a djin among its members, but if not, an outsider, almost always a relative, is asked to conduct the ceremony. Depending on the illness, several types of healing ceremonies are observed by the Sama Dilaut, but all initially involve only alliance unit members. If the illness is not particularly serious, some members of the unit may not attend. However, if the illness is serious, and especially if the afflicted is an adult, most members of the unit attend. If an adult is critically ill, all adult members of the unit attend, partly out of real concern for the patient and partly out of fear that if he dies, his spirit may punish those unconcerned.

One ceremony, the *magtimbang*, involves considerably more persons than those of the family alliance unit, although unit members plan and execute the ceremony. The ceremony is held for spirits that have allowed recovery from a critical illness and involves the distribution of goods to everyone in attendance. Although the family alliance unit plans and attends the ceremony, everyone in the moorage can attend and relatives of the recovered person are expected to do so.

Only the family alliance unit normally attends the ear-piercing operation (*magtabok*) performed on girls usually during infancy. The ceremony probably once had religious significance but now consists only of a minor operation performed by an older woman of the alliance unit. Women of the alliance unit attend the ceremony, but most men, except the father of the child and other men of the household, usually do not.

The superincision ceremony (*magislam*) for adolescent boys may involve only the family alliance unit, or, if elaborate, it includes additional relatives or even nonrelatives. If the family is poor or simply does not want an elaborate celebration, the ceremony is small and held in the family house or houseboat. Non-unit members, such as siblings or first cousins of the youth's parents, may attend and unit members are always there. Some play music before, during, and after the brief ceremony while others, especially girls and women, dance on the decorated boats. The djin who performs the simple operation is usually a member of the family alliance unit or a relative of the youth. More elaborate ceremonies include a distribution of rice and sugar to the entire moorage with music and dancing on the reef or nearby beach throughout the afternoon and evening. Such elaborate ceremonies are costly and although the parents of the youth are expected to bear the main expense, they sometimes call on relatives for assistance. Their siblings usually contribute to the celebration, regardless of whether they are members of their present family alliance unit—all probably have been members in the past and will be members again in the future. All share the limelight of the elaborate affair and all expect reciprocity when they superincise their sons. Usually only siblings of the youth's parents are asked to contribute.

A young man is dependent on his kinsmen for acquiring bridewealth at marriage. Even if he elopes and thereby avoids a large bridewealth, a cash settlement must be paid, which he normally does not have. Because most families are unable to afford the usual bridewealth of eighty to 100 pesos, parents call on siblings to assist. And even if the young man's family could afford to pay the entire bridewealth, tradition demands that others be asked for assistance. In one case, the groom's family paid less toward the bridewealth than any of the contributors; in another case, the groom's family paid over 75 percent of the total, with the remainder divided among the eight siblings of the groom's parents. Both cases are somewhat unique and most fall somewhere between them. As in all Sama Dilaut relations, reciprocity is expected: one contributes to a bridewealth what one received from the family's past bridewealth.

Division of the bridewealth received by the bride's family follows lines similar to those by which it was collected from the groom's family, that is, it is parceled out to the siblings of the bride's parents, with her parents receiving a larger share. Division among the parent's siblings is determined by the amounts they have contributed to past family ceremonies, but if family quarrels have separated siblings, they are not included. It is not unusual for a couple to contribute to a bridewealth and then a day or so later receive a share, possibly larger than their original contribution, from the same bridewealth. This would, of course, be the case if the bride and groom are first cousins; the actual transfer of goods and money always occurs even though much of it may return to the donors.

As the preceding discussion reveals, a family with only sons has considerably more expenses than a family with only daughters; sons require money for both superincision and marriage, whereas daughters have no comparable expenses. The Sama Dilaut recognize this imbalance but believe the nearly equal number of males and females in the kin group balances it over time. Nonetheless, a family with many sons is a drain on its kinsmen. A very exceptional, but illustrative case, is a family with eleven sons and no daughters. No money came directly to the family through marriages of daughters, although it shared in the bridewealth of the daughters of other members of the family alliance unit. As might be expected, superincision ceremonies in this family were extremely simple, and the four married sons had all eloped, thereby reducing their bridewealth payments. When each son married, another person was added to those who would contribute to the bridewealth of the next marriage. Most likely, elaborate weddings, the ideal of most Sama Dilaut, will be possible for the youngest sons. But thus far, marriage has been a drain on the family and its alliance unit.

Aside from economics, the family alliance unit has another important function at marriage. It is considered inappropriate for the parents of the bride and groom to directly involve themselves in the sometimes sticky business of negotiating the bridewealth. Consequently, all negotiations between the two parties are conducted by go-betweens (suku), siblings of the parents of the bride and groom. Once a youth has indicated his preferred bride, or his family has talked him into marrying their choice, siblings of his parents visit a household of the future bride's family alliance unit, never the household of the bride. At this time, after offering their proposal to the family, they leave a gift of family jewelry and other valuables. If the girl's family is interested, after long hours of discussion with the young woman's parents and after her consent, they return the gift to the household of the young man's relatives and ask the price they have decided on. If they are not interested in the marriage, they return the gift and ask for an unreasonably high bridewealth, which is interpreted as a rejection. But even if the proposed bridewealth is reasonable, the young man's family may try to negotiate a lower price. Eventually an agreement is reached. The future bride and groom and their parents are never present at these meetings, although the parents actively participate in the discussions before and after the meetings. Once the bridewealth has been paid, the wedding is held. The alliance unit members and other siblings of the parents arrange the entire affair. The bride and groom continue to play minor roles.

Death also demands the participation of the family alliance unit as well as other relatives. After an initial display of grief and mourning by the deceased's alliance unit, relatives less grieved by the death handle the funeral arrangements. One of these people, normally an uncle or an older in-law of the deceased (a woman if the deceased is female), washes the body and prepares it for burial. A wake is held throughout the night following the death. In the case of an adult death, most adults of the moorage visit the funeral boat to sing mourning songs. If the deceased is a child, only close relatives normally attend the wake. The following morning the body is taken to the cemetery islands for burial. The number and composition of the entourage of mourners vary greatly; in the case of an infant's death, only a couple of boats of family alliance members attend, whereas the death of an adult is mourned by several boats, including relatives of second- and third-degree collaterality. As with all Sama Dilaut ceremonies, the alliance unit organizes the activities and less intimate relatives, or even nonrelatives, attend the formal ceremony.

Death does not involve a great deal of expense for the survivors although some outlays of cash are necessary. It is most important that the shroud of white cloth be purchased. Usually, the immediate family of the deceased has the necessary cash; otherwise, members of the family alliance unit contribute to its purchase. Some families provide food for the mourners who accompany the corpse to the burial islands; in such cases, the family alliance unit contributes, although if the nuclear family of the deceased is fairly well off, it pays all expenses. If no one within the family alliance has the skills to make a gravemarker for the grave, members hire someone to make it.

125

Interpersonal Relations Individual personalities as well as the intimacy and duration of the contact among members determine relations within the family alliance unit. Normally the tie between siblings remains strong after marriage, although it tends to weaken as their children attain adulthood, marry, and form their own alliance units. Circumstances may separate siblings for months or years, but even after such long separations the sibling tie is usually reactivated. During the early months and years of marriage, the sibling tie occasionally overrides the marital bond. I observed many family quarrels when a spouse sided with a sibling rather than a mate, and I heard individuals chastised by siblings because they defended spouses rather than siblings. As the marriage bond lengthens, however, and loyalties are transferred to spouses, the sibling bond weakens. Uninvolved family alliance members act as mediators in the event of serious quarrels between spouses and between other persons in the alliance. If differences cannot be resolved, families leave the unit to join another one in the moorage or in a different moorage.

Among the adult members of the alliance unit, patterns of friendship and intimacy follow gender lines. Two types of sibling "in-law" relationships are recognized by the Sama Dilaut, namely the relationship between a person and his sibling's spouse and the relationship between a person and his spouse's sibling (the *ipal* relationship), and the relationship between two persons married to siblings (the *bilas* relationship). The nature of the relationship varies greatly among individuals, with perhaps the most significant variables being compatibility and the duration of the relationship. Compatible persons who work well together tend to remain in the same alliance unit and operate as a work group for long periods of time, perhaps until they break off to form alliances with their own married children. In such cases, intimate relationships develop which often override sibling ties. Two men who are married to sisters and belong to the same alliance unit for a long time develop sentiments and reciprocal relationships not unlike those between brothers. The same is true for men in the ipal relationship. Similar sentiments develop between women in the same relationships.

On the other hand, siblings may, for reasons discussed earlier, form different alliances and never act together in the same unit. In such cases obligations for mutual assistance are always present, but sentiments between siblings often weaken in favor of those persons more intimately involved in their lives. Also, family quarrels sometimes separate siblings for years or even a lifetime.

Relationships among children of the alliance unit are determined by the same variables. First cousins reared within an alliance unit form sibling-like relationships whereas those who never live together in an alliance unit are less intimate. These different relationships are reflected in the types of first-cousin marriages permitted. First cousins reared intimately together are improper marriage partners, whereas those reared separately can marry without qualms, unless they are patrilateral parallel cousins.

The Dakampungan

Dakampungan has two meanings among the Sama Dilaut. In its most general meaning, it is the totality of one's relatives traced lineally and collaterally, the so-called "personal kindred." But in a more restricted sense, it means a group of cognatic kinsmen, or more specifically a group of related family alliance units who regularly moor together at a moorage. To avoid confusion, I shall call the first group a "generalized dakampungan" and the second group a "localized dakampungan."

Structure of the Dakampungan Theoretically, the generalized dakampungan extends to all related persons, and in such a theoretical consideration all the Tawi-Tawi Sama Dilaut are probably members of one generalized dakampungan. Such a generalized dakampungan, of course, never meets as a group, and has little function beyond generating sentiments of obligation and reciprocity among members because they are kinsmen. Consequently, except as a term to describe the totality of one's relatives, the generalized dakampungan has little meaning to the Sama Dilaut.

The localized dakampungan, however, is quite a different matter. Seven such groups are found among the boat-dwelling Sama Dilaut of Tawi-Tawi: Tungbangkao has three, Tungkalang and Lu'uk Tulai have two each , and Lioboran and Lamiun have one each. Obviously these localized dakampungan are not closed kin groups since all members have kin ties that extend to other groups either in the same moorage or in different moorages. Furthermore, excepting the sedentary core of people found in each moorage, membership in the groups is constantly changing as families move in and out of the moorage. Each localized dakampungan is identified by a headman, or *panglima*, as well as by the moorage where the majority of its households are normally found. A localized dakampungan may constitute an entire moorage, or a moorage may have two or three such localized groups within it.

If a Sama Dilaut's parents are from different localized dakampungan, matters of circumstance determine which one he joins. Or he may find it unnecessary to claim membership in either, but simply use both at his convenience. More often, he identifies more closely with one of them because of the residence preferences of his parents. And upon marriage, he may choose to identify with his wife's localized dakampungan, which may be different from his own. Two important leads in determining a Sama Dilaut's kin affiliations are his participation in the *maggmbo' pai baha'o* ceremony, a first-fruits celebration held during the dry rice harvest season, and the man he recognizes as the panglima, or headman, of his localized dakampungan.

Sama Dilaut kin relations are revealed in the maggmbo' pai baha'o (from the word *mbo'*, meaning "grandparent" or "ancestor," and *pai baha'o* meaning "new rice") ceremony which is held in July or August at the beginning of the dry rice harvest season. Each household head acquires dry rice from land-dwelling Sama farmers. The rice is placed in a specially woven basket, which is then placed at the bow of the houseboat. That night members of the household sleep with their heads toward the rice. The following morning the rice is cooked, and taken by family members to a central household where other relatives have assembled with their own bowls of rice. The bowls, sometimes as many as twenty or thirty, are placed on the deck of the house or houseboat, following which a djin conducts a brief ceremony to call the ancestral spirits to partake of the rice and bless the living with good luck and health. Each family then takes its own bowl of rice home to eat at the next meal. All mooragers do not hold the ceremony on the same day and a family may participate in several ceremonies. The ceremony serves to reinforce ties among kinsmen, to remind them of their deceased kinsmen, and to socialize children into the kin group. Sama Dilaut claim that if the ceremony is not held, illness and death will occur and violent storms will visit the area.

A diagram of all the maggmbo' pai baha'o ceremonies of a season and the people participating in them would reveal the Sama Dilaut generalized dakampungan. Some Tawi-Tawi Sama Dilaut travel to Sitangkai to participate in the ceremony with kinsmen there, while some Sitangkai Sama Dilaut travel to Tawi-Tawi for the ceremony. Similarly, Sama Dilaut near Semporna, Sabah participate in some of the Sitangkai ceremonies with people from Tawi-Tawi. Groups participating in the ceremony comprise the bangsa, or subculture, as defined by these Sama Dilaut, namely the Sama Dilaut of Tawi-Tawi, Sibutu, and Semporna.

Each localized dakampungan recognizes a panglima whose chief function is arbitration. When disputes cross localized dakampungan lines in moorages which have several such groups, the panglima of the leading one handles the case. The position of panglima ideally passes from father to eldest son, but charisma and knowledge of *addat* (traditional law or custom) are more important in determining who holds the position. An old panglima at Tungkalang had several sons, none of whom wanted the position. At the old panglima's death, his eldest son was recognized as the new panglima and he was addressed by the title, but the younger brother of the panglima eventually assumed the position. People gravitated to him because of his natural charisma and interpretation of addat, and before long, he was recognized as panglima of the group. The eldest son of the deceased panglima did not object because he was uninterested in the position. Practical considerations of this sort more often determine succession than ideal patterns of inheritance.

The panglima settles disputes in the localized dakampungan, collects fines, and sometimes performs wedding ceremonies. His participation in these events is often minor, although his presence at a dispute gives official recognition to the disagreement. He fines offenders, but often the persons involved refuse to accept his decision and eventually settle the dispute themselves. Any fine he succeeds in collecting is divided with the offended party. I never saw or heard of any instance when the decision of the panglima was enforced against someone's will. If someone arouses too much antipathy in a moorage, he simply moves to another and returns after the incident is forgotten. If a case is particularly difficult, the panglima calls in other older men and women who are knowledgeable in addat to act as advisors, while serious problems are taken to law-enforcement officials in Bongao; however, the Sama Dilaut usually avoid such persons, most of whom they distrust.

Only in extreme cases is the panglima asked to settle disputes, since the members settle most disagreements within an alliance unit themselves. Consequently, disputes taken to the panglima are usually those that cross alliance units or deal with aspects of addat not widely known. The following cases illustrate the kind of disputes arbitrated by the panglima.

A Tungkalang Sama Dilaut man purchased a boat from a Sitangkai Sama Dilaut that was part of the bridewealth of the Sitangkai man's sister. Several months after the boat was sold, the seller became seriously ill. His attending djin claimed the illness was caused by the sale of the boat that legally belonged to the sick man's father. The Sitangkai man's relatives came to Tungkalang to buy back the boat in hopes the man would recover. When they arrived at Tungkalang, they offered a price less than the sale price, reasoning that the boat had depreciated during its several months of use by the new owners. The owners of the boat gave opposing reasons and argued that the price should be higher because they improved the boat after the purchase. For several hours the two parties argued as most of the mooragers dropped by to offer their views. Finally, they decided the panglima should handle the dispute. He was called to the boat and after listening to both sides, he recommended that the original sale price be returned for the boat. Dissatisfied with his decision, the owners said they would not return the boat unless the Sitangkai people met their price. After more discussion, the Sitangkai Sama Dilaut acquiesced and paid the demanded price.

Another case handled by the panglima concerned an elopement. In traditional style, two youths who wanted to forego the formalities of marriage stole away from their own houseboats to spend the night in the houseboat of the panglima. The following morning the parents of the couple went to the panglima's houseboat. No one was unhappy about the elopement and with the panglima acting as mediator, the parents negotiated a suitable bridewealth, after which the marriage ceremony was performed by the panglima.

The lengthiest case I observed concerned a dispute over boards. Two men were cutting boards in the forest near two other men who accused them of stealing some of their boards. The accused men adamantly denied the charge, and for several hours that night they argued with the accusers, at times almost coming to blows. Both parties finally agreed the case should go to the panglima. The following day, the men spent the entire day at the panglima's houseboat, arguing and defending their claims while other mooragers stopped by to express their opinions. The next morning, the case continued with more heated arguments. The panglima, realizing the men had become too emotional to act rationally, suggested they wait three days before continuing the case. The accusers refused to wait and said they wanted the boards returned immediately or they would go to officials in Bongao. But the panglima washed his hands of the affair and left the boat. The argument continued until finally a man related to both parties suggested that the accused men pay for the boards rather than involve the Bongao officials. After some reluctance, the two accused decided to pay part of the price and the case was dropped.

Another case concerned an argument between two sisters-in-law. One sent her child to the boat of the other, a member of a different alliance unit, to collect a debt which the latter had incurred several months earlier. The second woman, angry because the first had demanded the money through her child, accused her sister-in-law of sexual promiscuity before she was married. The accused demanded an apology, which her sister-in-law refused to offer. After several days of bickering, they took the case to the panglima, who met with the women and their husbands. After listening to both sides, the panglima decided the accuser should be fined ten pesos. The accused woman thought the fine too small and threatened to take the case to officials in Bongao, which she never did. The women remained enemies during my stay in the moorage, but the case was never renewed nor was the fine paid.

On another occasion, a launch traveling from Jolo to Bongao ran aground on the reef at Tungkalang. Sama Dilaut men from the moorage worked several hours with the crew and finally succeeded in freeing the launch. In appreciation for their assistance, the launch owner offered cash payment to the Sama Dilaut men. Some of the men thought they should not take the money because their assistance was a gesture of kindness offered to the unfortunate crew; others felt they had earned the money and should accept payment. During the argument, the moorage panglima was called and in a short time decided the men should not accept the money. Relatives of the panglima, those who originally refused payment, followed his decision while the nonrelatives of the panglima accepted the money.

The position of panglima carries a certain prestige although not much financial remuneration. Any money a panglima succeeds in accumulating is usually through his efforts at fishing or boatbuilding, and not through his duties as panglima. As revealed in the preceding cases, fines are often not paid even when levied and when they are paid, the small amount is divided with the offended party. The panglima has little power and it would be difficult for him to exert power even if he wanted to. The mobility of the scattered Sama Dilaut families discourages the development of any strong central political authority. If a panglima became inordinately demanding, the people under him would simply move to another moorage and a more tolerant panglima.

Title alone does not necessarily identify a panglima since the title is often extended to an older man as a term of respect for his age and knowledge of addat. In addition, certain Sama Dilaut men have received panglima appointments from the Office of the Sultan in Jolo because of favors they extended to local politicians. Consequently, a moorage may have several men who were appointed panglima in addition to the traditionally recognized panglima. These politically appointed panglima always acknowledge the priority of the traditionally recognized panglima.

Besides the panglima, each localized dakampungan has other specialists who perform primarily for group members but whose services may extend beyond the group, especially if their talents have gained some renown. These roles often overlap; for example, three panglima in Tawi-Tawi are also respected as outstanding djin and one enjoys additional renown as a master boatbuilder. An a'anambar ("medicine person") is found among most localized dakampungan. He or she has knowledge of plants and spells used in the treatment of wounds, headaches, stomach disorders, and other ailments. Normally, an ill person is first treated by an a'anambar, but if the illness persists, a djin is called for further treatment. Some djin rarely perform beyond their own alliance unit whereas others practice among the land-dwelling Sama and Tausug, and enjoy considerable fame throughout Tawi-Tawi. All localized dakampungan have several djin among their members who serve the needs of the group. Those most closely related are consulted first, but should illness persist, a more powerful, possibly unrelated djin may be consulted. Djin rarely charge close relatives for their services, but they sometimes charge nonrelatives, especially non-Sama Dilaut, a considerable fee. Each family alliance unit usually has at least one woman who acts as midwife, or *pandai*, but within each localized dakampungan, several older women are recognized as expert pandai and are consulted for difficult births. Some men known as imams know Arabic chants and recite them at curing ceremonies, funerals, and weddings. Three brothers who belong to the same localized dakampungan are the only imams among the Tawi-Tawi Sama Dilaut. Most localized dakampungan also have wood carvers among their members. These men execute the carvings on new boats and grave markers. As the djin, they never charge closely related people for their services, although they expect payment from distant kinsmen and especially nonkinsmen. Boatbuilders, too, are frequently called on by localized dakampungan members to assist in boatbuilding; except when helping closely related persons, they are always paid for their work.

Although the localized dakampungan never meets as a group, most of its members come together for important weddings, curing ceremonies, and superincisions.

Kinship Terminology Members of both the generalized and localized dakampungan are identified by kinship terms that reflect the cognatic principle of organization. The only persons within the generalized dakampungan who are distinguished by distinctive kin terms are members of the nuclear family. These terms are extended beyond the nuclear family only in cases of intimate friendships. The distinctive terms for the nuclear family reflect its basic independent role in Sama Dilaut society. The lack of terminological distinction between father's and mother's relatives reflects the cognatic nature of Sama Dilaut society.

Sama Dilaut kin terms are a combination of the so-called Eskimo and Hawaiian-type systems. Ego terminologically distinguishes his mother and father from their siblings, and parents' siblings are called by male and female terms that extend collaterally to all relatives of their generation. One term (the same one used for "ancestors") is used for all relatives in the second and ascending generations from ego. Within his own generation, ego distinguishes siblings from cousins, and further distinguishes collaterality of cousinship by suffixing first, second, or third to the term. Ego's own children are distinguished from nephews and nieces, but the term for nephew and niece is extended to the offspring of all kinsmen in ego's generation. All persons in the second and descending generations from ego are addressed by one term. Persons married to ego's spouse's siblings are called by a term that is also extended to include all persons married to kinsmen of ego's spouse's generation. Persons married to ego's siblings and collateral consanguines of his generation are called by a single term, as are those persons married to ego's consanguines of descending generations (including his own children's spouses). Ego calls all affines in ascending generations by a single term. Excepting the terms for mother, father, uncle, and aunt, Sama Dilaut kin terms are not gender specific, but gender may be indicated by suffixing *denda* (female) or *lella* (male). An apparently older term, *si'it*, makes no gender distinction between mother's and father's collaterals. The following discussion defines each Sama Dilaut kin term.

1. *Hundah* — ego's female spouse. This term is used both as a term of address and reference. Ego rarely refers to his wife by her first name. A wife is usually referred to as "my wife" ; if speaking to his child, as "your mother"; or if addressing her, as "hundah."

2. *Hallah* — ego's male spouse. This term is also used as both a term of address and reference. Ego rarely refers to her husband by his first name. A husband is usually referred to as "my husband"; or if speaking to her child as "your father"; or if addressing him, as "hallah."

3. *Unggoh* — mother. This term is used as both a term of reference and address.

4. *Ummah* — father. This term is used as both a term of reference and address.

5. *Babu* — parents' female siblings; female spouses of parents' siblings; any female collateral relatives of parents' generation; any female spouses of collateral relatives of parents' generation. Babu is used primarily as a term of reference. If ego is intimately associated with babu over an extensive period of time, it is used as a term of address. However, if there is little age difference between ego and babu, or if ego rarely associates with her, he refers to her by her personal name. Although the term may be extended to indefinite collateral limits, it is rarely used to address persons beyond parents' siblings except as a term of respect. However, as a term of reference, it is extended to indefinite collateral limits.

6. *Bapa* — parents' male siblings; male spouses of parents' siblings; any male collateral relative of parents' generation; any male spouses of collateral relatives of parents' generation. The uses of this term are identical to those for babu.

7. *Si'it* — any consanguineal relative of parents' generation. This term is rarely used among the Sama Dilaut, and apparently is an old term. Most young people cannot define it. Older informants, however, say it is an old term that describes persons in the babu and bapa categories. Among some Sinama-speaking people in Tawi-Tawi, the term is unknown whereas others say it is an old term simply meaning "kinsmen."

8. *Mbo'* — any consanguineal relative in the second and ascending generations from ego. Few Sama Dilaut can name relatives in ascending generations from their grandparents. Mbo' is extended collaterally to indefinite limits as a term of address and is frequently used as a term of respect for older persons unrelated to ego. The same term is extended lineally and collaterally to all of one's deceased ancestors. As a term of reference, it is used for any older relative.

9. *Danakan* — sibling. This kin term serves as a reference term. Occasionally it is extended to a close friend (relative or nonrelative) to indicate intimacy. Regardless of gender, an older sibling is referred to as *siaka* and a younger sibling as *siali*. Depending on age in relation to ego, siblings are addressed by one of the following terms or by their given names or nicknames.

10. *Otok* — youngest and oldest brother, or youngest and oldest son. Most commonly this term of address is reserved for members of the nuclear family although it is sometimes extended collaterally to cousins who stand in those age positions within their own nuclear families. When applied to the youngest child, it is used as a term of endearment (and is temporary if other sons follow him). It serves as a term of respect for the oldest son.

11. *Arung* — youngest and oldest sister, or youngest and oldest daughter. The use of this term follows that of otok.

12. *Kaki* — cousin. As a term of reference, kaki is used for any degree of cousin relationship. If there is need to specify degree of collaterality, suffixes indicating first, second, third, etc. are added. However, few Sama Dilaut can trace cousinship beyond second cousins, and although Sama Dilaut can theoretically trace cousinship to an infinite degree of collaterality, such relationships rarely need definition. A person beyond a first cousin falls into that large amorphous group called *kampun*, or kinsmen. Kaki is often applied to anyone known to be related to ego but whose exact relationship is unknown. In this second usage, it could perhaps better be translated as "kinsman" or "relative."

13. *Anak* — son or daughter. This term has the general meaning of child, but when used with a personal pronoun it becomes the reference term for son or daughter. Children are addressed by otok, arung or their personal names.

14. *Kamanakan* — sibling's child; child of any cousin in any degree of collaterality. Kamanakan is a term of reference; persons in this relationship are usually addressed by their personal names or by otok or arung, if they are in those age categories.

15. *Umpu* — any consanguineal relative in the second and descending generations from ego.

16. *Mattoa* — any affines in ascending generations from ego. Mattoa is a term of reference for relatives in these categories, but it is a term of address for spouse's parents. Other affines in spouse's generation are normally called by their given names whereas affines in higher generations are usually called mbo'.

17. *Ayuan* — any affines in descending generations from ego. Ayuan is a term of reference and rarely used in address.

18. *Ba'i* — the relationship between two couples whose children are married to one another. Also the term they call one another.

19. *Ipal* — any person married to a consanguineal relative of ego's generation or a consanguine of ego's spouse's generation. Most commonly used as a term of reference, ipal may also be used as a term of address.

20. *Bilas* — any person married to a consanguineal relative of ego's spouse's generation. Although the term may be extended to infinite collaterality, it is rarely extended beyond the first degree. The term is used as a term of reference and address.

As the preceding discussion reveals, Sama Dilaut kinship terms are predominantly classificatory. The grandparental and ascending generations are called by a single term. At one time, all members of ego's parents' generation (excluding the parents) were apparently called by a single term; now division occurs along gender lines. Excluding his own children, all members of the first descending generation from ego are called by one term as are all members of the second and descending generations. Affines are placed into even larger categories. A single term describes all affines in ascending generations from ego while another term describes all affines in descending generations from ego. All affines married to consanguines of ego's generation are called by one term.

The Moorage
Moorage Structure In each of the five Sama Dilaut moorages, one localized dakampungan is recognized as the leading kin group of the moorage. In most cases this group is the one that originally began mooring there, and others who later moored there recognize the priority of the first group. As noted, Tungbangkao has three such groups, Tungkalang and Lu'uk Tulai have two each, while Lioboran and Lamiun have one each . Although extremely informal, certain rights and prestige are enjoyed by these "first families." In the event of quarrels, others are sometimes chastised as "outsiders" even though they may have moored there for many years. The panglima of the original group is recognized as headman of the moorage, and although each localized dakampungan consults its own panglima for problems within the group, quarrels that cross group lines are taken to the moorage panglima. And should it be necessary for the moorage to be represented outside the community, the panglima of the first localized dakampungan would be the representative.

Lamiun illustrates how Sama Dilaut moorages originate. This moorage consists almost entirely of the married sons and daughters of two brothers and their female first cousin who began mooring there ten years ago after they were frightened away from a nearby village of land dwellers. Lamiun is known among Sama Dilaut as the home place of this particular localized dakampungan even though other Sama Dilaut have begun to moor there. Eventually other localized dakampungan will probably emerge at Lamiun if the present trend continues, but the founding group will be considered the "natives" of the moorage and their panglima will serve as the moorage headman.

A shift in power occurred between two localized dakampungan at Tungkalang. The original localized dakampungan was headed by a panglima who was a respected leader in his younger days. His siblings were equally respected in earlier years; one was a powerful djin, another a master boatbuilder, and still another was an expert fisherman. When I first met the family in 1963, they were old and somewhat senile. The headman himself had only one daughter, one of his brothers had eight children, and the other siblings had one or two children each. None of the younger generation had the skills or charisma of their parents. Some four years previous to my arrival, a localized dakampungan from a moorage now dispersed moved to Tungkalang. The adults of the new group were much like the leaders of the old group in their youth— charismatic and competent in a number of skills. The new localized dakampungan acknowledged the priority of the first group and paid proper respect to the old panglima. At his death they recognized the ascendancy of his oldest nephew to his position. The nephew was not qualified for the position, however; he was unlearned in addat, had poor judgment, and in general lacked the qualities of a good leader. After several unsuccessful cases, it became apparent to the mooragers that the man was not a proper headman. No one else in his family fared better, so the mooragers began to look elsewhere for someone to settle their disputes. The headman of the more recently arrived kin group was still fairly young, perhaps forty, but well versed in addat and a competent leader of his own localized dakampungan. Before long, mooragers began to seek his advice and by the time I left the moorage, he was recognized as the panglima of the moorage and his kin group was considered the leading localized dakampungan. The older members of the original localized dakampungan revealed some resentment at the shift in power, but realized they had failed to provide a competent leader for the moorage. The nephew of the deceased panglima continued to act as headman of his localized dakampungan, but his position of moorage leadership was lost.

Three different types of households are discernible within the localized dakampungan, namely sedentary, seminomadic, and nomadic. The house dwellers and a nucleus of boat dwellers that rarely leaves the moorage form the stable element of the population around which the other households cluster. These households are usually the immediate family of the moorage headman, married couples native to the moorage, and families who are primarily farmers or boatbuilders. The second group, the seminomads, are usually fishermen whose residence in the moorage is determined by the phases of the moon, or others who are in the moorage only part-time to garden or build boats. The third and smallest group, the nomads, is seldom in the moorage for longer than a few weeks at a time and includes people passing through the moorage en route elsewhere.

The moorage may be viewed as three concentric circles: the innermost circle is the sedentary population, the second circle the seminomads and the third the nomads. Overlaying these concentric circles are the localized dakampungan. Within these localized dakampungan, the family alliance units are a series of smaller circles, not concentric, but overlapping one another and overlaying the three major concentric circles since a family alliance unit may include sedentary persons, seminomads and sometimes even nomads. In addition, a member of an alliance unit may join another alliance unit in the moorage, conceivably in a different localized dakampungan. If another dimension is added to the above circles, it is possible to illustrate how the alliance units of one moorage eventually include members of other moorages, thereby revealing the web of kinship ties that connect the five Tawi-Tawi Sama Dilaut moorages.

Ideally, social stratification in a Sama Dilaut moorage follows a pyramidal structure that ignores localized dakampungan affiliation. At the top of the pyramid is the headman; on the second step are the djin and other leaders; on the third step are the permanent residents of the moorage, followed by the seminomads and ending with the nomads. There are exceptions, of course. For example, a seminomadic man, because of his success in fishing, may have considerable wealth which, coupled with a strong personality, may make him one of the most influential men in the moorage. Similarly, a very old man although still recognized as the moorage panglima, may be disregarded by the mooragers because of his senility. Some of the seminomadic fishermen may be wealthier than some permanent residents of the moorage, but are considered somewhat inferior because of their transitory position based on their nomadic way of life. Likewise, a djin, whose position may have high status, often leads a seminomadic life. A sense of prestige is rapidly becoming associated with house living, which will no doubt be a strong influence in accelerating the move to houses within the next few years as more Sama Dilaut embrace the house-dwelling habit.

Moorage Activities The localized dakampungan of the moorage join together for only two occasions, namely a ceremony to rid the moorage of disease-causing spirits and a communal fish drive practiced in the Bilatan waters. Although a large wedding celebration may attract the entire moorage to the evening activities, one or two localized dakampungan sponsor the affair and the other mooragers are observers. The curing ceremony and the fish drive, however, involve active participation and planning by all the mooragers.

During times of much illness, death, or unusually bad luck, a ceremony called pamatulakan is held to rid the moorage of the spirits believed responsible for the misfortune. Each family contributes an amount of money or goods toward the construction of a small boat (pamatulakan) to carry away the spirits believed responsible for the trouble. One family provides a sail, another outriggers, another food offerings, etc. Several men, representing all the localized dakampungan, construct the boat and fill it with offerings. Djin from the groups pull the boat through the moorage as they chant to attract the spirits. The boat is then taken to the open sea and set adrift with the troublesome spirits aboard.

The communal fish drives practiced at Tungbangkao also involve the active participation of most mooragers. As dicussed in chapter 5, at certain tides schools of fish are attracted to the Bilatan reefs. At this time, the moorage men, boys, and sometimes women leave the moorage in large flotillas for communal fish drives. Although most of the participants are related, kinship is not a prerequisite for joining the drives.

Intermoorage Relations Because of the kinship ties and frequent movements among the moorages, all five of the Tawi-Tawi moorages represent a single Sama Dilaut community. Moorages in close proximity have more contacts than more distant ones. Daily communication normally occurs between Lu'uk Tulai and Tungkalang, as well as between Tungkalang and Lamiun, and Tungbangkao and Lioboran. Contacts between the Sanga-Sanga moorages and the Bilatan moorages are less frequent, but the rich fishing grounds and the burial islands attract many of the Sanga-Sanga people to Bilatan. Sama Dilaut from Tungbangkao or Lioboran with business in Bongao often moor their boats at Tungkalang, rather than face possible mistreatment in Bongao. For similar reasons, Sama Dilaut from Lu'uk Tulai, as well as far-off Siasi and Sitangkai, usually prefer to stay at Tungkalang rather than Bongao. As a result, Tungkalang often has a large transient population.

The Tawi-Tawi Sama Dilaut recognize the Sibutu and Semporna Sama Dilaut as members of their bangsa, or subculture, while the Sama Dilaut of Siasi, Jolo, and Zamboanga are viewed as a different, albeit closely related group. Kinship ties verify the Sama Dilaut view; many kinship ties connect the Tawi-Tawi and Sibutu Sama Dilaut, as well as the Semporna and Sitangkai Sama Dilaut (Sather 1997, 19), whereas few ties extend northward to Siasi and Jolo.

THE SPIRITUAL REALM

The Tawi-Tawi Sama Dilaut believe in a host of spirits that are responsible for the fortunes and misfortunes of the world. Through trance and ritual, shamans (djin) are able to communicate with these spirits to sometimes restore harmony to human affairs. Ceremonies range from simple rituals performed by individuals to large gatherings involving most of the moorage. Although Sama Dilaut religion has obvious Islamic influences, much of it reflects the religion found throughout the islands prior to the coming of Islam. Thus, it provides a window to the religious past of the Sama people.

Origin Stories

The Sama Dilaut do not have an extensive oral literature dealing with religious matters, but like all people they have myths about their beginnings. The following is one of their myths about the origin of life and death:

> Long ago, in the early days of the world, Tuhan [God] told the people they must die. Either they could die like the moon and be reborn each month or they could die like the leaves of the tree and be replaced by new leaves. They chose the latter. Thus people die, but their descendants continue their family lines.

Another version of the same story offers a slightly different origin of life:

> In the beginning only two Sama Dilaut couples lived on earth. They were told they must die and were given a choice as to how death would occur. They could die like the moon and be reborn each month, or they could die like the banana plant, the roots of which produce new life. They chose the latter, and thus people die, but have children who continue their family line.

Another Sama Dilaut myth relates the origin of the various people of the world:

> In the beginning, only one man and one woman lived on earth. Eventually, they had two children. One child was thrown into the sea and his offspring became the Sama Dilaut. The second child was thrown onto land and his off-spring became the land people. Other children born to the couple were thrown in the four cardinal directions and their descendants populated the rest of the world.

The legend related in chapter 2 about the Sama Dilaut's departure from Johore and their subsequent drifting at sea tells the origin of the first shaman (djin). That portion of the legend is relevant to this context.

> For one week they drifted helplessly until finally the leader pleaded to Tuhan [God] for help. Within minutes, Tuhan sent down a saitan which entered the leader who became the first djin among the Sama Dilaut. The saitan instructed the leader to sail for two days toward the east.

In two of these stories, Tuhan (God) is mentioned as the prime mover. As the following discussion reveals, Tuhan is not important in the everyday lives of most Sama Dilaut, but he is generally regarded as the prime mover that created everything.

Spirits

The world of the Sama Dilaut is populated with countless supernatural beings. They are found in the sky, in the trees, on the beaches, under the ground, atop the mountains, on the sea, and beneath the sea. Sometimes they are visible, but usually they are not. Sometimes they speak, more often they are silent. They possess people and animals as well as inanimate objects. Often they are hideous and terrifying, but at other times they are beautiful and seductive. Some wander aimlessly, others never leave certain islets or locales. Some enter the sleep of humans and are responsible for bad dreams and nightmares. Some fly, some swim, some walk, and some run. Some are the spirits of once-living people whereas others have always existed as supernaturals. Some demand offerings of food, tobacco, or flags; others want to be left alone. None is by nature entirely benevolent.

No Sama Dilaut can name all the spirits that inhabit their world. They are simply too numerous. A few Sama Dilaut can list the different types of spirits and describe their unique characteristics, but most know spirits only in a general way. The more devout believers conduct small rituals to honor spirits during routine daily activities whereas others hold rituals only when faced with crises. A few even express disbelief in the spirits.

Although little consensus prevails on the specific number of spirits and their special characteristics, some consensus prevails on the different types of spirits. An investigation of Sama Dilaut religious beliefs reveals five general categories of spirits, namely (1) Tuhan, a supreme being who created the world, but rarely involves himself in human affairs; (2) saitan, supernatural beings who never lived as humans; (3) *ummagged*, spirits of once-living people, also known collectively as mboh' (ancestors); (4) *panggua'*, the remains of once-living people who occasionally come back to haunt the living; and (5) a collection of ghouls, monsters, and tricksters distinct from the above. Except for Tuhan, who is usually perceived separately from other spirits, these categories should not be considered mutually exclusive. Most Sama Dilaut are very casual in their use of the names and reveal considerable variation in their definitions of them.

Tuhan Sama Dilaut religion includes belief in a supreme being who created the world. This being, called Tuhan, is of minor importance in the daily concerns of most Sama Dilaut who have only vague and often contradictory notions about his role in human affairs. Some Sama Dilaut claim to know nothing of Tuhan, others say he is the god of the land people, while still others acknowledge him as part of their religious concerns. Among the Muslims of Sulu, indeed throughout much of Islamic Southeast Asia, Tuhan is used synonymously with Allah, but few Sama Dilaut use the names synonymously since they generally associate Allah with the religion of the land dwellers. Islam has doubtlessly influenced the Sama Dilaut concept of Tuhan, but the concept of a supreme deity most likely predates Islam since it is common to many indigenous religions of Southeast Asia.

Tuhan is always referred to as male, and his residence is assigned to some vague place in the sky. Some Sama Dilaut claim disbelief in Tuhan, but most consider him the creator and ultimate power behind everything, although they know little of him beyond that. Far less important to the Sama Dilaut than either the saitan or ummagged, Tuhan is rarely the object of ritual concern. I heard of no ceremonies specifically for Tuhan, nor of offerings made to him.

The Sama Dilaut disagree about the role of Tuhan in human affairs. Some believe he is removed from any concern. He created the universe and everything within it, and then left it to operate on its own. Others believe he is more actively involved. Some say Tuhan controls the saitan, and the saitan harm the living because of his will. Few Sama Dilaut regard Tuhan as a benevolent being.

Some, in fact, believe the opposite and claim that if Tuhan were all-powerful, he could stop the evil deeds of the saitan if he chose to do so. He does not, so he must not be too kindly disposed toward people. One woman told me Tuhan watches the behavior of humans and sends saitan to punish them when they misbehave. Only one person associated the ummagged with Tuhan, claiming they are sometimes his messengers. Many Sama Dilaut use Tuhan and fate interchangeably as explanations for events they cannot control.

Saitan The word saitan applies to a large category of spirits that can cause illness, bad luck, and other kinds of misfortune. Saitan have existed since the beginning of time and were never humans. One Sama Dilaut claimed, however, that the spirits of evil land-dwelling people sometimes become saitan. The name is obviously Islamic in origin, but the belief in such spirits no doubt predates the arrival of Islam in Tawi-Tawi, since similar spirits are found in most indigenous religions of Southeast Asia. They were probably part of Sama religion long before the arrival of Islam, and as the islanders became Muslims, the Islamic name was transferred to the local spirits.

Saitan are encountered day and night, but are most commonly seen at night, especially during the period of bulan matai ("dead moon") when the nights are darkest. The best way to avoid misfortune with the saitan is to stay away from places they are known to inhabit. Although most saitan wander freely throughout Tawi-Tawi, some tend to congregate or live individually in certain locations called *tempat*, such as tiny islets, distinctive trees (especially the *nunuk* [*Ficus*

Fig. 55 Tempat inhabited by saitan

microcarpa]), unusual geological formations (such as strangely shaped rocks) and seas with treacherous riptides or strong currents (fig. 55). If these places must be visited, the resident saitan should be given offerings, such as betel, tobacco, cigarettes, bits of food and small green, white or yellow flags (*panji*).

If disturbed, saitan sometime cause illness and misfortune, but often they interfere in human affairs simply because they are temperamental. Most Sama Dilaut death and illness are attributed to saitan. They also enter people's heads and cause mental illnesses. Two shipwrecks in Tawi-Tawi were attributed to saitan. Once a ship passed too closely to an islet inhabited by saitan and they caused it to go aground. At another time, a saitan appeared in the form of a beautiful woman and lured a ship's pilot onto a reef. Saitan inflict illness on those who express disbelief in them, and if people speak disrespectfully of them, they retaliate by causing sore throats and laryngitis. Saitan have traditional tastes and do not like change. They brought illness to one household because the dwelling was partitioned into rooms rather than retained as a traditional one-room house. A boatbuilder painted the prow of his boat a nontraditional color and suffered consequent illness from the offended saitan. They also dislike unclean surroundings, and one household experienced frequent illnesses because the saitan disapproved of their slovenly housekeeping habits. An old woman always kept the waters around her houseboat clear of seaweed and debris so the saitan would not be displeased. Saitan do not approve of mechanical gadgets either, and several times when my tape recorder, camera, and outboard motor failed, their malfunction was attributed to saitan.

Although it is difficult to escape saitan bent on harm, amulets sometimes discourage them. Infants are especially vulnerable to saitan, but if boughs of citrus trees are placed on the houseboat of a newborn child, they stay away. Also, a charcoal spot on a baby's forehead as well as special necklaces and bracelets will provide protection from saitan. When a child's head is shaven to deal with the lice and sores that occasionally plague children, a small patch of hair is always left on the fontanel to protect it from saitan. A branch of black coral wards off saitan, as does a burning lamp or a dog barking at night. Sleeping on the side assures that one's sleep will not be disturbed by saitan.

Small flags of yellow, white, or green appeal to saitan in different ways. Sometimes they are left as offerings at tempat, places where saitan reside, but at other times they are placed on houseboats to deter saitan, as at Tungkalang, where boats once flew flags to keep away saitan believed responsible for an outbreak of cholera. Flags are sometimes displayed in the wake of storms to discourage approaching saitan carried by the wind, especially the south wind.

Ummagged All living beings have ummagged (some Sama Dilaut say inanimate objects have them also), but those most important to the Sama Dilaut are the ummagged of once-living people, known collectively as mbo', or ancestors. Many ummagged are known by the personal names they had as living friends and relatives, and the respect such people warranted in their lifetimes should be extended to them after death. One should never speak disrespectfully of ummagged (some say their names should not even be mentioned) and one should periodically share good fortune with them in the form of small offerings. In return for this proper treatment, the ummagged occasionally assist the living. But if such respect is not shown, they may bring harm to the offenders.

The Sama Dilaut disagree as to where the ummagged is located in the living body. Some say it is located in the heart or liver while others claim it is in the stomach. If the body is struck soundly, the ummagged may be dislodged and cause illness. It may even leave the body and cause fainting. The ummagged sometimes leaves the body during sleep and its adventures are remembered as dreams. At death, the ummagged withdraws from the body, lingers near the place of death for a short period, and then dwells on the cemetery island where its grave is located.

For the most part, the ummagged reside contentedly on the cemetery islands. Much more localized than the saitan, they only leave the islands to punish offenses or to assist djin in curing ceremonies. In their benevolent moods, they bring good fortune to the living, but more typically they involve themselves in human affairs to punish misbehavior. The ummagged of people who died young are sometimes jealous of the living and harm them out of spite. Ummagged bring dreams to sleepers and give them messages by entering their opened mouths. Because ummagged are primarily nocturnal beings, the Sama Dilaut approach the cemeteries with little apprehension during the daytime, but avoid them at nighttime.

If a Sama Dilaut offends an ummagged, the result is illness, misfortune, or even death. To atone for the offense, offerings are given the ummagged at home or at the cemetery. If Sama Dilaut are near the cemetery islands, perhaps on a fishing trip, they often stop to leave small offerings to the ummagged of recently deceased relatives. Suitable offerings are similar to those given to saitan, namely tobacco, food, betel, cigarettes, or flags.

Panggua' Panggua' are not spirits like saitan or ummagged but corpses that return to haunt the living. The chief reason panggua' appear is that their bodies were not properly bathed before burial. Panggua' may also return to haunt people who dealt with them unfairly when they were alive or who failed to mourn their deaths properly. People who were evil during their lives sometimes return to haunt the living. One informant told me that panggua' are particularly fond of cooked squash and will appear if it is left in the houseboat overnight.

Panggua' are seen in boats, houses, trees, and reefs, but are most often encountered on land at night. I knew only one person who claimed that panggua' appear during the daytime. They assume various forms and colors. Some say panggua' look exactly like corpses when wrapped in their white shrouds. Others describe them as partially decayed bodies, with rotting flesh and offensive odors. Sometimes they appear as skeletons. One man saw a panggua' that looked like an octopus, while another man saw one that was a black blob with holes for eyes.

Encounters with panggua' sometimes frighten the ummagged from the body and result in illness or fainting. Some people have bouts of bad luck after seeing panggua'. Most panggua' are content to frighten people, but death from an encounter is not unknown.

Offerings are not made to panggua'. The best way to avoid them is to treat all people respectfully, mourn the dead at funerals, and bathe corpses properly before burial. But some panggua' simply enjoy haunting the living and do so even if they were not mistreated.

Some people become panggua' while still alive. Such people are called *panggua' allum* ("live ghosts") or sleepwalkers. If people harbor incestuous thoughts, ummagged sometimes take their bodies on nocturnal adventures while they sleep.

Ghouls, Monsters, and Tricksters In addition to the above supernatural beings, the Sama Dilaut believe in a host of ghouls, monsters, and tricksters who occasionally harass them. Some Sama Dilaut claim these are types of saitan, but others view them differently from saitan. Belief in some is widespread whereas others tend to be localized. The following list is not intended to be exhaustive, but rather illustrative of the beings within this category.

A *mananokoban* is a hideous monster that lives in the forest. If it attacks a person, death follows in half a day.

A *galap*, usually encountered at night, is terrifying to see and causes death by heart attack.

A *barbalan* looks and behaves like a normal person, but at night it takes the form of a bird, attacks people, and sucks their blood. According to the Tawi-Tawi Sama Dilaut, many barbalan are found among the Yakan people of Basilan island.

A *gansuang* is a gigantic monster-like creature that tears people apart and eats them.

A *babangan* is a flaming being that appears at night. If the flame touches a person, death is instantaneous.

A *kaliawan* is a small spirit, usually encountered in the forest, which encourages people to fly, but once high in the sky, they fall to their deaths.

A *bagganan* lives in the sea, often in the Siasi waters. It drowns unsuspecting fishermen.

A *manolokot* is a large monster with dark skin, no hair, and only one leg. Encounters result in headaches, general illness, and sometimes death.

A *bagongan*, sometimes called *timbalon*, causes insanity when encountered.

Offerings are not made to these supernaturals, nor are they important in the spiritual concerns of most Sama Dilaut. Their habitats are avoided, although it is not always known where they might be found. If one becomes ill as a result of an encounter, the traditional healing methods of the djin are usually effective. I met only two Sama Dilaut who encountered such beings. Most know them only through stories they have heard, some do not believe in them, while most assume a more agnostic stance.

Magic

The traditional anthropological distinction between religion and magic generally applies to the Sama Dilaut: religion is a system of beliefs and rituals directed to the appeasement of forces and beings beyond human control, whereas magic is an attempt to manipulate processes to bring about desired results, or to ward off undesirable influences by wearing amulets. Sama Dilaut magic is of two general types, namely anting-anting, the wearing of protective amulets, and kabolan, the recitation of spells and formulas to bring about desired ends.

By far the most common magic used by the Sama Dilaut is anting-anting, amulets of various sizes and materials worn on the body or kept in the house or boat. Such amulets include strangely shaped, or unusually colored stones, shells, and pieces of wood that are woven in strings and worn as bracelets or necklaces; charmed earrings, bracelets, or necklaces placed on infants and small children; and strips of shrouds worn as bracelets to ward off the spirits of the recently deceased.

Anting-anting offer various types of protection. They protect children from the many harmful spirits believed to prey on them, assist fishermen by luring fish to their nets and hooks, assure success in love, provide protection from the bullets or blades of enemies, give immunity to poisons and various ailments, and discourage spirits from approaching homes and individuals. The popularity of the different kinds of anting-anting depends on their effectiveness. For example, a man with a stubborn wound that would not heal tried many types of anting-anting. Finally, a djin advised him to tie a gold ring on a black ribbon and wear it around his neck; he did so and within days the wound healed. Soon other members of the moorage were wearing gold rings on black ribbons to heal their sores and wounds.

The following incidents illustrate the effectiveness of anting-anting. One man said his anting-anting was so powerful that when he was struck twice on the head by a bladed weapon, he suffered no injury. A fisherman showed me scars on his body resulting from wounds inflicted while dynamiting fish; he claimed that without his anting-anting, the explosive would have killed him. Another man said he was able to make the wind blow with his anting-anting. A young man with a special anting-anting from Borneo said that when a man attacked him with a stick, his anting-anting turned the stick on the attacker. A young woman who wore a special string necklace made by her grandfather was protected from would-be seducers. Another woman carried a special stone when she collected firewood for protection against land spirits. An old man demonstrated the strength of his anting-anting by striking his arm soundly with a knife, and no injury resulted.

Much less widespread among the Sama Dilaut is kabolan, the recitation of special chants and spells to bring about desired ends. This magic can be used for purposes as varied as those of anting-anting. Kabolan spells can drive away evil spirits, aid in curing illness, facilitate the delivery of a baby, or improve one's luck in love. For instance, if a man gathers sand that a woman has stepped on, ties it in a white cloth, places it in his houseboat, and recites a spell over it, the woman will develop a great itching on her feet that will not be relieved until she goes to the man's boat where she can be easily seduced. Other spells are believed to increase or decrease the wind's velocity. One man claimed to know a spell that would eliminate the smell of a decomposing body. Only one type of fishing kabolan is used regularly by the Sama Dilaut. Most Sama Dilaut do not employ magic in fishing and are well aware that successful fishing is the result of following time-tested methods. In shark fishing, however, most fishermen sing songs that are believed to attract the shark and offer protection to the fisherman. As noted earlier, this type of fishing is the most dangerous of all Sama Dilaut fishing.

Both anting-anting and kabolan must be purchased to be effective. The more powerful the magic, the higher its price. One man paid 100 pesos (a great sum for a Sama Dilaut) for his anting-anting, whereas another bought his for only three pesos, some incense, two pounds of rice, and a glass float from a fishing net. Various precautions are taken to insure the success of the magic. One man told me his fishing anting-anting was ineffective if someone slept in the boat while he fished. Another said the power of his anting-anting would be lost if he urinated or defecated while wearing it. A young mother claimed the magical necklace worn by her baby would be weakened if submerged in water.

Although anting-anting and kabolan are used principally for protection by the Sama Dilaut, they can also be used for malevolent ends. The Sama Dilaut consistently claimed that sorcerers are not found among them but are common among the land dwellers, a reflection of their view of the land people. Certain villages and islands (especially Sibutu island) are well known to the Sama Dilaut for their sorcerers who use magic to bring about illness, misfortune, and even death. Such sorcery usually involves the recitation of chants, but sometimes objects are treated and left in the presence of unwary victims. Land people occasionally direct their sorcery toward the Sama Dilaut, as in the following cases. A Sama Dilaut man sold a boat to a land-dwelling Sama who refused to pay for it on the agreed date. After attempting to collect his money, the Sama Dilaut suffered dizziness and nausea when he returned home. He decided the man was using kabolan to make him ill, so he went to a djin who knew a kabolan that would counteract the spell. Another Sama Dilaut claimed an infection on his foot was caused by the sorcery of a land dweller who disliked him.

Sama Dilaut magic is not a realm of ritual and belief separate from religion. Magical amulets and chants are often used in the context of ceremonies directed toward spirits; less often, a religious ritual is performed to make the magic more effective. Anything that offers protection from a potentially dangerous world appeals to the Sama Dilaut, and magic therefore has wide appeal.

The Djin

Central to Sama Dilaut religion is the djin, or shaman.[1] The djin, who may be male or female, communicates with spirits to discover causes of illness or misfortune. In addition, he or she officiates at all rites of passage to invoke and appease spirits.

Although all Sama Dilaut djin share certain views of the spirit world and perform similar rituals, each is nonetheless somewhat distinctive. One becomes a djin in various ways. More often than not, a djin's father or mother was also a djin and much of his knowledge was learned from his parent. Frequently, several children of one family are djin. Becoming a djin, however, is not strictly a matter of inheritance. The children of some powerful djin never become djin, whereas some people whose parents were never djin somehow become djin.

One of the most powerful djin in Tawi-Tawi, a woman in her middle sixties, inherited her djin powers when her grandmother died. After the grandmother's death, the saitan with whom she regularly communicated began communicating with the granddaughter. Her grandmother had already taught her some rituals and the saitan taught her more. At the time I knew her, her daughter was assisting in ceremonies, and she claimed that after her death the daughter would inherit her powers. A powerful male djin told me he was never interested in becoming a djin until his father died. One night while he was sleeping, his father's spirit came to him and told him to become a djin. Shortly thereafter, he became seriously ill; the saitan began visiting him and when he recovered, he became a djin. Another man became critically ill and while his father, a djin, was treating him, the saitan told the father to teach the son his djin skills when he recovered. The father did so and the son eventually became a djin. Another man became a djin after a serious illness at the age of three. The saitan causing his illness said they would leave his body only if the parents (who were not djin) promised that the child would become a djin when he reached adulthood. The parents made the promise and the child recovered. When he reached his early twenties, the saitan again came to him and he has been a djin ever since. Most typically, then, the saitan decide who becomes a djin, and quite often the saitan select the children of deceased djin. A female djin told me Tuhan decides which people will become djin. After selecting them, he sends saitan to communicate with them. Some djin have a special saitan who remains with them throughout their lives to provide contact with the spirit world. Frequently, these personal saitan are also called djin.[2]

When a patient is brought to a djin for treatment, she must first determine which spirits are causing the illness. The ways to determine this are as numerous as the djin, since each has a method somewhat unique. One djin used the following diagnostic technique. When someone came to her for treatment, she first determined if she could help the person by lightly placing a sewing needle in a white bowl of water. If the needle sank to the bottom, the case was beyond her powers. But if the needle floated, she could treat the illness. To discover the cause of the illness, she then placed a small stick in the same bowl of water. She stirred the water with her finger and if the stick settled in a position pointing in the direction of the cemetery islands, she knew an ummagged was causing the illness. But if the stick pointed toward islets believed inhabited by saitan, then these spirits were responsible for the illness. Next, the djin questioned the patient carefully about his illness and any behavior that might have offended the spirits. Usually the patient, the patient's family, or the djin could think of something that might have offended a spirit.

In order to treat illness, the djin needs cooperation from the responsible spirits. They must be contacted to discover why they are causing the illness and how it can be eliminated. This is achieved in various ways. All djin begin ceremonies by burning incense, the smoke of which is believed to attract spirits if accompanied by prayer incantations. If incense is not available, a smoking wood coal will suffice. Some djin sprinkle perfume over the patient and themselves in order to attract the spirits. Green, white, and yellow are favorite colors of the saitan, and consequently, the djin and the patient often wear clothes of these colors to attract spirits. Small flags of the same colors are sometimes displayed to invoke spirits. Several male and female djin told me that their long hair attracts the saitan, and if they cut it they will lose their powers. Because some saitan like dancing, the djin sometimes dances until possessed by a saitan who then reveals the remedy for the illness. One djin told me that when she wants to contact the saitan, she puts on her green and yellow djin clothes and calls to them in the Tausug language. If they do not appear, she calls in Malay, and if they still do not appear, she calls in Sinama. When a saitan appears, she sends it to discover the cause of the illness. She said it was like sending a letter, only faster. Another djin said that if he wears Western-style trousers, the saitan will not come to him. Some claim the saitan like cleanliness and if their boats or houses are not kept immaculate, they will not appear. Special chants attract some saitan, and it is only through such chants that the djin can communicate with them. Some saitan are very traditional and do not come to djin who live in houses with partitions. Other saitan visit only houseboats and avoid houses altogether. Therefore, some djin must conduct ceremonies in a houseboat to contact the saitan even though they may be house dwellers. One djin built a

Fig. 56 Dancing djin

special addition to his house where he kept the various paraphernalia he used in curing. When he wanted to communicate with the saitan, he sat in the room until they spoke to him. Several djin said that if they want to communicate with saitan, they sleep and the saitan appear in their dreams.

Many djin communicate with saitan through a trance brought on by a dance or a chant (fig. 56). With or without the fast accompaniment of drums and gongs, the djin dance until the spirits possess them, at which time they fall into a trance and the spirits answer questions they have posed. Some djin recite special chants in a language only they can speak until they fall into a trance and communicate with the spirits. Some lie quietly in a trance whereas others shake convulsively. Some babble in the language of the saitan, which can only be understood by another djin who translates for the congregation. Some djin write messages on paper or white cloth in a script which only they can write and read. They then go into a trance and upon awakening, they interpret the writing as a message from the saitan. Some have notebooks of such writing inherited from other djin, which they interpret after going into a trance.

Djin describe the trance experience differently. Some say it is devoid of physical feeling because their spirits have left their bodies to visit the spirit realm. Others who become possessed by saitan experience pain when the spirits enter their bodies. One man compared the trance sensation to a cool wind blowing over his body, while another said the entrance of the saitan was like a gentle touch on his arm. Djin do not consume intoxicants or hallucinogens to bring about a trance. However, one type of djin drinks seawater prior to communicating with saitan. Called *duata* and most commonly a woman, this djin communicates with sea saitan who demand the seawater. The communication occurs while the seawater is in the duata's stomach, following which it is vomited.

Most djin do not charge for their services since their clients are usually relatives. Many claim their skills are gifts from the spirits or Tuhan, and they are obligated to help the sick. They are, however, almost always given gifts for their services. The most respected djin are widely sought for their assistance, sometimes even by non-Sama Dilaut, and it is understood that they will be paid for their services. One djin told me he was paid three to five pesos for minor ceremonies. Another djin, an elderly woman, received dishes, candles, twenty-four pesos, seven gantas of rice, a bag of young coconuts, and several items of clothing for an elaborate curing ceremony she conducted for a land-dwelling Sama family.

Each family alliance unit usually has at least one djin among its members, and more typically several. Ages of djin vary. The youngest I met was a man in his mid-twenties while the oldest was probably in his early seventies. Generally, the older djin have greater status and are sought more frequently than younger ones. I observed no status differences between males and females. Individual abilities rather than gender determine status. Among the Tawi-Tawi Sama Dilaut, the djin work individually, only occasionally assisting one another at large ceremonies. No djin are full-time practitioners. They conduct ceremonies when the need arises, and the rest of their lives are indistinguishable from other Sama Dilaut. Many djin hold positions of leadership in other arenas of Sama Dilaut life and are among the most respected members of the community.

The djin's powers are usually limited to their lifetimes, and consequently djin are treated like others when they die. Exceptions are those who were especially powerful during their lives, whose spirits are considered very temperamental and must be dealt with cautiously. Sometimes the body of such a powerful djin is buried apart from the traditional communal Sama Dilaut graves. The body may even be buried away from the main cemetery. I knew of two such isolated graves in Tawi-Tawi which were a short distance from the main cemetery and covered with white finger-coral. Receptacles for offerings and small green and white flags were placed in the crevices of the coral, and each had a canopy of white cloth, stretched over four poles, to shield it from the sun. Such graves, called tempat, are visited periodically to seek the assistance of the spirits of the deceased djin.

Few Sama Dilaut discount the importance of the djin, although intensity of belief varies. Some firmly believe in the djin's powers and never question their abilities, acknowledging though that some are more powerful than others. Other Sama Dilaut, especially younger ones familiar with Western medicine, openly doubt the abilities of the djin and seek their assistance only when pressured to do so by the family. I met one man, very traditional in other respects, who told me that all djin were charlatans and that their curing successes were sheer coincidence. His views, however, were the exception. Most Sama Dilaut agree that the djin are helpful in combating certain ailments, but if their methods do not work, they are amenable to other treatments, as the djin themselves usually are.

The Imam

"Imam," a title obviously borrowed from Islam, is used rather indiscriminately among the Sama Dilaut to refer to anyone who conducts rituals for life-cycle ceremonies, such as weddings and superincisions. Consequently, djin are sometimes called imams when they perform wedding ceremonies, but are called djin when they conduct curing ceremonies. I knew only three Tawi-Tawi Sama Dilaut men who were known as imams and not also considered djin. The three men were brothers who learned Arabic chants from their father who had learned them from a land-dwelling Sama imam. None of the brothers claimed to be djin and all considered their ceremonies different from those of the djin. According to them, the djin treat illness through contacts with saitan, whereas they cannot contact saitan, but rather know Arabic chants that make certain ceremonies effective because they please Tuhan and discourage saitan. The chants themselves have magical powers that assure success.

The chants are memorized and usually recited without the aid of the *Qur'an*; in fact, one of the imams does not even own a copy of the *Qur'an*. The imams do not understand Arabic, and therefore do not know the meaning of the chants and cannot translate or even identify specific words in the *Qur'an*. They claim the *Qur'an* is a sacred book, but their copies are old and ragged and given no special value. The same chants are used for all ceremonies they conduct, namely ceremonies of curing, burial, marriage, and superincision. Djin usually assisted the imams and frequently superseded them in the ceremonies I witnessed. For most Tawi-Tawi Sama Dilaut, these imams play minor, if any, roles in their lives. The three imams conducted ceremonies only for their own kin groups

Curing Ceremonies

The ceremonies held for the Sama Dilaut spirits are many and multifaceted, and participation in them ranges from a single individual to the entire community. Ceremonies are conducted to ward off and cure illness and misfortune and to thank the spirits for their assistance. In addition, rites of passage at birth, adolescence, marriage, and death demand obeisance to the proper spirits. As a result, not too many days pass in a Sama Dilaut community without a ceremony of some sort. Some ceremonies are unique to certain moorages or kin groups, whereas others are conducted by all Tawi-Tawi Sama Dilaut. But even those found among all Sama Dilaut have their individual stamp dictated by moorage and family traditions, and the idiosyncrasies of the officiating djin.

Ceremonies are ideally held in the early morning, but necessity does not always allow this. The material objects used in all curing ceremonies are similar. The djin sometimes wears special clothes, namely green trousers and white blouses for men, and yellow sarongs and green blouses for women. The household's best mats are spread on the deck or floor to accommodate the participants, while incense is always lighted in a small white bowl or a coconut half-shell, the smoke of which summons the spirits. If incense is unavailable, a smoking wood coal suffices. When the djin lights the incense, the ceremony begins. In many ceremonies, (especially those concerning ummagged) a green coconut, a glass of water, and a bowl of cooked or uncooked rice are regular fixtures (fig. 57). One djin told me that the coconut and water are gifts from heaven while rice is the favorite food of the spirits. Depending on the ceremony, additional food may be prepared. A betel-nut box containing the traditional ingredients and sometimes cigarettes are placed on the mat for spirits during the ceremony and for the participants who share them after the ceremony. Some families have brass urns and bowls inherited from ancestors and associated with their spirits, which are brought out for important ceremonial occasions. Some ceremonies are conducted before the *hainan*, an ornately, curvilinearly decorated bar, about four feet long, hung to one side in the interiors of some houseboats and houses. Associated with ancestral spirits, the hainan is painted

 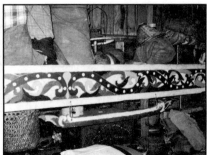

Fig. 57 Magmbo' ceremony offerings   Fig. 58 Hainan

green, red, yellow, blue, and white (fig. 58). The posture for prayer (dua'a) is the same for all ceremonies. Participants sit on mats in a circle around the material objects. The djin begins the ceremony by calling the spirit or spirits. As participants follow him, he rests his hands on his crossed legs with palms upward. Then, at the appropriate time, hands are turned palms downward and then again upward. The symbolism of the palms-upward position is to receive blessings from the spirits while the palms-downward position is to ward off evil. At the conclusion of the prayer, the hands are lifted briefly to cover the face.

During the ceremony, the spirits consume the spiritual essence of the offerings and at the conclusion, the participants consume the material offerings. The consumption serves to unite the participants with the spirits and to renew ties among themselves.

Few Sama Dilaut ceremonies are solemn, hushed occasions. Although the participants direct their attention to the ritual activities, others in the house or houseboat may be talking in the background while children continue their play. Unless such activities disrupt the ceremony, no one is disturbed by them.

If the ceremony is one of thanksgiving for the recovery of a sick person, the ceremony is concluded by the djin bathing the recovered person in seawater followed by a rinse in fresh water. A brief prayer usually accompanies the bathing, which is believed to cleanse the person of the former illness.

Individual Ceremonies The simplest Sama Dilaut ceremonies consist of small offerings made to spirits by one or two persons, or perhaps a nuclear family. The offerings are requests for assistance, payments for assistance or favors granted, or simply to keep one in harmony with the spirits. Appropriate offerings are bits of tobacco, betel, food, a cigarette, or small white or green flags.

If a fisherman or a family is passing an area where spirits are believed to reside, such as a cemetery where ummagged are found or an islet where saitan are known to dwell, a small offering is left to show proper respect for the spirits. Sometimes a spirit appears in a dream and asks for an offering, and the sleeper complies upon awakening. As the offering is left, a short prayer is uttered acknowledging respect for the spirit. Sometimes such places are visited to seek a spirit's assistance, or to pay a spirit for help already provided. The following are examples of such ceremonies. A man caught in a storm while out fishing became frightened and asked the ummagged of his recently deceased father to help him to safety. The storm subsided and the man made it safely home. The following day he went to the cemetery island where his father was buried and left a small offering at his grave in appreciation of his assistance. One night a woman and her husband were fishing and unintentionally drifted near an islet inhabited by saitan. The woman apologized to the saitan for their intrusion and promised to bring them an offering the following day if they did not punish her and her husband for their transgression. They returned home without mishap, so the following afternoon the woman left three cigarettes and two small white flags on the islet. In another case a young Sama Dilaut man experienced a string of misfortunes, including bad luck in fishing, a stolen boat, a quarrelsome wife, and an unusually fussy baby. To seek remedy for his problems, he visited the grave of his grandmother, left a small offering, and asked her to restore harmony to his life.

Individual ceremonies such as these are conducted for minor concerns. For more serious problems, the Sama Dilaut consult specialists from among their relatives to conduct appropriate ceremonies. When illness occurs, the Sama Dilaut first seek their traditional herbalists for treatment. Each kin group has at least one such person, called a'anambar ("medicine person"), who knows the herbs appropriate for various illnesses. If this treatment is ineffective, or if the ailment is obviously caused by spirits, then the afflicted seeks the assistance of a djin who conducts the appropriate ceremony to the spirits responsible for the illness.

Magmbo' The ceremony most central to Sama Dilaut religion is the magmbo' ceremony. The root word, *mbo'*, means "grandparent or ancestor," and magmbo' can be translated as "ceremony for ancestors." The ceremony is held on various occasions, sometimes to request that normalcy be returned to troubled times. It is also held to request the protection of spirits during hazardous journeys or to ask that spirits desist from causing illness or misfortune. And once a year, the special pai baha'o magmbo' ceremony ("new rice ceremony for ancestors") is held to honor all ancestors and insure the continuance of balance and order in the world. Although the reasons for magmbo' ceremonies are similar throughout all Sama Dilaut communities, their ritual and content are somewhat varied, revealing the tastes of the officiating djin, family preferences, and different local traditions. Except for the elaborate pai baha'o magmbo', to be discussed later, the magmbo' ceremony is usually attended by members of the family alliance unit with perhaps a few other closely related persons in the moorage.

As noted, the magmbo' ceremony is often directed to a general group of ancestral spirits to request that normalcy be restored to difficult times. Such was the reason for the following ceremony, which involved the participation of a family alliance unit.

> Two family members had diarrhea, a child in the family recently died, bad weather made fishing difficult for almost a week, a strong wind swept through the moorage and lifted the roofs from several boats, and the fishing boat of one family drifted away during the night and was found only after a day of searching. Members of the group decided a magmbo' ceremony was needed to restore normalcy. A djin officiated at the ceremony, which was held in his houseboat. A young coconut, a small bunch of bananas, and a bowl of cooked rice were placed on a banana leaf in the center of the boat. Incense was lighted and as family members crowded around, the djin addressed the ancestral spirits, requesting assistance in solving their problems. Following the ceremony, participants returned to their houseboats. That night, the djin and his family slept with the food from the ceremony placed at their heads. The next morning, the participants in the ceremony returned and the djin repeated his requests to the spirits. The ceremony concluded with all participants eating together.

Magbusang A ceremony called *magbusang* is held to remove a disease-causing curse (*busang* means "curse") placed by a particular deceased relative. Some Sama Dilaut say such a ceremony may be directed toward a saitan believed responsible for the curse, but all magbusang ceremonies I witnessed were directed toward deceased relatives. Reasons for holding a magbusang ceremony are varied. One ceremony was held for a man made ill by his deceased mother because he had not properly mourned her recent death. A child became ill because her deceased brother resented his premature death and was jealous of her life. A woman suffered illness because she inadvertently offended a powerful djin. The djin had not wished the illness, but her behavior toward a person with his supernatural power could not go unpunished by the spirits.

Magbusang ceremonies are held in the house, the houseboat, or at the cemetery. Offerings include rice, cassava, fish, bananas, coffee, cigarettes, or betel. During the ceremony, the sick person promises to perform certain acts if he or she is allowed to recover. For example, one man promised the offended spirit that if he recovered, he would travel to Bongao and leave appropriate offerings at a sacred Muslim grave atop Mount Bongao.[3] A critically ill woman promised to abandon house living and return to her houseboat if she was allowed to recover. More often, promises of food or tobacco are made to the spirit during the ceremony. Typical of the many magbusang ceremonies I witnessed is the following summarized from my field notes.

> A young woman with a very painful toothache came to G, a djin. She had tried the traditional herbal remedies to no avail, and after suffering for several days, she thought a spirit might be responsible for her pain. G questioned her about recent deaths in her family and discovered her grandfather had died two months previously. He further questioned her and her family about her relationship with her grandfather and asked if she might have done something to offend his spirit. After some discussion, a family member remembered the young woman had laughed at a picture of the old man taken shortly before his death. On hearing this, the djin said the grandfather's spirit was punishing her with the toothache since it is improper to laugh at the infirm and elderly, and especially at the deceased. The djin recommended that betel and food be placed on the grave of the deceased man, and then he accompanied the family to the nearby cemetery to do so. With family members in attendance and the patient beside him, he told the spirit that the young woman had not intended disrespect, and offered the betel and food in penance. He then requested that the patient be relieved of her pain. The group dispersed and returned to their homes. The next day the toothache was gone and the cure was attributed to the actions of the djin.

Sinumangit Another ceremony for ancestral spirits is called *sinumangit*, or, as one Sama Dilaut translated it, "feeding the dead." Some say the ceremony is held when deceased relatives appear in the dreams of the living and request food. Upon awakening the following morning, the dreamer contacts a djin to perform a ceremony. Family members contribute food and spread it on a mat. With smoking incense, the djin calls the spirit who requested the food. After the spirit has consumed the spiritual essence of the food, the participants consume the material part.

Some Sama Dilaut hold the sinumangit only in response to a spirit's request for food in a dream while others hold it whenever an ummagged appears in a dream. The following is a description of a sinumangit from my field notes.

> The sinumangit was held because L, the present headman and brother of the old headman who recently died, had a bad cough that would not go away,

a cough similar to that the old headman had at his death. The djin at the ceremony decided L's cough was caused by the deceased headman's spirit who was jealous of his title being passed on to his brother. In the center of the room on a mat were a dish of bananas, some cookies, several cassava cakes, cups of coffee, an opened betel box, and a dish of smoking wood coals. M, niece of the deceased, who was assisting the djin, held clothes of the deceased headman over the smoke. After the clothes were smoked, they were placed on the mat beside the other items. The djin, a son-in-law of the deceased, then began a long prayer asking the spirit to allow L to recover and assume the title of headman. He told the spirit that L would abandon his house and return to houseboat living if he were allowed to recover. Other family members were seated around the mat, and they, too, made brief requests that L be allowed to recover. The djin made more requests for L's recovery and after sitting for several moments with his eyes closed, he informed the group that the spirit of the old headman told him that he approved of L's succession to his position. Following more prayers, L donned the clothes of his deceased brother while everyone in attendance was served food. The ceremony then concluded and the participants dispersed.

Magjanji If the disease-causing spirit continues to inflict illness on the living, perhaps eventually causing death, the individuals involved feel no obligation to carry out the promise made in the curing ceremony. On the other hand, if the patient recovers, the recovery is attributed to the spirit and the living must fulfill their promise to avoid the return of the illness. Such a ceremony to fulfill a promise to a saitan or an ummagged is called a magjanji, and like most Sama Dilaut ceremonies each is somewhat distinctive. The nature of the ceremony, of course, depends on the nature of the promise made in the curing ceremony. In the case of the man who promised to visit the sacred grave atop Mount Bongao, he was required to visit the grave and leave appropriate offerings. Many sick people promise to leave gifts at the cemetery and for this reason many magjanji ceremonies are held at the grave of the spirit believed responsible for the illness or misfortune. Gifts are left on small islets believed inhabited by saitan in fulfillment of promises to those spirits. The following is a description of a magjanji at a grave.

This morning I went to the cemetery at Bunabuna'an with B and his family for a magjanji. B's daughter was seriously ill and the family djin blamed it on the spirit of B's father who for some unknown reason was angry with the family. B promised the spirit that if his daughter were allowed to recover, he would leave appropriate offerings at the grave. The child recovered, so today we went to the cemetery. Before leaving our boats to approach the grave, the four adult men of our group changed into new clothing. At the grave, the djin poured seawater over the gravemarker. He then put incense in a coconut half-shell and held it in various places over the grave to attract the spirit. Next he chanted to the spirit, asking it to send no more illness to the child and to grant her good fortune. A small board was removed from the foot of the grave, providing an opening to the interior. Two bundles of betel nuts were placed in the grave and the board was replaced. The child's father then threw several handfuls of rice over the grave as he told the spirit he had fulfilled his promise of betel and therefore it should no longer cause illness to his daughter. Before leaving the cemetery, the family placed small offerings on the graves of other relatives, unaccompanied by prayer or ritual.

Magtimbang The nature of the promise made to the disease-causing spirit depends on the seriousness of the illness. If the illness is relatively minor, the promised ceremony is a small one, such as the magjanji in the preceding illustration. However, if the illness is serious and many attempts have been made to cure it, then the patient promises to hold a more elaborate ceremony if recovery is allowed. One such ceremony is the magtimbang, which means "to weigh, or to balance." The ceremony is found throughout Tawi-Tawi among both the Tausug and the Sama, but it varies somewhat as to why, when, and how it is conducted. For the Tawi-Tawi Sama Dilaut, it is held in fulfillment of a promise to spirits that have allowed recovery from a serious illness. These spirits may be either saitan or ummagged. Regardless of the spirits, the procedures in the ceremonies are much the same.

After the patient's recovery, the magtimbang is held in the early morning shortly after sunrise, the time of most important Sama Dilaut ceremonies. The recovered individual is placed in a sling at the end of a pole tied to the rafters of a house or a specially constructed support on a boat by a rope at the center. At the other end of the pole is another sling into which are placed items such as coconuts, firewood, rice, sugar, bananas, and containers of water, until they balance the person's weight. A djin then chants to the spirits as he turns the pole counter-clockwise three times. He then unwinds the pole to its starting position, still chanting. The recovered person is removed from the sling and the items that balanced her weight are distributed to everyone in attendance. The following account describes one of the more elaborate magtimbang I saw.

> The woman featured in the ceremony was dressed in djin clothes. A wooden pole, about two-and-a-half meters long, was hung from the rafters of the house by a rope tied at its center. Mats were spread on the floor, and directly under the rope, at the center of the pole, was a tray containing three bowls of rice

topped by three triangular coconut cakes, a glass of water, and an opened betel-nut box. Hung on the pole at the center were a gallon jug of water and several gold coin bracelets. Draped over the pole on either side of the rope were brightly colored sarongs. A sling made of a new sarong was attached to either end of the pole. The woman was assisted into one of the slings by a djin and his assistant. Her weight was balanced in the other sling by a dozen coconuts, two pots of cooked rice, a bunch of bananas, and some firewood. After a balance was achieved, the djin and his assistant stood at either sling while another djin placed burning incense near the articles on the mat where he sat. The woman's husband stood beside the djin while her father stood beside the djin's assistant. Seated around the mat were about twenty men and women. The djin and his assistant turned the sling as they slowly walked counter-clockwise, taking turns chanting to the spirit, thanking it for allowing recovery. As they walked, several male relatives of the woman came forward and placed peso bills in the shirt pockets of the djin and his assistant. After three turns, the two djin requested that everyone at the ceremony be granted good health and fortune. The sling was then unwound to more chants until it reached its starting position. Several people from the audience came forward to embrace the woman before she was helped out of the sling. The items in the sling and the food on the mat were distributed to the people in attendance, following which they dispersed.

Magla'ankuliah The magla'ankuliah ceremony involves the removal of foreign objects from the body of a sick person. The objects, placed in the body by offended spirits, are believed responsible for illness or abnormal behavior. One man told me that nails and bits of glass were once extracted from his body by a djin. I saw the ceremony only twice, both times at Tungbangkao, where it was attended by the family alliance units of the afflicted parties. The following is a description of one of the ceremonies I witnessed.

M's youngest son, about two years old, had been sickly for the past two months. He and another son, about a year older, who had been particularly unruly for the past week, were taken to M's uncle, a djin, shortly after dawn this morning. About a dozen people, relatives of both the mother and father of the children were at the houseboat for the ceremony. Seven white plates of rice and a white dish containing smoking wood embers were placed on a mat in the center of the houseboat. M and his wife sat opposite the djin, each with a child on his/her lap. The djin began the ceremony by speaking very softly to the spirits. As he spoke louder, he asked the saitan to allow the children to recover and then closely examined the palms of both. He told the parents the illness was in the older boy, but was affecting the behavior of both children. He took the older boy and placed him on his lap. After massaging the boy's chest briefly, he began sucking loudly on his breast. After several moments, he stopped and spat a wad of red fibers into a coconut half-shell. He announced that the fibers had been placed in the child's body by a saitan and were responsible for the abnormal behavior of both children. Now that they were removed, he said the children would recover. The rice was then eaten by everyone present, following which the group dispersed. The father gave the djin a peso for conducting the ceremony.

Ta'u-Ta'u The Sama Dilaut at Tungkalang conduct a ceremony I never saw or heard of elsewhere. The ceremony consists of transferring a disease-causing saitan from an ill person to a djin and then to a specially carved wooden image, called ta'u-ta'u, which is armed with miniature guns and knives. The image is then placed with similar images in a special *nunuk* tree (*Ficus microcarpa*) considered very dangerous because of the presence of saitan. I was told the weapons on the image protected it from harm, although why the invulnerable saitan needed protection did not seem illogical to the Sama Dilaut. The following account from my field notes describes the ceremony in greater detail.

For several days, H had been ill. Her old mother, a djin, decided H was ill because she walked too near a tree believed inhabited by saitan while she was collecting firewood on the beach. Thus a ta'u-ta'u ceremony was held to rid H of the saitan causing her illness. Eight adults and three children gathered at H's houseboat shortly after sunrise. H sat with the djin on a mat covered with small containers of food, cigarettes, and betel. A coconut half-shell held smoking incense. Between them was a crudely carved, wooden, anthropomorphic image, about a half-meter tall. Similar to some of the markers found on Sama Dilaut graves, it was asexual and had legs, but no arms or facial features. Attached to its torso were two small wooden swords, and a girdle of green cloth was tied around its waist. The ceremony began with the djin asking the saitan to allow H to recover. She massaged H's body vigorously as she spoke to the spirit. After several minutes of massaging, she closed her eyes, gave several convulsive shudders and held the image to her body. After shaking for several minutes, she relaxed and asked one of the men in attendance if the boat was ready. He replied that it was and we crawled onto the deck of the houseboat where a fishing boat was tied. Seated in it were two men who began playing gongs after being instructed to do so by the djin. The djin stepped into the boat, still holding the ta'u-ta'u carefully. Five other people, including myself and the husband and brother-in-law of the patient, followed her into the boat. The sick woman remained behind. I was told I should not spit, laugh, urinate, defecate, speak loudly, or look backward en route. Two of us paddled as the musicians played and the djin danced. We left the moorage and paddled to the Sanga-Sanga shore, where we anchored the boat on the beach. We disembarked and followed the djin down a path for perhaps twenty-five meters until we reached a large nunuk tree. As the gongs continued, the djin spoke to the ta'u-ta'u, flattering it and asking it to remain in place as she carefully placed it in a crotch of the tree. She also placed several small green and white flags in the tree as well as small offerings of rice and cassava. Seven ta'u-ta'u were scattered throughout the tree, ranging in height from a half-meter to a meter. Some were armed with small wooden knives and guns. Two were painted, one white and the other black. All had legs, but most had no arms. A few had penises. Noses and ears were pronounced on some, but other facial features were missing. Placed among the images were about a dozen small flags, all white or green, except for two orange ones. Green or white girdles were tied around the waists of some of the images and some were engulfed in the growth of the tree. In addition to the ta'u-ta'u, a species of green lizard, about thirty centimeters long, also inhabited the tree. I was later told they were friends of the saitan. Unlike most Sama Dilaut ceremonies, the brief ceremony at the tree was very solemn. No one spoke but the djin. After the ceremony, we left in silence and returned to the moorage.

Kipalat Selamat Like many people, the Sama Dilaut occasionally have disagreements that result in family rifts. Kinsmen are important in all aspects of a Sama Dilaut's life, and to sever ties with them not only disrupts the normal flow of social intercourse but also angers the ancestral spirits. Therefore when such rifts occur, efforts are made by less involved persons to bring the feuding relatives together. Once the quarrels are breached, harmony is formally restored with a kipalat selamat, or peacemaking ceremony. The ceremony is also conducted to restore good will between unrelated people, but the cases I witnessed involved only kinsmen.

Family feuds are not uncommon among the Sama Dilaut. Most are easily resolved after the heat of the argument has dissipated, but others may last for several weeks, months, or even years. Unless the rift has seriously disrupted the social or economic activities of the groups involved, little effort is made to bring about a reconciliation between the quarreling parties. However, if the disagreement has seriously hampered normal social or economic intercourse, less involved relatives attempt to bring about a reconciliation. These people meet separately with the disputing parties to discuss the grievances of each. Several meetings and perhaps several months may pass before reconciliation is achieved. When both parties are ready to set the disagreement aside, the negotiating group arranges the kipalat selamat.

The paraphernalia of the ceremony are similar to those in other Sama Dilaut ceremonies. Mats are spread on the floor of the household hosting the event. In the center of the mats are placed a glass of water, a green coconut, rice, and smoking incense. A djin sits before the incense with the quarreling parties on either side of him. Other persons, closely related to the disputants, complete a circle around the mats while additional family members crowd in to observe. The djin begins the ceremony by commenting on the renewed friendship and asks the disputants to shake hands. All persons involved in the quarrel shake hands with one another, often displaying great emotion as they embrace. Next, the djin lights incense and asks the family spirits to witness the reconciliation and bless everyone with good fortune. Following the brief ceremony, food is served and the entire group eats together with the djin and the former enemies. The following field notes describe a kipalat selamat ceremony I witnessed at Tungbangkao.

I and his brother-in-law G quarreled several months ago over the division of fish. The quarrel did not go beyond their immediate nuclear families, but the two families refused to associate with one another despite the fact that they live as neighbors within a section of the moorage. For several weeks, the sisters of I and G tried to convince the men to reconcile, probably prompted by the approaching wedding of the daughter of one of the sisters. The sisters believed the ill feeling of the dispute displeased the family spirits and would bring misfortune to the marriage. They were successful in bringing about a reconciliation that would be sealed with the kipalat selamat. The ceremony was held at one of the sisters' homes and although the two women were responsible for the reconciliation, they had little participation in the ceremony. As we approached the house, I heard gongs and drums. Musicians were playing on the deck and three young women were dancing. Several women in the outdoor kitchen greeted me. Everyone was very happy. We were late and the ceremony was about to begin as we entered. I was invited to sit beside the djin conducting the ceremony. On either side of us were I and G, the brothers-in-law whose disagreement was being settled. They looked sheepish and did not participate in the banter and chatter of the rest of the group. Others crowded into the room to observe as the wives of I and G sat directly behind them. In the center of the mats, a large tray contained cooked rice, three coconuts, a glass of cooking oil, a glass of water, a dish of salt and small peppers, and several peso bills. The djin signaled the beginning of the ceremony and announced that I and G had resolved their differences and were friends again. He then gave a short lecture on the importance of relatives getting along with one another and told the two men and their families to clasp hands. They did so with much embracing and shedding of tears while the rest of the audience voiced their approval. Everyone sat again and the ceremony resumed. The djin lit incense and offered a prayer to the ancestral spirits requesting good health and good fortune for all. Following the prayer, the djin told I and G to consume the water and rice. Women then brought in additional food and everyone ate. After a half-hour or so of eating and socializing, the group dispersed.

Kata-Kata Certain Sama Dilaut men know how to chant kata-kata, or healing chants. These are long, memorized chants that take two to three nights to complete with one or two hours of chanting each night. The kata-kata must be recited without error to avoid offense to the ancestors. They relate the long-ago adventures of heroes who traveled to faraway places where they encountered strange and marvelous characters. Considered very sacred by the Sama Dilaut, these chants belong to the domain of the ancestors. Some of the land-dwelling Sama of Tawi-Tawi tell the same stories as folk literature and do not regard them as particularly sacred, but to the Tawi-Tawi Sama Dilaut, they are extremely sacred and have the power to heal.[4] (The text of a kata-kata chant is reproduced in the appendix.) Kata-kata are used in a variety of contexts. Most commonly, they are chanted in the presence of a sick person whose illness is attributed to the acts of ummagged, or perhaps saitan. The words themselves are believed to have healing properties, and after being in the presence of kata-kata chanters for several hours, the spirits responsible for the illness depart and the patient eventually recovers.

The ceremony begins as members of the sick person's localized kindred gather in a house or houseboat with a djin. Bowls of food, always including rice, are placed on a mat between the djin and the patient. The djin then lights incense, invites the spirits to participate, and begins to chant. He seldom chants for more than two hours a night during which he takes breaks to rest his voice and drink water. However, it may take several nights of chanting to exorcise the disease-causing spirits. The ceremony is very sacred and the audience is extremely attentive, speaking in whispers and only when necessary. Because interruptions bring illness and other misfortune to those in attendance, fussy babies and noisy children are removed from the ceremony. The following summarizes a ceremony I witnessed at Tungbangkao.

K invited me to attend a kata-kata ceremony in his houseboat this evening. When I arrived after sunset, about ten men and women were seated on mats. K's sister, the sick woman for whom the ceremony was being held, was lying at K's side and looking very ill indeed. No food or drink was present. K told me earlier that many different treatments had been tried on his sister, and tonight he was going to chant kata-kata to drive away the stubborn saitan causing her illness. K was dressed in his djin clothes and the others were dressed in finer clothing than they normally wear to ceremonies. K began the ceremony by lighting incense and speaking to the spirit, asking it to refrain from bothering the woman. He then began chanting. His intonation and the speed at which he recited the chant made it difficult to understand the words even though I can generally follow the gist of most Sinama conversations now. He chanted for about forty-five minutes before stopping to smoke a cigarette and drink water. I heard no talking during the entire time he chanted, unlike at most Sama Dilaut ceremonies where people converse in the background during ritual. After his break, K chanted for another half-hour before stopping for the night. He concluded the ceremony with another appeal to the saitan, and told the group that if the woman failed to improve the next day he would chant the following evening. After a short period of socializing, the group dispersed.

For one more evening, K chanted. The procedure was the same as that on the first evening. After the second evening, the woman showed signs of recovery and K deemed it unnecessary to continue the kata-kata.

Malud A localized kindred at Tungkalang occasionally holds a ceremony called malud.[5] Three brothers from this group who know Arabic chants are known as imams who occasionally conduct malud ceremonies for sick people within their kin group. This ceremony consists of the recitation of Arabic chants throughout the night in the presence of the patient. Sometimes malud are held in fulfillment of promises to spirits who have allowed recovery. The ceremonies I witnessed among the Sama Dilaut began after sunset and were held for curing rather than fulfillment of a promise to a spirit. The imam offers the usual incense, food, cigarettes, and betel to the spirits as they are invited to the ceremony. The sick person is present, together with other concerned relatives. The three imams then take turns chanting from memory, sometimes holding a battered copy of the *Qur'an* before them. The two ceremonies I saw lasted about three hours, with occasional short breaks as people came and went throughout the night. The ceremonies concluded with a final request that the spirits allow the patient to recover. Saitan were believed responsible for the illnesses of the people treated in the ceremonies I saw, but I was told that a malud could also be held for Tuhan or ummagged.

Pamatulakan Only two Sama Dilaut ceremonies involve the participation of the entire moorage, namely the pamatulakan and the pai baha'o magmbo'.

165

During times of much illness believed caused by saitan, the pamatulakan ceremony is held to rid the moorage of its misfortune. Members of the different families in the community construct a boat varying in length from a half-meter to two meters. Some build the hull, others the sail, and still others the oars. Ta'u-ta'u images equipped with miniature guns and bladed weapons are sometimes placed in the boat. The women of the moorage prepare food for the boat as well as small flags of white, green, and yellow, the saitan's favorite colors. When completed and loaded with its cargo, the boat is pulled among the houseboats by several djin representing the different kin groups of the moorage who take turns calling to the saitan believed responsible for the illness. After canvassing the entire moorage and attracting the disease-causing spirits, the boat is taken to the open sea where it is set adrift with its undesirable cargo. The following account from my field notes describes a ceremony I observed at Tungkalang.

> Today several djin from the moorage met and decided a pamatulakan should be built to rid the moorage of the saitan responsible for the misfortunes of the past few weeks. It has been unusually cold, rainy and stormy making it difficult for fishing. In addition, many people are suffering from colds and two children in the same family died last week. Last night two women had a raucous quarrel that ultimately involved several members of their families, and this morning a boat was missing from the household where I am staying. Old M, the most prominent djin in the moorage, supervised the project and instructed several different families to make the different parts of the boat. My household was responsible for the hull, perhaps because the head of the household is a boatbuilder. A neighboring family would make the sail, another family the outrigger, and another the oars. In the late afternoon, the parts were collected and assembled by three djin. The assembled boat was about a meter long. Four women, representing households different from the ones that built the boat, brought small amounts of food, betel, cigarettes, and small green and white flags to place in the boat. The djin then changed into their djin clothes and pulled the boat through the low tide waters visiting each household as they took turns chanting invitations to the saitan to board the boat and enjoy the gifts. After the entire moorage was visited, they tied the pamatulakan to a fishing boat that they paddled to the edge of the reef where they set the small boat adrift on the current of the rising tide. They then returned to the moorage, changed into their normal clothes, and resumed their usual activities.

Magmbo' Pai Baha'o The most extensive of all Sama Dilaut ceremonies, the magmbo' pai baha'o ("new rice magmbo'"), requires the participation of all

Tawi-Tawi Sama Dilaut as well as some of their kinsmen from outside the area. The ceremony is held each year during the dry rice harvest, usually July or August, and probably dates to a time when rice was more central to the Sama Dilaut diet than it is now. Some Sama Dilaut believe that if rice is eaten from the new harvest prior to the ceremony, misfortune will befall the community. Households acquire dry rice for the ceremony from land-dwelling Sama farmers or from the Bongao marketplace. A container is made from the bark of a tree called *kayo* mboh', meaning "tree or wood of the ancestors." The bark is cut into a strip about twenty centimeters wide and joined together to form a circle about thirty centimeters in diameter. The bottom is laced with wide webs of rattan. Rice stalks and leaves are placed in the bottom of the container, which is then filled with unhusked rice. The container is placed at the bow of the houseboat or under the hainan of the house if it has one. On the same night members of the household sleep with their heads toward the rice.

Fig. 59 Magmbo' pai baha'o ceremony

The following morning the rice is husked, cooked, placed in a white bowl, and molded into a conical shape. Family members then take it to a central house or houseboat where other relatives have assembled with their own bowls of rice (fig. 59). The bowls, sometimes as many as twenty or thirty, are placed on the deck of the boat or the floor of the house where a djin conducts a brief ceremony to call the ancestral spirits to partake of the rice and bless the living with health and good fortune. Taking small portions of rice from each bowl, the djin mixes them in an empty bowl. He then offers the combined rice to the children present, each of whom takes a small bite. Families then take their bowls of rice home to eat at the next meal. Not all families hold the ceremony on the same day, and a family usually participates in several ceremonies conducted by its different relatives. The ceremony serves to reinforce ties among

167

living kinsmen, to remind them of their ties to deceased kinsmen, and to socialize the children into the group of living and deceased kinsmen. Sama Dilaut believe that if the ceremony is not held, illness, death, and violent storms with rough seas, strong winds, and heavy rains will visit the area.

If all the magmbo' pai baha'o ceremonies of the season and all the people participating in them could be diagrammed, the network of Sama Dilaut kinship would be revealed. Some Sama Dilaut travel south to Sitangkai to join ceremonies with kinsmen there, while the Sitangkai Sama Dilaut occasionally travel to Tawi-Tawi for ceremonies. Sama Dilaut near Semporna sometimes participate in Sitangkai ceremonies with people from Tawi-Tawi. The people participating in this web of ceremonies, namely the Sama Dilaut of Tawi-Tawi, Sibutu, and Semporna, consider themselves a bangsa, or subculture, distinct from others in Sulu.

Life-Cycle Ceremonies

Like many people, the Sama Dilaut call on religious specialists to assist them through the stages of their life cycle. For the Sama Dilaut, these stages are birth, an ear-piercing ceremony for young girls, superincision for adolescent boys, marriage, and death. The scheduling of these ceremonies is determined somewhat by Sama Dilaut fishing cycles which result in the gathering of many houseboats in certain moorages at certain times of the month. After several days of intensive fishing, families rest from their activities to hold ceremonies. At such times, superincisions, wedding, curing, and ear-piercing ceremonies are held on the same day or within days of one another. The elaborateness of the ceremonies depends on the affluence and preferences of the families involved.

As with curing ceremonies, the paraphernalia used in these life-cycle ceremonies become predictable after one has witnessed several. Prior to the ceremonies, which always begin in the early morning, participants are bathed in seawater poured from a white bowl and then rinsed in fresh water as they face the sun.[6] They are then dressed in their finest clothes and make-up is applied to their faces, especially for superincision and wedding ceremonies. Umbrellas are always held over the central figures of the ceremonies as they move from place to place. Drums and gongs provide music and often women (and sometimes men) entertain the people by dancing. Boats and houses hosting the ceremonies are decorated with brightly colored hangings, sarongs, flags, and even fishnets. As with curing ceremonies, confirmed house dwellers frequently return to their boats for life-cycle ceremonies, believing it more acceptable to the spirits to have the ceremonies in the boat. Firecrackers are often exploded at weddings and superincisions to add to the festivities. Incense, or wood embers, in a white bowl or coconut half-shell is used to invoke the spirits. Cooked food, especially rice, is always present. During the ceremony, spirits consume the spiritual essence of the food and at the conclusion of the ceremony, the participants consume the material food. At some of the larger weddings and superincisions, uncooked rice and sugar are distributed to all households in the moorage.

The degree of religious concern during these ceremonies ranges from a mere nod to spirits during the ear-piercing ceremony to a constant concern with spiritual matters throughout the funeral activities. Threads of commonality run through ceremonies of the same type wherever they are conducted, but as with curing ceremonies, each is somewhat distinctive, reflecting family traditions, moorage differences, or the idiosyncrasies of the officiating djin.

Like the curing ceremonies, Sama Dilaut life-cycle ceremonies are similar to those of other Muslim groups in Sulu.[7] These similarities reflect not only an ancient common cultural tradition but also the more recent influence of Islam. The following discussion summarizes the general features of Sama Dilaut life cycle ceremonies.

Birth Pregnancy and birth are times of potential danger for the mother and child. Death at childbirth is common among Sama Dilaut women and the infant mortality rate is extremely high. Several mothers I interviewed had lost so many children in infancy, they could not remember the exact number. Common causes of infant death are diarrhea, respiratory disorders, and intestinal parasites. Most of these deaths are attributed to the actions of spirits, and for this reason pregnancy and birth are occasions when special attention is paid to spirits. The Sama Dilaut have naturalistic explanations for the difficulties of pregnancy and birth (Nimmo 1970), but the problems believed caused by spirits are the most difficult to control.

If a woman does not become pregnant within a reasonable time after marriage, a magmbo' ceremony may be held to request assistance from the ancestors. Other than its rationale, the ceremony is no different from those previously described. If the expectant mother is experiencing difficulties, other ceremonies, such as a magbusang, may be held to request the ummagged or saitan to refrain from causing problems . In addition to these ceremonies, a host of traditions prescribe proper behavior for pregnant women. For example, a pregnant woman should not laugh at a deformed person or her child will be born with the same deformity, or if she sees clouds pass over a full moon, she should bathe immediately to insure a safe delivery. Some women believe they should not eat sweets during pregnancy, otherwise the fetus will harden and make delivery difficult. Many believe the houseboat is the appropriate place for birth, even though they may be full-time house dwellers.

The birth is attended by a midwife (pandai) and her assistants, who are always close relatives of the mother, as well as a male or female djin who is also usually a close relative. The midwife assists in delivery while the djin offers prayers and food over incense to the various spirits in attendance. The prayers request that the delivery pain be eased, that the child be blessed with good health and longevity, and that the mother be allowed to recover and bear many more children. The prayers continue after the infant is delivered and during its seawater bath followed by a rinse in fresh water. The djin offers cooked rice to the spirits, after which the mother and those in attendance, including the new-born infant, are given a small portion to eat. Amulets in the form of bracelets and necklaces prepared by the djin are sometimes placed on the infant, although often this is not done until some danger to the child is sensed. Also a black spot of charcoal (sinagan) is frequently placed in the center of the infant's forehead as an additional protection against malevolent spirits. A gift, usually a small amount of money, is given to the midwife at this time; failure to do so may bring illness to the child. The afterbirth, believed by some Sama Dilaut to be the infant's undeveloped twin, is placed in a coconut shell and disposed of by the father, either by burying it on land or in the reef under the house or boat of birth. Some say that if it is placed in the sea, the child will become a good swimmer. When burying the afterbirth, the father should look neither left nor right, otherwise the child will become cross-eyed. One family told me the infant would become ill if fish were roasted in the houseboat during the week after birth. Some Sama Dilaut believe the hammock-like cradle of the baby should be pink or green for protection against harmful spirits. Boughs from citrus trees are placed on the house or houseboat to keep away evil spirits that might prey upon the infant. After the umbilical cord falls from the child's stomach, it is tied to the cradle. When it falls from the cradle, its disposal depends on the gender of the child. If the child is a boy, it is taken to the open sea and thrown over-board so he will become a good fisherman. If the child is a girl, the cord is placed in a pandan tree, the leaves of which are used for mat making, so she will become a good mat maker.

Children are not named until they are several weeks or even several months old. Some say naming too soon will result in bad luck or even death for the child. The name of a boy generally takes the suffix of his father's name; for instance, the four sons of Masarani are Mastarani, Sugarani, Armisani, and Motorhani. Less frequently the suffix of a girl's name takes the suffix of her mother's name. The name usually identifies the gender of the child. Children are sometimes named after significant events. A child born in a household where I was staying was named Inglisani because at the time, the family was enthusiastic about learning English. A child born in another household where

I stayed was called Motorhani after the family's fascination with my new out-board motor. One family honored me by naming their son Harisani. In addition to the given name, a Sama Dilaut usually has a nickname that sometimes re-places the given name. Nicknames reflect personality traits such as "Happy," physical traits such as "Tall," or natural phenomena such as "Shark" or "Moon." Sometimes, if a child is sickly, her name is changed in the hope that the new name will improve her health.

Magtabok A special ceremony called magtabok is held for young girls when their ears are pierced. Sometimes the ceremony is performed when the child is only a few weeks old while other families wait until the child is four or five years old. Seldom is the ceremony delayed beyond that age. It is the least important of all life-cycle ceremonies in terms of the attention it receives. The rationale for performing it varies from family to family; some claim it is important to hold the ceremony when a child is young so earrings or plugs can be inserted to protect her from malevolent spirits. Two ceremonies I witnessed for infants were held because the children were sickly and the families believed the ceremony would improve their health. Others say the ears are pierced for cosmetic reasons so the child can wear earrings to make her more attractive.

As with all Sama Dilaut life-cycle ceremonies, the elaborateness of the magtabok depends on the family hosting it. For some it may be a very simple ceremony attended only by the child's parents, a djin, and perhaps an older woman versed in the proper method of piercing ears. Sometimes the latter two persons are the same. As most Sama Dilaut ceremonies, the magtabok is held in the early morning. The child is first bathed in seawater, followed by a rinse in fresh water. She is then dressed in new clothes and sometimes make-up is applied to her face. The djin gathers several strands of her wet hair, puts them in his mouth, and blows on them as he offers prayers. He then makes a brief invocation to family spirits over incense, asking for good health and fortune for the child. The person performing the operation rubs the child's ears between her thumb and forefinger until the lobes are numb. Then a large, threaded needle or perhaps a threaded piece of fire-hardened wood is passed through the lobes. A piece of string is left in the hole to prevent it from healing shut. The child cries during the operation, as do the female attendants who empathize with her pain. Following the ceremony, specially prepared food, always includ-ing rice, is offered to the spirits, after which those in attendance eat it. Such a simple ceremony may last no more than fifteen or twenty minutes and may be attended by only three or four people. More elaborate ceremonies involve the participation of fifteen to twenty people. Prior to the elaborate ceremonies, boats are decorated with brightly colored sarongs and banners (*tipas-tipas*) and paraded throughout the moorage as musicians and dancers perform on them. Following the ceremony, the family distributes uncooked rice and sugar to households as the little girl is paraded around the moorage in a decorated boat. The most elaborate ceremonies I saw were held in conjunction with other ceremonies (such as weddings and superincisions) and were for older girls, whereas the simpler ceremonies were held individually for infants.

Magislam A magtabok ceremony of the simpler sort may pass almost unnoticed by the moorage, but such is never the case with the magislam ceremony held for boys during their adolescence. Although the word magislam, meaning "to become a Muslim" or "to make one a Muslim," is obviously of Islamic origin and is the same name used by the Muslim people of Sulu for a similar ceremony, the Sama Dilaut ceremony most likely predates Islam in Sulu. Male genital operations are found among both Muslim and non-Muslim peoples in insular Southeast Asia and appear to be an ancient cultural practice. Furthermore, unlike the Muslim operation, the Sama Dilaut operation is not a true circumcision in that the foreskin is not removed, but rather superincised. Some Sama Dilaut told me a comparable ceremony was once held for girls, but I never witnessed such a ceremony or interviewed anyone who could describe it. One man told me it consisted of shaving the pubic hair prior to the wedding ceremony, but this was denied by other informants. Some Muslim groups of Sulu once held ceremonies for young women at adolescence and possibly the tradition of those ceremonies inspired the stories I heard among the Sama Dilaut.

Some magislam ceremonies are very elaborate and families save for years to finance them, whereas others are much simpler and demand a more modest outlay of money. The ceremony is the highlight of a young man's life and announces to the moorage that he has reached manhood and is ready for its responsibilities, including marriage. Frequently, brothers and cousins share the same ceremony. As in the case of the ear-piercing ceremony, the magislam is usually held at a time when other ceremonies, such as weddings or curing ceremonies, are scheduled in the moorage.

Whether held by itself or as one of several ceremonies, it is a time of festivity and celebration. Moorages hosting the celebration greatly expand in population. For example, the little moorage of Lioboran normally has about twenty houseboats, but during an elaborate magislam celebration I witnessed, that number grew to 160. When such large numbers of houseboats gather, it is a festive time for everyone; adults visit old friends and relatives, adolescents size up potential sexual and marriage partners, and children play with new playmates.

After the family decides when and where the magislam ceremony will be held, word is spread throughout the Tawi-Tawi Sama Dilaut community. A day or two prior to the ceremony, the host family decorates its house or houseboat and plays music on drums and gongs. As boats begin to arrive for the ceremony, more musicians join the group and additional boats are decorated. Children and teenagers gather on the nearby beach to play games while adults visit back and forth among their houseboats, usually laden with catches from recent fishing activities. At elaborate celebrations, the host family distributes gifts of sugar and uncooked rice to all the households in the moorage. More often, however, such gifts are limited to close relatives directly involved in the celebration. The youth being superincised has no special role in these activities and is indistinguishable from other teenage boys at the gathering.

During the evening before the ceremony, dancing is performed to the accompaniment of gongs and drums on a nearby beach, on an exposed reef, or on the large deck of a house. Lanterns are placed on poles as young girls begin the dancing. After the young girls have danced, the women follow, and then the men. After the dancing, adults and children retire while the teenagers and young unmarried adults stay on for romance and singing throughout the night.

Early the next morning, the magislam ceremony is held. A djin bathes the youth in seawater from a white bowl and asks the ancestral spirits to give him health and good fortune. The youth's male relatives play drums and gongs as female relatives dance. An umbrella is held over the youth during his bath while firecrackers are exploded to add to the festivities. Following the sea bath, he is rinsed in fresh water and taken to the house or houseboat where he is dressed for the ceremony. His costume is frequently very elaborate, consisting of a new sarong (or perhaps trousers), a new shirt, and a special headgear decorated with flags made of peso bills (fig. 60). If someone in the family has a wristwatch, he

Fig. 60 Youth dressed for magislam ceremony

adds it to the boy's costume. His face is covered with white powder and his hairline and eyebrows are outlined in charcoal. In some of the more elaborate preparations lipstick is applied to his lips and dotted on his face. Sunglasses and nail polish often complete his costume.

Prior to the operation, a magmbo' ceremony is held for the ancestral spirits. If the magislam is being held near one of the burial islands, this ceremony is sometimes conducted at the grave of family members; more typically, though, it is held in the houseboat. For most boys, this is their first active participation in a religious ceremony. Incense is lighted as bowls of food, always rice and sometimes fish, are spread on a mat. The youth sits with the djin on mats while his close relatives gather around. The djin again asks for the benevolence of the spirits and the operation takes place. The youth sits astride a large gong. The djin raises the youth's sarong and places his penis on the knob of the gong. Then he slips a piece of bamboo between the glans and foreskin and incises the foreskin with a knife or a piece of split bamboo. The nature of the incision varies, depending on the tightness of the foreskin. Sometimes it is a small nick; at other times a considerable incision is made so the foreskin hangs on either side of the glans. It is inappropriate for a youth to react to the pain and most of them do not. Wood ashes are rubbed into the wound to stop the bleeding and the penis is wrapped in white cloth. Following the incision, the youth again joins the djin on mats before incense and bowls of food. The djin asks the ancestral spirits for benevolence, good fortune, good health, and long life for the youth. Following the prayer, he and the youth eat some of the food and then share the remainder with others in attendance. After the food is consumed, the ceremony is concluded. Games and music continue throughout the day as houseboats depart for fishing or their home moorages.

Magkauwin The Sama Dilaut marry young, often at fourteen or fifteen years of age, when they have achieved the status of *bujang* (young woman) and *subul* (young man). Not uncommonly, parents arrange marriages between their infant children, and if the families remain amiable, and if the young people have no objections, the wedding, or magkauwin, takes place at a later time. Boys never marry before their magislam, or girls before their first menstruation.

Parents encourage their children to choose spouses from relatives and close friends. Parents sometimes select spouses for their children, but the youth are never forced into a marriage they find distasteful. As noted, relatives are the ideal mates and the only tabooed ones beyond the nuclear family, parents' siblings, and grandparents are patrilateral parallel cousins who are considered more closely related than other cousins because "their fathers have the same semen." Also, marriages between two people, related or unrelated, who have nursed from the same woman or were reared together intimately are considered incestuous (*sumbang*). However, even marriages between these people and between patrilateral parallel cousins are permitted if a ceremony is held to erase the incest associated with such a union. To conduct the ceremony, the couple wishing to marry travel to the open sea with a djin who, after asking the ancestral spirits to approve of the marriage, throws certain valuables, such as a gong, coins, or jewelry, into the sea. If the ceremony is not performed, it is believed that the children of the marriage will die, and storms, droughts, tidal waves, and other catastrophes will visit Tawi-Tawi. Should a couple marry without performing the ceremony, the community must drown them. No Sama Dilaut I knew, however, ever heard of this happening.

After a bride is selected, relatives of the parents of the groom-to-be meet with the proposed bride's family to discuss the potential marriage and the bridewealth (*dalaham*). At this meeting, called *magpahanda*, the young man's family leaves a decorated box, called *ba'ul*, containing items of value, such as jewelry or new clothes, with the proposed bride's family after suggesting a price for the bridewealth. The proposed bride's family then discusses the offer and returns the ba'ul and its contents to the young man's family with their answer. The young couple and their parents are never directly involved in these meetings although the parents always participate in the discussions before and after the meetings. Several meetings may be necessary before the amount of the bridewealth is settled.

After the bride wealth is negotiated, another magpahanda is held. The young man's relatives visit the family of the proposed bride to give a portion of the cash payment in a brightly decorated ba'ul. They are served refreshments and the ba'ul is placed in the center of the circle of participants. Traditionally, betel chew was offered to the group by the host, but now both betel and cigarettes are distributed and the group chews and smokes together. The payment is then formally presented to representatives of the family of the bride-to-be. The amount is discussed and the date for paying the remainder of the bridewealth is decided. After further conversation, the group disbands. A second meeting is held shortly before the wedding to pay the balance of the bridewealth.

The wedding takes place any time following this meeting except during the month of *Ramadan*, the Muslim month of fasting; however, some Tawi-Tawi Sama Dilaut marry even during this month. The length of the engagement period is determined by the time it takes the groom's family to accumulate the bridewealth; this may be only a few days or as long as a year. The young man's parents and their siblings contribute to the bridewealth. The bridewealth varies greatly, depending on the affluence of the families involved, but typically it consists of about 100 pesos, two or three 100-pound bags of rice, a fifty-pound bag of sugar, and several cartons of cigarettes. In addition, a small houselike structure, called a *maligai*, is filled with gifts (*sokat*) and given to the bride's family. If it is the second or third marriage of the bride, the bridewealth is considerably less. If some doubt arises about the compatibility of the young man and his future in-laws, he sometimes stays in their residence during the engagement period to test their compatibility. Ideally, sexual intercourse does not occur between the young couple during this period, but in reality it sometimes does. If personality conflicts develop, the wedding is cancelled.

A Sama Dilaut wedding is one of the most colorful events in Tawi-Tawi. The day before the celebration begins, when many houseboats have congregated in the moorage, several boats belonging to relatives of the groom sail to Bongao to purchase goods for the wedding. The boats are brightly decorated with flags, colorful sarongs, fishing nets, and lighted lanterns (fig. 61). Musicians play gongs and drums while girls and women dance on the prows. In the early morning of the first day of the celebration, boats of the bride's relatives, decorated in similar fashion, with dancers and musicians, parade throughout the moorage, visiting relatives and picking up paraphernalia for the ceremony. The next morning, shortly after dawn, when the groom's boats are spotted coming from Bongao, the bride's boats go to the edge of the moorage three abreast, with musicians playing inside and women dancing on the prows. When the groom's boats are about a quarter-mile from the moorage, the bride's boats move slowly toward them. The boats draw closer together and a mock battle ensues as the passengers throw sugarcane, firecrackers, bananas, and other such items at one another amid much laughter and joking. When the boats are very near one another, they stop and the groom's center boat pulls away from the others and gently touches its prow to the prow of the bride's forward boat, as loud music, exploding fire crackers, shouting, and dancing reach a crescendo. The bride's boats then turn around and escort the groom's boats into the moorage. Once inside the moorage, the boats disperse and move throughout the moorage waters for an hour or so, the occupants playing music and collecting items for the wedding. The relatives of the groom then distribute rice and sugar to the moorage households, each receiving about two pounds of rice and a pound of sugar, if the bridewealth is large. Otherwise, only close relatives receive the gifts. The musicians retire to the reef or beach where they play for the remainder of the day.

At dusk, everyone in the moorage gathers on the reef or beach, dressed in their finest clothes and jewelry to participate in the *tagungi'ian*, the celebration held the night before the wedding ceremony. The relatives of the bride spend the evening supplying adults with betel or cigarettes. As the musicians perform, children play games, men and women gather to gossip and joke, while teenage

Fig. 61 Wedding boat

Fig. 62 Bathing of groom

Fig. 63 Bride escorted to wedding boat

Fig. 64 Bride and groom

boys play volleyball, wrestle, or tease the teenage girls who coyly congregate near them. As darkness descends, kerosene lanterns are hung on poles above the musicians, mats are spread out, and the dancing begins. Normally, girls and women, single or in pairs, dance ahead of the men. Men and women rarely dance together.

While the dancing takes place, young unmarried couples may seek the privacy of nearby bushes for sexual encounters. It is a night of general license and not infrequently fights break out between people who carry the relaxed mood too far. Eventually the adults wander back to their households, leaving the night to the young people who play music in shifts until dawn. The bride and groom are usually absent during the nighttime activities—indeed, beyond the actual wedding ceremony, they play only minor roles in the two-day celebration.

The following morning at dawn, three boats are again decorated, one each for the bride and groom, and the third for the wedding ceremony. The bride and groom are paraded throughout the moorage in their special boats, eventually arriving at the home boats of their respective future in-laws, where they are bathed in seawater by a djin, followed by a rinse in fresh water (fig. 62). Umbrellas are held over them during their baths while dancers perform to drums and gongs and the djin chants to ancestral spirits to protect their health and insure their good fortune. Following their baths, they enter the houseboats,

177

where they are dressed in new clothes and family jewelry (fig. 63). White powder is applied to their faces, and their eyebrows and hairlines are outlined in charcoal; lipstick and red dots sometimes decorate their faces. Each wears an elaborate headdress, often covered with jewelry and money.

When their toilets are completed, usually around noon, the groom is carried on the shoulders of male relatives to the wedding boat or house where his bride is waiting for him, hidden behind a curtain. Sometimes the final cash portion of the bridewealth is given to the bride's family at this time, but more commonly it has already been delivered. The groom sits on mats with his father, his future father-in-law, and a male djin, while other close relatives cluster around. The djin lights incense, takes the groom's right hand in his own over the incense, covers their hands with a cloth, and recites a prayer to ask for blessings from ancestral spirits. The djin then taps on the curtain hiding the bride, and with much laughter and joking tries to pull it from the hands of the women who hold it to conceal her. Eventually, the curtain is removed to reveal the bride. The djin then directs the groom to kneel behind the seated bride. He takes the groom's right forefinger and touches it to the center of the bride's forehead and then above her right breast, following which he seats the groom beside the bride. Throughout the entire ceremony, the wedding couple are very solemn and never smile, appropriate behavior for a Sama Dilaut bride and groom (fig. 64).

The newlyweds are then carried to the nearby exposed reef or beach on the shoulders of male relatives, followed by the male attendant of the groom and the female attendant of the bride who have been with them throughout the morning. On the reef, they are placed on mats near the musicians, surrounded by most of the moorage dwellers. First, the bride's attendant dances with a woman from the crowd; then the bride and groom dance together; finally the groom's attendant dances with a man from the crowd. After the last dance, the bride and groom are carried to the boat where they will spend their first night, and all festivities cease. Boat decorations are removed, the musicians retire, and the rest of the afternoon is like any other afternoon in the moorage. It is not unusual for two or even three couples to be married at the same time. They are usually closely related to one another, and although the general celebration is held in common, ceremonies are conducted separately for each couple.

Sometimes if a couple do not want to wait until money is available for the bridewealth or if their parents object to the match, they elope to the boat of the headman where they spend the night. The following morning, their families meet with the headman, decide on a suitable bridewealth, and the wedding ceremony is held. There may be some music, dancing, and decorated boats, but usually an elopement passes with little fanfare. No stigma is attached to an elopement; it is simply a quicker and easier way to marry. In fact, some parents prefer to have their sons elope, since the bridewealth for such marriages is considerably less.

Death Death is a common occurrence in a Sama Dilaut moorage. Although well aware of some of the natural causes of death, the Sama Dilaut attribute most deaths to the actions of spirits, even some deaths that appear to be the result of natural causes. Most deaths occur among infants who die from various stomach and respiratory disorders. Among adults, tuberculosis, malaria, childbirth, and occasionally cholera are common causes of death.

As soon as death occurs, female relatives of the deceased begin wailing a mourning refrain, which is soon picked up by other women in the moorage. Those closest to the deceased fall into fits of grief, kicking, screaming, flailing their limbs, and breaking objects within reach. Others must often restrain them to prevent injury to themselves or destruction of property. Such fits may last an hour or so, during which the persons mourn themselves to exhaustion. Meanwhile older relatives, distant enough to be uninvolved in mourning, oversee the preparation of the corpse and subsequent rites. One of these people of the same gender as the deceased washes the corpse, usually with seawater followed by a rinse in fresh water. The bathing must be done to prevent the spirit of the dead from returning to haunt the living. The hands of the corpse are crossed over its stomach and white cloth is stuffed into its apertures. Perfume and powder are sprinkled over the body, and money representing the deceased's share of the family wealth is sometimes placed on its chest. The body is then wrapped in a white shroud and several new sarongs, and placed in the center of the house or lengthwise in the houseboat with the head toward the bow as friends and relatives gather for the wake, or *tinulkinan*, which lasts throughout the first night after death. A mirror is placed on the chest of the corpse to keep away evil spirits who are frightened when they see their image in the glass. As long as the corpse remains in the moorage, no one fishes in order to avoid illness and additional death. One family told me that if fish is roasted within a week after a death, the person who roasts the fish will also die; other ways of cooking fish present no problem. Rice powder, or any available white paste, is sometimes applied to the faces of children to protect them from the spirit of the deceased. In general, the moorage is very subdued as long as the corpse is present. Noise, loud laughter, and other ceremonies are inappropriate at this time.

Throughout the night, mourners visit the corpse, sing songs to it, and occasionally fall into fits of mourning. If the deceased is an adult, most people in the moorage visit the corpse, but if the deceased is a child, mourners are generally limited to close relatives. The wake is not particularly solemn, and considerable talking and joking occur among those not singing. The Bajau have no fear of the corpse itself, although the spirit is believed to be potentially malevolent at this time. Thus, most of the songs flatter the spirit and recall its good qualities. Persons who were on unfriendly terms with the deceased display the greatest grief in order to redeem themselves since it is believed that the spirit may seek revenge for their past behavior. The singing continues throughout the night as mourners come and go.

The following morning, boats are prepared for the journey to Bunabuna'an or Bilatan Po'on, the burial islands where all Tawi-Tawi Sama Dilaut are interred. Burial elsewhere is unthinkable to the Sama Dilaut, who often told me that all Sama Dilaut are buried on these islands because "the bones of our people cannot be scattered," an explanation that always struck me as somewhat ironic for a people who spend their lives scattered throughout the Tawi-Tawi waters. If the deceased is a small child, only one or two boats of close relatives travel to the cemetery island, but if the deceased is a well-known, respected adult, a large flotilla of perhaps fifteen to twenty decorated boats with dancers and musicians accompanies the body. More commonly though, boats are undecorated, with no music and dancing, although mourning songs are always sung throughout the journey.[8] Depending on winds and currents, the boats normally reach the cemetery island from the Sanga-Sanga moorages by late afternoon or sunset. From the Bilatan moorages, the trip only takes an hour or so. When approaching the cemetery island, the Sama Dilaut do not point at them in order to avoid bad luck or even death.

After reaching the burial island, the boats anchor offshore and unless it is still daytime, the graves are not visited since it is believed that spirits are at the graves at night. Mourning songs continue throughout the night while the women wail their endless refrain. Not infrequently, the men take advantage of the overnight anchorage to do nighttime fishing, and some mourners even stop to fish en route to the cemetery. One man claimed that sleepers never direct their heads toward the stern of the boat for fear that they will be the next to die. The following morning at dawn, part of the funeral party goes to the cemetery to prepare the grave.[9] Ideally the coffin of an adult man is made from his houseboat; more commonly, however, the coffin is made from a small dugout. The houseboat is not destroyed to build a coffin but a small piece of the houseboat is sometimes left with the corpse.

Typically, Bajau are buried with the relatives they interacted with most frequently during their lives. However, if a recent burial has occurred in the grave of these relatives, burial takes place elsewhere rather than disturb the grave, not out of fear of the spirit, but rather to avoid the stench of the recently interred corpse. One can even be buried with in-laws if these were the important people in one's life.

The grave is enclosed by a roof of corrugated tin supported by four corner poles and is decorated with wooden markers elaborately carved in abstract curvilinear motifs. Carved anthropomorphic figures, birdlike figures, and white cloth canopies are found on the more elaborate graves. Beneath these markers, the grave is covered with wooden planks over which a thin layer of sand is sprinkled. When a new burial takes place, the sand, grave markers, and planks are removed and the grave is rearranged to make room for the new corpse. Deteriorated grave goods are discarded, while those still usable, such as bottles and toys, are sometimes taken by the grave makers; however, goods belonging to recently interred corpses are never removed. Old bones encountered while preparing a new burial are often identified by name, cleaned, stacked in a pile until the grave is readied, and then replaced. Recently interred corpses are never disturbed unless absolutely necessary. All who assist in making the grave and handling the corpse are given a small piece of the shroud to tie around their wrists to protect them from the potential malevolence of the disturbed spirits. The preparation of the grave is not a particularly solemn occasion, and joking and laughing intersperse the activities.

On the boat, the corpse is wrapped in a mat. As it is lifted from the funeral boat to be carried to the grave, siblings, parents, children, and the spouse of the deceased pass under it twice as they scream and weep. Sometimes firecrackers are exploded at this time. The corpse is then carried to the grave followed by the wailing mourners. As it is lowered into the grave, mourners sometimes jump in to join it or attempt to tear down the grave structure in their grief. Some say the corpse should be placed in the grave with its head directed to the east, but not all corpses are interred this way. Grave goods left with the corpse include food, water, cigarettes, and such personal property as dishes, clothing, and fishing equipment. Bottles of the mother's milk and cradle bars are often left with infants. I saw explosives placed in the grave of one man who was killed while using them in fishing. Valuables such as jewelry and money are sometimes left with the corpse. Grave goods are often broken to release their spirits. Some Sama Dilaut say the goods are left behind to assist the spirit in the spirit world, others say they are left because they belong to the deceased, and still others say they are left so they will not be in the household to remind survivors of their loss. One man told me it was a waste to leave the goods since they could be better used by the living.

Shortly before the grave is covered, a ceremony called *magsangbaihian* is held. A djin steps into the grave and opens the wrapping around the nose of the corpse. After placing a coconut shell of incense nearby so the smoke enters the corpse's nostrils, he recites a prayer asking the spirit to be content and not to send illness or misfortune to the survivors. Planks are then replaced over the grave and covered with sand. At times, if the deceased is an adult male, a small boat or even the prow of his houseboat is placed atop the grave. The final rite is a libation of water poured over the grave by the djin as she again asks the spirit to refrain from harming the survivors. At one funeral, the djin concluded the ceremony by placing sharpened bamboo sticks about six inches long in crisscross arrangement on the grave to prevent ghosts from entering it.

After the initial grief displayed at death, further mourning is fairly ritualized. By the time the corpse is buried, the survivors are usually weary of the mourning ritual and the presence of the corpse. Most Sama Dilaut are reluctant to mention the name of a recently deceased person; some say it is insensitive because it reminds survivors of their loss, while others say it will call back the spirit. Several Sama Dilaut told me the houseboat of the deceased should be abandoned after his death. I never saw this happen, although I did see several houses abandoned after the deaths of family members because house dwelling was believed responsible for their deaths. A bereaved spouse has no formal period of mourning, but generally waits a year before remarriage.

THE AESTHETIC REALM

The Tawi-Tawi Sama Dilaut do not regard the arts as a domain separate from their other activities; on the contrary, song, music, dance, carving, and the other arts are intimately integrated into the patterns of their everyday lives. However, I have chosen to discuss the arts as a separate chapter because I find it disruptive to discuss them within the contexts of fishing, social organization, religion, and other places where they occur. An exception is boat art, which I discussed in the context of boatbuilding (chapter 4).

Songs dominate this survey of art. Not only are they the most pervasive Sama Dilaut art form, but they were of personal interest to me when I conducted fieldwork. Extensive though this discussion of songs may seem, it is nonetheless limited because it concentrates on lyrics and cultural context. I lack the knowledge to discuss the songs from a musicological perspective. For that reason, also, my discussion of instrumental music is limited.[1] The discussion of dance deals primarily with its cultural context while the discussions of grave art and mat making are more complete. When I left Tawi-Tawi in 1967, I planned to return to research Sama Dilaut arts in greater depth, but before I was able to return, their traditional arts were significantly altered. Rather than leave the Sama Dilaut artistic record blank, I offer the following discussion, limited though it is.

Songs

Virtually every Sama Dilaut is a singer of songs. Some, of course, are better singers than others, but all can sing the appropriate songs for the occasions dictated by their culture. And Sama Dilaut culture has songs for almost every occasion. The births of infants are heralded by the magical chants of the assisting djin. Mothers' lullabies early become familiar to babies, and when children have mastered the rudiments of their language, they become singers of their own songs. Teenagers compose ballads to court would-be lovers and to while away the empty hours of youth. Later in adulthood, wind and fishing songs are added to their musical repertoires and their mature minds turn with new interest to the long chants a few of the elders know. And when the Sama Dilaut die, their deaths are mourned with songs by surviving kinsmen and friends as funeral boats transport their bodies to the burial islands at Bilatan.

Each song-type can be recognized by its distinctive melody. However, within these musical structures, each singer improvises according to his or her creativity. The lyrics are, for the most part, original and not sung from memory. Certain stock images and phrases recur in the songs, but each has the individual stamp of its singer. The originality of the lyrics varies with the artistry of the singer.

Songs serve various functions in Sama Dilaut culture, the most obvious one being entertainment. In a society with no radios, books, television, or movies, songs provide important entertainment. Much Sama Dilaut singing occurs during leisure hours or during travel, when songs offer diversion.

Most importantly to the Sama Dilaut, some songs serve the functions for which they are consciously used. For example, lullabies soothe babies to sleep, shark songs bring success in shark fishing, kata-kata chants help cure the sick, and funeral songs placate the spirit of the deceased. To the outside observer, the songs may appear irrelevant to the situations that call for them, but the Sama Dilaut tell of many occasions when the songs have fulfilled their overt cultural functions and their claims cannot be discounted. The greater security the shark songs provide to the fisherman of this dangerous fish no doubt contributes to his success in fishing. Similarly, the patient who knows that the most powerful of all chants, the kata-kata, is being performed for her is more psychologically prepared for recovery than she who feels that nothing is being done for her illness. And the mourner who sings proper songs to the spirit of the deceased is less likely to become ill than he who has not mourned properly.

Sama Dilaut songs are also an important medium for the dissemination of news. Because most Sama Dilaut do not read or write and have no access to radio or television, they learn all news by word of mouth. Usually this is through conversation, but often it is through singers who sing of current events such as a quarrel with an in-law or a big catch of fish. Other more spectacular events, such as a shipwreck or the capture of a pirate, may fire a singer's imagination when she sings the long tenes-tenes ballads.

Some song types serve the important function of providing a socially approved channel for the expression of subjects that are normally taboo. A child sings about his anger toward his parents through lia-lia without fear of punishment, but he would never voice such anger through everyday speech. While singing binua to her baby, a mother may tell of her hard life with her in-laws, but she would breach Sama Dilaut etiquette if she made the same complaints to her neighbor during conversation. A youth may sing a tenes-tenes of his love for a young woman of the moorage, but he would never announce such feelings through speech. The songs, then, provide a safety valve, an approved channel for the expression of otherwise repressed feelings.

Sama Dilaut songs are also important agents of social control. It is not uncommon for a Sama Dilaut who feels mistreated to sing his or her case to the moorage. One evening, I heard a young wife sing loudly to the entire moorage about the injustices she suffered from her in-laws. The moorage listened sympathetically and several people later chastised her in-laws for their behavior. Within days, the in-laws rectified their behavior, partly because of the moorage's reaction to the woman's song. No one cares to hear his faults sung to the moorage, and partly because of this, one is more careful not to offend others.

The songs also have educational and enculturational functions. Most are laden with Sama Dilaut cultural values, such as the way to court a sweetheart, the proper behavior toward relatives, and the courage that befits a man when confronted with danger. The same values permeate other aspects of Sama Dilaut culture and the songs are another reminder of the proper way to behave.

Binua Lullabies, or binua, are sung at any time to soothe the sleepy or fussy baby, but they are most commonly sung in the moorage during evening hours. The Sama Dilaut baby normally sleeps in a hammock-like cradle suspended from the roof of the house or houseboat, and as the mother sings, she swings the cradle. The creaking sound of the swinging cradle provides the only accompaniment to her song. The lullabies have a plaintive quality, and often recall the mother's bittersweet, melancholy experiences. The song is addressed to the child and her name is usually mentioned in the first line or so, but the text typically consists of the mother's personal thoughts and reminiscences. If she wishes the moorage to know of some event, she may sing loudly so all can hear. The lullaby gives her license to speak of people and events she would not mention in normal conversation. If someone wishes to respond to her musical statement, she can do so through the same medium. As a result, a repartee of musical comments sometimes drifts across the waters between houseboats. More often, however, the mother sings the song to herself, of things personal she wishes the moorage to know. She bares a part of herself normally concealed and her neighbors listen quietly, perhaps sympathetically, but do not discuss it in everyday speech. The following are examples of the binua. The name of the singer and the recording date follows each song throughout this chapter.[2]

My daughter I sing a song of sleep to you.
I am weary, but still I swing your cradle.
When the moon came out tonight, it shone like a
    bright coin.
The mountain on Siasi is very small –
    There, the Chinese are flying kites.
Siasi is very, very far.
Sleep soundly like a bird, my child.
                  (Akirina 1966)

I sing a lullaby.
We sail all our lives and our bodies become weary.
It is to you I am singing, my daughter.
We suffer from great poverty,
But it is our fate to lead this life.
We have no fine mats to sleep on, nor robes to
    wear; we sleep with nothing.
You are a beautiful child, but you are also a fickle
    child.
If I should die, you probably would not cry for me.
Mount Bongao is very small, and atop it is the *lagondi*
    tree that gives eternal youth.
Should I die while you are still young, I wish you a
    good life.
                  (Nurusia 1966)

Go to sleep, my child.
Go to sleep, my child.
I am so weary of singing to you.
I am so weary of singing to you.
Midnight is almost here, and you are still awake.
The moon is now directly above, and you are not yet
    asleep.
Go to sleep now as I place you in your cradle.
                  (Musulaini 1965)

Lia-Lia Songs called lia-lia are sung by small children. The Sama Dilaut offer no definition of lia-lia other than a name for this type of children's song. It could be called a "spite song" or an "anger song," since it is often sung during those moods. When children become angry at playmates or family members, they sometimes retire to a secluded spot to vent their displeasure through song. As the mothers who sing lullabies, the children who sing lia-lia have a license denied them in speech. They sing comments about friends or family they would speak only at risk of punishment. Although Sama Dilaut children have much freedom, respectful behavior toward parents and adults is early instilled in them. But there are times when adults frustrate children. Since they cannot speak badly about adults without punishment, a way to retaliate is through song, and Sama Dilaut children use their unique song tradition in this way. Parents usually pretend they do not hear the songs; indeed children sometimes seek lonely spots where no one can hear them, but if they are within listening range the parents listen to what the children have to say.

The following examples illustrate the lia-lia songs.

> Lia, lia, lia.
> I am angry with you, mother.
> You will not let me play on the beach.
> Other children have good mothers who let them play on
>   the beach.
> But my mother does not like me.
> I wish I had another mother.
> I wish I could go away.
>   (Bangsaria 1965)

> Lia, lia, lia.
> I do not like the children at this moorage.
> Tomorrow I will go away from this moorage to Lu'uk
>   Tulai.
> My father is a handsome man;
> He is better than the fathers of the other children
>   here.
> Tomorrow he will take me to Lu'uk Tulai,
>   Because I do not like the children here.
>   (Kambar 1965)

> Lia-lia.
> I am angry with you.
> I remember my father, a handsome man.
> Hear my song, my friend.
>   (Maria 1965)

187

Tenes-Tenes Tenes-tenes is another song-type widely sung by Sama Dilaut children, as well as teenagers and young adults. A very versatile song-type, it is sung on various occasions. While at play, a child may burst into a tenes-tenes, singing about whatever comes to mind or sight. While fishing, sailing, or paddling, teenagers use the song tradition to sing about travels, fishing, or the scenery. At evening in the moorage, teenagers sometimes sing tenes-tenes to announce their love for someone. And sometimes, it is used to tell long stories about local events, such as a shipwreck or a shootout with pirates.

The name tenes-tenes has no meaning to the Sama Dilaut other than a name for a song-type. "Ballad" is perhaps the nearest English equivalent. The length and tempo of the song depend on the mood or message of the singer, but all tenes-tenes follow the same musical pattern and each begins by announcing a color for the song, such as "My song is of blue colors," "My song is of green and red stripes like the sail," or "My song is of the colors of the sunset." The colors have no particular symbolism, nor are they consistent images throughout the song.

The tenes-tenes sung by young children is most commonly a series of remembrances or images that come to mind during play. One day as I wandered the exposed moorage reef, I came upon an eight-year-old girl playing by herself as she loudly sang a tenes-tenes. No other children were around, so I asked her to sing into my recorder. The following is one of her songs.

> My song is of blue colors.
> Yesterday my father went fishing, and caught many
> > fish.
> Tomorrow we will sail to Lioboran, and my father
> > and brother will fish there.
> The trees on the island are very tall.
> I often remember my friends who live at Lu'uk Tulai.
> I hope you are enjoying my song.
> My mother has wavy hair and yesterday she bought a new
> > sarong.
> When I grow up I shall have a lover and be married.
> This is the end of my song.
> > (Bangsaria 1965)

The tenes-tenes sung by teenagers are the most colorful. During paddling or sailing, teenagers often sing duets back and forth to one another, or one may sing while others interject musical comments into his song. Young people sometimes sing to themselves when fishing alone to help pass the time. Some of the best musical improvisation I heard, however, was during the songfests of Sama Dilaut youth. These impromptu affairs occur when several youth gather in a houseboat, usually during the evening hours. One begins to sing, others answer, and soon young·people in neighboring boats join them. On such occasions, someone usually furnishes a *gabbang*,

Fig. 65 Gabbang player

a xylophone-type instrument made of bamboo slats and played with two rubber-tipped mallets (fig. 65). While someone, usually a young woman, plays the gabbang, others take turns singing, never in unison because each song is the original creation of its singer. The songs usually have a romantic flavor, since it is a time when a youth may appropriately tell peers of his love for someone. The name of the person is never mentioned and often the sentiments are expressed in stereotyped images and phrases, but everyone knows what is being said to whom. As with other Sama Dilaut song traditions, the words of the musical statement would never be stated so publicly in speech.

Young people also sing tenes-tenes during activities at sea. One evening while fishing with a group of Sama Dilaut, I heard a teenaged boy and girl sing tenes-tenes to one another as we paddled the shallow waters. Their songs consisted of stock phrases and images of love and romance. Personal names were never mentioned, but everyone knew the youth were expressing their love for one another. On another occasion, I was paddling to a neighboring island with teenaged boys in four different boats. During the entire trip the boys sang tenes-tenes ranging from love affairs to fishing experiences. Some songs were solos while others were musical repartees with the entire group participating. The following songs are typical of this type of tenes-tenes.

My song is of the many colors of the sail.
As I left home this morning, I was talking to a
    certain girl.
We have been in love since we were small, and now
    she is almost a woman.
Once I lay next to her and laid my legs over hers.
I told my mother she should go to the headman,
    so we could be married.
My sister is wearing a sarong as she is playing
    the gabbang.
My sister and I were invited to sing and play at
    a wedding.
This will be my last time to sing because I am
    very tired.
I will even go to the spirit world with my lover
    after we die.
I have given much food to my lover.
Someday I will marry her.
My lover is almost crazy in her love for me.
The home of my lover is far away, but I will sail
    to see her.

                    (Basilhani 1965)

My song is of many interwoven colors.
You hear me.
I was going to Cagayan, but my lover cried so much I
    decided not to go.
I am embarrassed to sing to you because my voice is not
    very good.
I shall go to Palawan.
When I return, I shall have a woman for my wife.
If I have good luck in fishing, I will ask the parents
    of the woman for the hand of their daughter.
I will suffer from the heat of the sun and the dew of
    night, so long as I can travel to see my lover.
If you do not become my wife, all my gifts to you will
    have been in vain.
Even though I am far away, you will remember me when
    you see my gifts.

                    (Hajibulan 1965)

My song is of many colors.
This is my first time to have a lover.
I have not seen you for three months, and now you
　　have a husband.
After I went home, I could still see your image before
　　me.
Since we first fell in love, you have grown taller
　　than I.
You have not returned the gifts I gave you when we
　　were in love.
You live far from me and the wind is too strong for
　　me to go there.
I will never get the gifts I gave you.
　　　　　　　　　　　　　　(Landisani 1965)

Sometimes a tenes-tenes is sung as a long narrative ballad in which the singer relates an actual incident that occurred in Tawi-Tawi. This type of tenes-tenes is most highly developed among the land-dwelling Sama of Tawi-Tawi, the most talented of whom travel up and down the archipelago performing at weddings, circumcisions and other celebrations. These balladeers are usually young men and women in their late teens or early twenties. The listeners know the singer has altered the event somewhat for the sake of art, but nonetheless much of the ballad is accepted as fact and disseminates news of recent events. This type of tenes-tenes is not highly developed among the Sama Dilaut, although a few youths sing the musical stories.

During my first trip to Tawi-Tawi in 1963, a pirate named Amak was captured after harassing southern Sulu for almost two years. Landisani, a Sama Dilaut teenager, saw Amak's body after the pirate had a shootout with the Philippine Constabulary, and combining Amak's experience with other stories he had heard about the pirate, Landisani composed the following tenes-tenes. (He is one of only three Sama Dilaut I met who sang this type of tenes-tenes.) The following song is short compared to the songs of the land-dwelling professional balladeers, who sometimes keep an audience's attention for one or two hours.

My song is of the many colors of the sail.
The home place of Amak, the pirate, is at Paranang in
　　the forest.
On his way home from Bilatan, Tahanan was robbed by
　　Amak.

Amak took money from the home of Tahanan only and not
from the other houses in the village.

Tahanan gave Amak more than 100 pesos, but he wanted
more.

Tahanan said he had no more money.

Amak put his gun in the window and shot Tahanan while
he was in the doorway.

Amak then went to his own house in the forest and
slept peacefully with his companions.

While Amak was sleeping, the Philippine Constabulary
rangers surrounded him.

A sergeant and a captain were the leaders of the
rangers.

All the rangers from Batu-Batu went to Paranang
to kill Amak if they could find him.

In all, there were nineteen rangers who attacked Amak.

As the rangers approached the camp of Amak, they
walked very quietly.

Amak heard a barking dog, so he went slowly outside.

He did not know the Philippine Constabulary rangers
were near.

Amak's brother saw the rangers and told Amak they
should run away.

However, Amak told his brother the rangers were
American soldiers who would not harm them.

Then Amak realized they were Philippine Constabulary
rangers.

He was naked and took cover in the house and began to
fire at the rangers.

Captain Tanang was the leader of the rangers.

Captain Tanang sneaked up to the house of Amak.

He was so close to Amak that Amak almost stepped on
his hands.

But the Captain did not move.

Amak loaded his rifle and began firing at the rangers.

Amak was killed and taken to the jeep by the rangers
and then to Batu-Batu.

The body of Amak was very white.

He had curly hair and was blind in one eye.

At about 2 A.M., the rangers threw Amak's body on the
        wharf at Batu-Batu.
The body was then placed outside the Philippine
        Constabulary camp.
Dew fell on the body since it was not covered.
At nine the following morning, a picture was taken of
        Amak's body.
Before taking the picture, a Philippine Constabulary
        officer placed Amak's rifle, kris and bullet
        belt next to his body.
In the afternoon Tinah carried the body of Amak on his
        shoulders.
But Amak was so heavy that he was dropped in the
        middle of the road.
Amak was taken to his home place at Paranang.
No one likes to pass Paranang Island because it is the
        home of pirates.
The body of Amak was beginning to rot, so the imam
        bathed and buried him.
Amak smelled like a dried fish.
The imam did not offer prayers for him because he was
        afraid it would displease the Philippine
        Constabulary rangers.
He only bathed him.
Amak's two widows were crying in the door of the
        house.
They sang mourning songs all night long.
When Amak was alive, he did not eat and became thin
        like an American's son.
He wore Cutex on his fingernails.
One time Amak went to Borneo with his companions.
They met some Chinese at sea.
Amak and his companions robbed the launch of the Chinese.
They also pirated some goods from a Malayan ship.
They went on further and met an Indonesian ship.
The smoke of the ship was like the smoke of incense.
They fired machine guns at the Indonesian ship, but it
        outran them and went to Borneo.
Later the Indonesian navy caught some pirates and took

them to Borneo where they cut off their hands and
ears to mark them as pirates.
The British cut off the heads of pirates to warn
others.
The punishment was for offenses these men
committed against the Chinese and Malays.

(Landisani 1966)

Kalangan Baliu Kalangan baliu, or "songs of the wind," are sung almost
exclusively by Sama Dilaut men, although women occasionally sing them. They
are sung during the idle or lonely hours of fishing and sailing trips, usually at
night. When heard over the dark waters, the songs have a lonely, melancholy
air. Most often a man sings his songs alone, but sometimes he sings with a
sailing companion or a friend within hearing distance in another boat. Although
the singer often uses stock phrases and images, the songs are not sung from
memory, but rather are creations of a mood. Despite their name they are not
sung to call the wind and I met no Sama Dilaut who seriously believed the songs
could bring the wind. Invariably brief, they consist of a single image or a series
of vignettes, often unconnected except in the mind of the singer. Themes and
images reflect the sea home of the Sama Dilaut.

Changing, shifting winds,
Tell Salamdulila,
Do not forget me.

(Enang 1967)

White sails.
Sailing from Kangan.
A smooth sea.

(Anonymous 1966)

The whirling wind strikes the prow;
The flying wind.

(Suluhani 1966)

White sails.
Sailing to Sitangkai.
Single file.

(Masarani 1966)

O south wind,
You bring the dark clouds.
Like a ripe jackfruit are you: on the surface alike
and smooth, but inside, varied and many.

(Laja'udden 1966)

O wind.
You blow the waves–and my heart–
into a thousand pieces.

(Anonymous 1966)

Now blows the north wind.
Tell her the truth:
I never loved her.
My heart is always angry,
Like a ship on a rough sea.

(Jalai 1967)

Kalangan Kalitan Another song-type sung even more exclusively by men is the kalangan kalitan or "shark songs." During the southeast monsoon, Sama Dilaut fishermen seek sharks in the waters to the west of Sanga-Sanga island. After baiting large hooks, they shake coconut-shell rattles in the water as they sing dirge-like songs to attract the sharks. The songs are brief and tend to flatter the shark. Some Sama Dilaut claim the songs have no magical qualities and are sung only because it is traditional to do so. Nonetheless, few Sama Dilaut fish for sharks without singing the songs. It is significant that musical, magical aids of this sort are used only in shark fishing, the most dangerous of all Sama Dilaut fishing. The following are examples of the kalangan kalitan.

Datu Shark,
Your fin is handsome and looks like a flag in the sea.
I have thrown my baited hook into the deep sea
        especially for you.
Come and take my gift.

(Hajibulan 1966)

I am shaking my rattle to call you.
I know you are under my boat, waiting to take my bait.
Come now and take my bait and hook.

(Anonymous 1966)

195

Datu *Pandana* [female shark]:
My bait is thrown into the sea.
The two of us, my brother-in-law and I, are fishing.
(Samsalani 1966)

Datu *Talung Badji Tabulan* [a species of shark]:
I throw my baited hook into the deep sea.
I throw my baited hook to the bottom of the sea.
(Laja'udden 1966)

Why, shark, have you not come to eat my bait?
If you are a *Kalitan Mangalih* [a species unfit for
    eating], do not take my bait.
Why do you not come to taste my bait?
The brightly colored red and white line of my hook is
    newly bought from the store.
Why *Kalitan Talong Badji* [a favorite eating shark] do you not come to
    my hook?
You are so good to eat.
(Masarani 1965)

Kalangan Kamun Among the edible sea life found on the great reefs of
Bilatan is the kamun, known in English as sea mantis or *Squilla sp.* It is a
pinkish crustacean that reaches lengths of twenty-five centimeters and is greatly
prized for its succulent flavor. The kamun lives in the natural holes of the reef
in male and female pairs. During low tides, trapping the animal is a popular
pastime for Sama Dilaut boys and sometimes men. A special baited trap is made
to snare the animal and while the boys wait for the trap to spring, they sing
kalangan kamun (kamun songs) to pass the time. Unlike shark songs, these
songs are not believed to have magical qualities but rather are sung simply as
entertainment. Normally, the male kamun (*lantig*) is caught first and while the
boys wait for the female (*balu*) to take the bait, they sing songs to entice her.
The songs are frequently comic.

Kamun, I give you food.
Catch my bait as it comes inside your hole.
Kamun, I am giving you food, so why don't you take it?
(Timpa 1966)

196

Kamun, tell your mate: "Do not talk anymore. Here is
      our food. We will go together through our door."
Kamun, I have given you all kinds of food, even cassava.
Many of your friends already have nice white rattan
      around their necks.
I brought this rattan all the way from Palawan for
      you.

(Landisani 1966)

Kamun, come and take my bait.
Your husband has already taken it and likes it.
You take it, too, and join your husband.

(Mastarani 1966)

Balu, I place my noose in your hole.
Take my bait, Balu.
Do not be ashamed.
I already have your husband.

(Anonymous 1966)

Kata-Kata As discussed in the previous chapter, long chants known as kata-kata are traditionally sung by the Sama Dilaut for healing the sick. Considered extremely sacred and belonging to the domain of the ancestors, the chants must be recited without mistake to avoid offense to the spirits. The men who know kata-kata are all djin. I met no women who knew the chants. All kata-kata chanters paid others to teach them the chants, and they therefore insist on a small payment before chanting, otherwise everyone involved will suffer misfortune. The texts of the chants usually deal with heroes who travel to faraway places, experience unusual events, and encounter strange people. Some kata-kata are heavily influenced by Islamic traditions. An evening of chanting typically consists of several tangentially related stories. Kata-kata are extremely difficult to translate because of the occasional words and phrases the chanter himself does not understand, which he usually explains as the language of the ancestors. In addition, lapses in the chanter's memory sometimes result in confusion. Some of the land-dwelling Sama of Tawi-Tawi tell the same stories as secular folk literature but to the Tawi-Tawi Sama Dilaut, they are the most sacred of their oral traditions.

Salbaiyani was a renowned chanter of kata-kata. Because of our friendship, he told me I could record his kata-kata the next time he was asked to chant. Several weeks after his promise, a man of the moorage became

197

critically ill. The traditional curing methods were tried on him, to no avail. As a final attempt to dispel the saitan causing his illness, Salbaiyani was asked to chant kata-kata.

The atmosphere was subdued when I arrived at Salbaiyani's houseboat for the curing session. Salbaiyani was dressed in his finest clothes. Sitting beside him on the household's best mat was the sick man, and sitting around them in circular fashion were his close kinsmen. Salbaiyani lighted incense in a small white bowl between him and the patient. He spread his arms with palms upward on his crossed legs and for several minutes asked the spirits to acknowledge the power of the kata-kata, to take pity on the sick man and allow his recovery. Then he began to chant.

His words were lengthy and displayed a wide tonal range. Because the words sounded distorted and my knowledge of Sinama was still limited, I could understand only a few of them. Only later, after laborious hours of transcribing my tapes with Salbaiyani, did I understand the story. He chanted for about two hours, stopping only twice for a drink of water. When he stopped for the night, another petition was made to the spirits believed responsible for the illness and the small group dispersed. For one more night the ceremony continued. The appendix contains the text of the kata-kata chanted by Salbaiyani during the first evening of the ceremony.

The kata-kata is obviously two different stories. Typically, if a story is not long enough to fill an evening, the chanter adds another to it. The first story is typical of many Sulu tales about the long-ago adventures of culture heroes in faraway places, which for the most part predate Islam in Sulu. The second story about the child's visit to heaven has obvious Islamic roots. Islam is hardly mentioned in the first story whereas it flavors the second. Subsequent nights of chanting would include similar stories held loosely together by a narrative thread. Such chanting would continue until the djin concluded either the patient would recover or was beyond the power of kata-kata.

Kalangan Matai Death is another occasion for singing traditional Sama Dilaut songs . As soon as news of a death is heard, the women of the moorage begin wailing a dirge-like refrain. With other members of the moorage, they crowd around and within the death boat as the deceased is bathed and wrapped in a shroud of white cloth. Normally the corpse remains in the moorage overnight and is transported to the burial island the following morning. During the night, mooragers visit the funeral boat to mourn the deceased and sing kalangan matai ("songs of the dead").

The songs usually flatter the deceased and express sorrow over the death. Most songs spring from genuine grief, but some are inspired by the belief that the spirit of the deceased will return to haunt the offender if proper sorrow is not expressed at death. Consequently, even if someone openly disliked the deceased during his lifetime, he will mourn dramatically at his death. In fact, the loudest mourners are often those who were on unfriendly terms with the deceased.

The following songs were recorded during the funeral of a man, about thirty-five, whose sudden death was attributed to the anger of offended spirits.

His brother-in-law who sincerely loved him sang the following song:

> You were my brother-in-law, my best friend.
> When you were alive, we fished together.
> You were always generous and always gave away
> more fish than you kept.
> How shall we continue to live now that you are
> gone?
>
> (Salani 1966)

His wife:

> My father is dead.
> My mother is dead.
> My sister is dead.
> My brother is dead.
> And now my husband is dead.
> How, then, can I live?
>
> (Abira 1966)

A cousin with whom the deceased never got along:

> You were the best fisherman.
> Everyone in the moorage loved you.
> I respected you more than any man I know.
> You were a good father and husband.
> Now you are gone, but I will see that your wife
> and children have fish.
> You and I were like brothers.
>
> (Sawani 1966)

His aged mother:

> You are gone now and I am alone.
> But you are not alone.

> With you in your grave are your father, brothers
> > and sisters.
> And soon I, too, shall join you.
> > > (Laiha 1966)

At another funeral, a man sang the following to his brother-in-law who was killed while dynamiting fish:

> I will not stop using dynamite,
> > so I can soon be with you.
> > > (Samsalani 1966)

At still another funeral, a man sang to his dead wife:

> Why are you so late?
> You said you would come for me two days
> > after your death.
> Still, I wait.
> > > (Ganti 1966)

Instrumental Music

Four musical instruments are used by the Sama Dilaut, namely gongs (*agong*), skin head drums (*tambul*), a set of small gongs (*kulintangan*) and an xylophone-like instrument (*gabbang*). The first three instruments comprise the orchestra that provides music at important Sama Dilaut events, such as the evening celebrations that precede weddings and major superincision ceremonies. The gabbang is not part of the orchestra but is played solo or accompanies singers. The description of the Sitangkai Sama Dilaut orchestra by Martenot and Maceda (1980) applies to the Tawi-Tawi Sama Dilaut orchestra:

> The orchestra is composed of: (1) a set of seven to nine small gongs placed horizontally on two cords which are stretched over a low frame (*kulintangan*); (2) three hanging gongs (the narrow-rimmed *bua*, the wide-rimmed *pulakan*, and the *tamuk*, the largest of the gongs); (3) and a drum (*tambul*).[3] The drum is a long bronze cylinder with a goatskin head, equipped with lateral tensors and a vibrator . . . The melody is carried by the *kulintangan*. The other instruments provide background color or rhythm.

The full ensemble is the ideal orchestra, but frequently only two gongs, or even one, accompany the other instruments. The gongs are played with large wooden sticks capped with cloth or rubber strips; the kulintangan and the drum are each played with two wooden sticks. If sticks are unavailable, any piece of

200

wood of appropriate size is substituted. Martenot and Maceda claim that in Sitangkai only men play the gongs and only women play the kulintangan. That gender division generally holds true in Tawi-Tawi also, but I occasionally saw women play gongs and men play the kulintangan. Both sexes play the drums.

I have no data on the different kinds of music played by the orchestra, but Martenot and Maceda discuss eight different pieces played by the Sitangkai Sama Dilaut, namely (1) *Tagunggu'*: "the simplest and also the most frequently performed gong music"; (2) *Titik to'ongan*: "the prime representative of Sama [Sama Dilaut] orchestral music. An orchestra is hardly ever set up without playing it"; (3) *Titik tabawan*: "This piece is played on the occasion of wedding celebrations and of dances of possession, when it is reserved for women"; (4) *Limbayan*: "This piece is played only during wedding celebrations, where the only dancers are women; it owes its name to the slow and graceful swinging motion of the dancers' arms"; (5) *Tariray*: Another piece that is played during wedding celebrations for women dancers. It has a "syncopated rhythm"; (6) *Sambulayang*: "this is a purely orchestral piece played simply for the pleasure of the music and is not accompanied by a dance"; (7) *Titik Jin*: This piece accompanies the dances of djin during the full moon when they become possessed. "The drum plays a major role; its roll must be sustained enough to allow the possession . . . to take place"; (8) *Lellang*: "This piece generally concludes the dance of possession and is reserved for the organizer of the dance."

With the exception of the last two, these pieces are probably also found among the Tawi-Tawi Sama Dilaut, given the close cultural ties between the two communities. The large gatherings of djin that dance every three months under the full moon in Sitangkai are not found in Tawi-Tawi; consequently, the pieces for that occasion (7 and 8) are not played in Tawi-Tawi.

Most musical instruments appear quite old and I was told they are the property of the ancestors and held in special esteem. No special care, however, seems to be given the instruments. Not all families own musical instruments, but all families have kin connections to families who have them. Many Sama Dilaut can play the instruments, but some are, of course, more talented than others.

At simple ceremonies, such as the ritual bathing of the bride and groom, relatives of the couple play drums and gongs as the djin pours water over the youths. Such players are usually members of the immediate family of the wedding couple and their musical abilities are often limited. However, at the evening celebrations that precede weddings and important superincisions, the most talented musicians are sought to play in a full orchestra to accompany the dancers. The musicians play the entire evening with members of the audience occasionally relieving them. If the musicians are not close relatives of the family sponsoring the event, they are sometimes paid but more often the family provides them reciprocal favors. One or two days preceding large celebrations, the full ensemble practices during the afternoons and early evenings to announce the upcoming festivities to the moorage. The same instruments are played in the decorated boats during the pre-wedding activities as well as in occasional funeral entourages.

Gongs and especially drums frequently accompany the dances of the djin. Some djin dance to the rapid beat of these instruments to achieve a trance. One djin I knew accompanied himself on a drum as he danced into a trance; others dance into a trance to drums and gongs played by others.

Fig. 66 Children and orchestra instruments

Music is not formally taught. Prior to ceremonies, after musicians have set up their instruments, children are often allowed to play them (fig. 66). As they grow older, those with musical interests relieve musicians at celebrations, and through imitation and practice some of them eventually become accomplished musicians.

The gabbang is less commonly played and is owned by only a few families (fig. 65). A xylophone-type instrument composed of seventeen bamboo slats placed on a resonance box, it is played with two rubber-tipped mallets. Sometimes another player accompanies by striking the box with a stick. The gabbang usually concludes the evening pre-wedding celebration. When the dancing ends and the musicians have packed away their instruments, teenagers set up a gabbang. As adults and children disperse to their households, the young people sing into the night and early morning to the accompaniment of the gabbang. The gabbang is also played during the early evening hours when young people gather in households for impromptu songfests. A young woman or man plays the gabbang as others sing tenes-tenes.

Dance

Unlike singing, which can be done almost any time and any place, dance (*angigal*) is reserved for special occasions. Different types of angigal are performed in different contexts, namely (1) dances performed as entertainment at evening celebrations for weddings and superincisions, (2) dances performed at ceremonies, and (3) dances performed by djin during possession.

Except for some of the animated dances of the men, the movements of Sama Dilaut dance are subtle and confined to a small space, such as the prow of a boat, a mat in a houseboat or a small arena surrounded by viewers at celebrations. In most cases, the dancer performs to an audience crowded around her on all sides and her performance must be in the round. Slow circular steps of her bare feet on slightly bent legs turn her body so all in the audience can view her performance. Toes and heels are slowly raised from the ground to accent the natural lines of her foot. The movements of her feet and legs are extended into sinuous but subtle hip movements that extend into her torso. The most animated movements are always in the arms and hands of the dancer, which are extended outward from the body with occasional waving gestures above the head and downward toward the knees. Additional movement occurs in the hands and the upwardly curved fingers. Neck and head movements are very limited and are usually a continuation of the movements of the torso. Facial expressions are always sober and unchanging. Some dancers use *bola-bola*, strips of wood held like castanets that sound by hitting against the palm of the hand.

The dance costume depends on the dancer and the dance context. If a woman intends to dance at the evening celebration preceding a wedding or superincision, she wears her finest sarong and blouse, as well as rings, bracelets, and brooches. Her hair is oiled and secured tightly in a bun at the back of her neck, which frequently displays a brightly colored plastic comb. Some women coat their faces with rice powder and most wear lipstick. Dancers frequently attach long curved aluminum nails to their upper fingers like rings. Women who did not plan to dance but decide to do so after attending the celebration, wear their everyday clothing, although they often wear their best garments for such celebrations. Women and men who dance at minor ceremonies, such as the bathing ceremony of the bride and groom, wear clothes indistinguishable from others at the ceremony, which may or may not be their finest garments. The djin often wear special clothing while dancing—green trousers and white shirts for men, and green sarongs and yellow blouses for women. Many, however, dance in their everyday clothes.

Celebrations On the eve of a wedding or a superincision, a celebration called *tagungi'ian* is hosted by the families sponsoring the ceremony. Activities begin at sunset, when pressurized kerosene lanterns are hung to illuminate the arena where the celebration will take place, which may be a beach, an exposed reef, or the deck of a large house. Musicians arrive with their gongs, drums, and kulintangan. As they set up their instruments, mats are spread to cover an area approximately three square meters where the dancers will perform. The musicians warm up as mooragers gather for the celebration. The first dancers are usually children who dance on the mats as the crowd assembles. Some dance seriously while others play with much laughter, shouting, and encouragement from their playmates. Dancers have no formal instruction, and it is through such play as well as observation that children learn to dance. After the crowd has congregated, the dancing begins in earnest as young adult women step forward. Most of these dancers have planned to dance at the celebration—some have been asked to do so by the host families—and have dressed in their finest clothes for the occasion. The land dwellers and the Sitangkai Sama Dilaut sometimes hire professional dancers to perform at these occasions, but I never heard of this among the Tawi-Tawi Sama Dilaut. No applause is given to fine performances, but the rapt attention of the crowd signifies a greatly appreciated dance. For about an hour or so, the dancers perform, almost always solo, to the accompaniment of the musicians. Especially fine performers are sometimes rewarded by admirers who step from the crowd and place a peso bill on the dancer's person or perhaps on the mat before her. Following the best dancers of the community, other women dance. The female portion of the program concludes with comic dances by old women who exaggerate the movements of the earlier dancers. Sometimes old men join the women, to the delight of the crowd.

Fig. 67 Kuntal dance

Next come the men's dances, which are similar to the women's dances except for their greater animation. Someone usually suggests that two men dance the *kuntal*, a fight-dance (fig. 67). Peers coax the reluctant men, who have prob-

204

ably had a series of disagreements over the past weeks, into the dance arena. As the orchestra plays, the men pretend to fight in dance movements by striking at one another in slow motion without making body contact. With the increased tempo of the music, the dancers make light physical contact with their strikes. As the tempo accelerates further, they strike one another soundly with closed fists, but always to the beat of the music. The dance evolves into a serious fight as the combatants hit one another in earnest, sometimes falling down but always getting up and resuming the fight to the beat of the music. Eventually someone decides the fight has gone far enough and signals the musicians to stop playing, at which time the kuntal ends. Sometimes, however, the men continue to fight and must be separated by others. The dance serves the important function of allowing men with a history of disagreements to resolve their conflict in a culturally sanctioned way. If the men engaged in a fistfight in the moorage, they would be chastised and probably fined by the panglima, but it is culturally appropriate for them to fight out their differences in the kuntal.

The *silat*, another men's dance, is a ritualized fight with bladed weapons. Among the land dwellers this dance is performed with a kris, but the Sama Dilaut use whatever blade is available, usually the *bolo* or wooden sticks. It is much more ritualized than the kuntal as the men hit their blades or sticks together to dance movements. The evening usually concludes with comic dances by an old man or old woman, or perhaps both.

Ceremonial Dancing Dancing is part of many Sama Dilaut ceremonies for they believe that dancing honors the initiates and pleases the ancestral spirits. During weddings, superincisions, and some curing ceremonies, women and sometimes men dance while initiates are bathed by the djin. Drums and gongs usually provide accompaniment.

Musicians also play drums and gongs as dancers perform on the prows of the decorated boats that parade through the moorage during wedding and superincision festivities. The dance movements are similar to those of the women's dances, although more limited because of the restricted performance space.

Dancing also concludes the wedding ceremony. After the ceremony, the bride and groom are carried on the shoulders of male kinsmen to a nearby exposed reef or beach where mats are spread for them as musicians play and guests crowd around them. The bride's attendant dances a brief dance after which the bride and groom dance together or separately (fig. 68). The groom's attendant then dances and the celebration is concluded. This is the only occasion when men and women dance together, except during the comic dances of the elderly at the evening celebrations.

Fig. 68 Bride's dance

Dancers also sometimes perform on the prows of boats that transport corpses to the cemetery islands. They dance to the accompaniment of gongs and drums as the boats depart the moorage and then again as they arrive at the cemetery island. Such dancing is not common. Of the many funeral entourages I accompanied, I saw dancing only twice.

Djin Dances Some djin dance to attract the spirits that assist them in healing ceremonies. These djin dances (angigal djin) follow the basic movements of the other dances, but frequently are much more animated, especially those of the men. The movements depend on the nature of the possession, which varies from djin to djin. Some djin change into special costumes before dancing, others do not. The dances begin in the subdued fashion of the traditional angigal, but when the djin becomes possessed the tempo changes. For those who experience a violent possession, the dance becomes very animated and sometimes the djin must be restrained by others to prevent injury to himself and spectators, or to prevent destruction of property. I once saw a djin plunge overboard during his possession before he could be restrained. For other djin, especially women, the possession and dances are more subdued. Some imitate the flights of birds or spirits, as their bodies seem to lift from the dance arena. Not all djin go into a trance after possession. Spirits speak to some djin as they dance while possessed; others fall into a trance after possession, during which spirits communicate with them.[4]

Grave Art

The carvings on Sama Dilaut boats are equaled, if not surpassed, by the carvings on gravemarkers in the Sama Dilaut cemeteries. David Szanton conducted a survey of art throughout the Sulu Archipelago and concluded that the finest carving he saw in all of Sulu was a gravemarker in the Sama Dilaut cemetery on Bunabuna'an Island (1963, 40). I did not conduct such a survey, but I would concur that some of the finest carving in Sulu is found in Sama Dilaut cemeteries.

All Tawi-Tawi Sama Dilaut bury their dead on the islands of Bunabuna'an or Bilatan Po'on, two small coral islands to the west of Bilatan Island. Small, flat, and only a few feet above sea level, both islands are planted to coconuts claimed by nearby Sama farmers. The cemetery at Bilatan Po'on is the smaller of the two, with only ten communal graves. Located near the shore and visible from the sea, it initially appears unkempt although it is used regularly. Muslim Sama graves, located to one side of the Sama Dilaut graves, are no longer used and belong to "the people of long ago."

The cemetery at Bunabuna'an is located about sixty meters inland at the terminus of a path that leads from the shore. The cemetery consists of some thirty-six communal graves within an approximately twenty-five square meter area. A Muslim Sama cemetery is located nearby and like the one at Bilatan Po'on, it is neglected and no longer used.

Most Sama Dilaut have relatives buried on both islands and I found no consensus as to which cemetery is older. The Sama Dilaut only know that their ancestors established the cemeteries long ago.

At first glance, the cemeteries appear neglected. Weeds, fallen fronds, and coconuts are not cleared unless they lie directly on the graves. When graves are filled to capacity, they are allowed to deteriorate since those buried in them have been forgotten. However, graves of recently interred corpses are regularly maintained. When the deceased are visited, roofs are repaired, past offerings are removed, new offerings are left, leaves and branches are cleared away, new gravemarkers are added, and old carvings are sometimes repainted.

The Sama Dilaut have no fear of the graves during daytime, but avoid them at night. Noisy children and their boisterous play are not tolerated, but otherwise no special behavior is demanded at the gravesite.

Sama Dilaut graves are called *kubul* (fig. 69). A typical grave consists of a cavity excavated one to two meters below ground, about two meters square. The sides are sometimes lined with planks, less often with coral stones. When a new corpse is placed in the grave, old bones are cleaned and rearranged, and deteriorated grave goods are discarded. Bodies of adults are placed in coffins made from old dugout boats or, like children's bodies, simply wrapped in mats and deposited in the grave. Several wooden beams across the top of the excavation support sheets of corrugated metal. Boards are placed over the metal and a layer of about ten centimeters of sand is spread over the boards. Sometimes a low wall, also called kubul and thirty centimeters high, surrounds this crypt. This wall was traditionally made of coral blocks, but concrete is now the prestige material for its construction. At each of the four corners of the kubul, poles about one-and-a-half meters tall support a gabled or hipped roof. Sometimes these poles are carved, but more often they are not. Corrugated metal is the preferred roofing material now, but in the past the roofs were thatched with coconut fronds and many still are. The more elaborate roofs, whether hipped or gabled, have winged bird-like finials (*laiung-laiung*). One elaborate grave on Bunabuna'an has a hipped metal roof topped by a cupola (*maligai*) which in turn has a hipped metal roof topped by a birdlike wooden finial. This structure above the grave is called *lumah-lumah* (small house).

Fig. 69 Grave. Bunabuna'an island

Beneath the roof and within the lumah-lumah is a rectangular frame called *kanlil*. Carved and painted horizontal boards about twenty-five centimeters wide on all four sides support its carved corner poles, which are about a meter high. The carved motifs on these boards are similar to those found on the hulls of boats, such as *dau'an-dau'an* and *sambili-sambili*. Within the kanlil are gravemarkers (*sundok*) and grave offerings. Easily distinguished from female markers, male gravemarkers are three dimensional, columnar, and often topped with a knob (fig. 70). Sather (1968, 105) reports that the Sama Dilaut of Semporna deny any phallic symbolism in the markers, but this is not the case with the Tawi-Tawi Sama Dilaut who often called my attention to their phallic resemblance. Female markers tend to be flat, triangular or ovular in shape, two-dimensional (fig. 71), and carved in curvilinear floral and wave-like patterns. The female sundok are often topped with *surai*, or comb-like motifs. Like the kanlil, the sundok are painted in red, blue, yellow, green, and white, favorite colors of the Sama Dilaut. Within these basic patterns, the sundok reveal a great deal of variation. Sometimes the male marker is carved in the form of a human

Fig. 70   Male gravemarkers. Bunabuna'an island

figure (ta'u-ta'u) which occasionally stands in a boat. Other male sundok are horses (*kura-kura*) and birds (*manuk-manuk*). Although female markers initially appear more uniform, they too reveal a great deal of variation on closer examination. Sundok range from one-third of a meter to a meter in height, and are made for adults and older children, but not usually for infants. In addition

Fig. 71   Female gravemarkers. Bunabuna'an island

to the gravemarkers, receptacles for offerings as well as small green and white flags (panji) are placed within the kubul.

Ideally when an adult man dies, the prow of his houseboat is left at his grave. In reality, this is seldom done since his family usually needs the boat for their home; nonetheless, several prows are found on the graves at both Bunabuna'an and Bilatan Po'on. The broken cradle bars of infants are frequently left on the graves, as well as other personal belongings of the deceased, such as household utensils or fishing gear. Perfume is periodically poured over sundok as offerings to spirits, and the empty bottles are left on the graves. Graves of powerful djin or other important individuals are sometimes draped with white cloth.

The artists who carve the gravemarkers are the same men who create the carvings on boats. Salbaiyani and Kayani were two respected carvers of sundok during my stay in Tawi-Tawi. As boat carvers, these men are paid for their work; failure to do so would bring misfortune from the ancestral spirits. The men charge close family members very little, but more distant relatives and unrelated people are expected to pay more.

Two graves at Bunabuna'an are significantly different from the others. They are covered with piles of white finger coral about a meter high and decorated with small green and white flags. A white cloth canopy supported by four poles shelters one of the graves. I was told they are the graves of powerful djin who because of their great spiritual power warranted individual graves at death. To my knowledge, they are the only individual graves at the cemeteries.

Mats

The spare time of most Sama Dilaut women is spent weaving mats (*tepo*). These mats, about one by two meters in size and of double thickness, are used for sleeping and ceremonies. The top mat (*diam*) usually has a colorful woven pattern and is sewn onto a slightly larger plain bottom mat (*lapis*). Mats are made throughout Sulu, and some islands, especially Laminusa Island near Siasi island and Ungus Matata in eastern Tawi-Tawi, are known for their mats' fine design and weave. Sama Dilaut women are less concerned with design and weave and consequently their mats are less highly regarded.

The long narrow leaves of a palm called pandan are used for mat making. The Sama Dilaut use two types of pandan, both of which grow wild on nearby islands. One has spines along the leaf edges while the other does not. The spineless one is preferred since the removal of the spines entails more work, but both are used equally. The ribs and spines of the leaves are removed and the resulting halves are rolled into coils. Tied to prevent uncoiling, they are submerged in a large pot of water and boiled. Following their removal from the boiling water, they are flattened by pulling them over the edge of a stick and allowed to dry in the sun. If they still have too much color, they are boiled again, after which they are dried and drawn through a special metal-bladed gauge (*jangatan*) that cuts them into strips, the width depending on the tool. They are again spread in the sun to bleach for a day or two, after which they are soaked overnight in cold water and spread out to dry. By now the natural color is gone, the strips are soft, and they are ready for dyeing. Marine products and plants collected from island forests were once used for dyes, but now commercial dyes purchased in Bongao are preferred. Favorite colors include red, blue, yellow, purple, and pink. The mat maker chooses her colors, and dyes the leaves in hot water. The dyed leaves are then spread in the shade to dry to prevent fading. The preparation of the leaves for weaving takes about a week, longer if there is no urgency.

Fig. 72 Mat making

Weaving begins in the middle of the proposed mat and moves outward (fig. 72). As the mat grows larger, the weaver places a rock or other weight on the finished section to hold it in place. Strips are rarely long enough to reach the edge of the mat, so additional ones must be woven in to continue the pattern. When finished, the edges are turned under and the patterned mat is sewn onto a plain undyed mat, the edges of which have also been turned under. The patterns described by Szanton (1963, 60) are the common ones found among the Sama Dilaut, namely stripes, varicolored squares, checkers, and zigzag.

The dyed, patterned mats are made of finer strips and are reserved for ceremonies and special guests. The common sleeping mats of the family are usually undyed, unpatterned, and made of wider strips.

EPILOGUE

For centuries, the Sama communities of Tawi-Tawi maintained a harmonious relationship with their environment and one another. Different communities occupied different ecological niches that resulted in different economic specializations. Some were farmers and others were fishermen. Some manufactured pottery, wove fine mats, or excelled in music and dance. Others were overseas traders while still others were master boatbuilders. They traded their specialized products to satisfy individual and community needs. Certainly it was not a closed, unchanging system, but the changes that occurred over the centuries were gradual enough for the Tawi-Tawi people to adapt without significantly altering their basic patterns of interdependence. The Tausug arrived, as did Islam and a sultanate that demanded occasional tribute from all the communities. Overseas traders came from the Middle East, India, China, and Europe. Spain and the United States established colonies but eventually departed, and a world war marched through the archipelago. The basic patterns of interdependence varied with the changing times, but they persisted. However, during the past three decades, the consequences of a secessionist war and the introduction of seaweed aquaculture catapulted the people of Tawi-Tawi from their traditional past into a very different present and an uncertain future.

Recent Tawi-Tawi History

The Muslim secessionist movement in southern Mindanao and the Sulu archipelago was one of the most significant events in the Philippines during the past three decades. The movement resulted in a virtual civil war that only recently abated into a tenuous and somewhat sporadic truce.

Power struggles are certainly nothing new in the Muslim provinces of the Philippines. Long before Europeans arrived, conflicts between and within the different Muslim sultanates were common. The arrival of the Spaniards and their determination to wipe out Islam not only antagonized the individual Muslim groups but provided an incentive for them to occasionally join forces against the invaders. The history of Spain in the Philippines is punctuated by battles between Spaniards and Muslims as Spain attempted to extend its sovereignty and trade into the southern islands. The Spaniards established garrisons in Jolo and built a small fort on Bongao Island where they retained troops for a short time, but they were never successful in gaining a permanent foothold in Sulu beyond Jolo town. They eventually abandoned their attempt to dominate Sulu and established a truce with the Muslims during their final years in the Philippines.

When the Americans took over the Philippines in 1898, they discovered that Filipinos throughout the archipelago were none too happy about the arrival of another colonial power, and a bloody chapter in Philippine history was written before the United States established control. When Americans visited the Sulu Islands, Muslims were claiming sovereignty and it took several more years of bloodshed before the Americans worked out a truce with them. After the initial battles, the period of American rule in Sulu was relatively peaceful. It was, of course, interrupted by the arrival of the Japanese in 1942 when once again Sulu was invaded by a foreign power. A major Japanese base was established in Jolo and another at Sanga-Sanga, where local residents were forced to build an airstrip. Resistance fighters were active in Tawi-Tawi and other parts of Sulu throughout the Japanese occupation, and they helped the Allied Forces liberate the islands.

The Philippines gained independence from the United States after the war in 1946, but once again the people of Sulu witnessed an outside power move in to govern them. This time it was the Christian Filipino government in Manila. It was not until 1957 that Sulu elected its first governor.

During the late1950s, the Philippine government implemented a resettlement program to move Christians from heavily populated sections of Luzon to seemingly empty areas in the Muslim provinces. One such resettlement was on Tawi-Tawi Island, which at that time was thinly populated. Muslims, of course, held traditional claim to the land and resented the Christians who came to occupy it. Conflicts developed almost immediately, and the resettlement project was eventually abandoned.

Resentment toward the national government grew. Large garrisons of Philippine Constabulary were established on Jolo Island and to a lesser degree in Tawi-Tawi to deal with the Muslim "problem" as perceived in Manila. One of those problems was the smuggling of goods between Sabah and Sulu. In Sulu eyes, this was an ancient trading tradition that existed long before the establishment of the current national boundaries drawn by the colonial powers. But to the national government it was lost revenue and further evidence of Muslim troublemaking.

Economically, Sulu lagged behind most of the Philippines. High rates of illiteracy and few job opportunities beyond the Christian-controlled government and military sectors kept much of the population at a poverty level. To the growing number of discontents, it seemed that money the government succeeded in collecting from Sulu remained in Manila and was never used for local projects. Muslim youth increasingly attended colleges in Manila as well as newly established colleges in their own provinces, such as the Notre Dame of Jolo. Some received scholarships to study in the Middle East, especially Egypt. Away from home, they gained an awareness and resentment of their status as second-class citizens in their own land. These youth and their sympathizers provided the leadership for the growing resistance to legislation from Manila and the presence of the Philippine military who were considered oppressors rather than peacekeepers. The rise of Islamic nationalism around the world also contributed to the growing discontent of local Muslims and their increased desire to determine their own future. The Moro National Liberation Front (MNLF), an armed resistance group, was forged from the growing discontent in the Muslim provinces and aimed at greater self-government for the Muslim provinces. Their clashes with the Philippine military eventually received support from sympathetic Muslim nations.

The confrontations with the Philippine military escalated into a major battle in February 1974, when MNLF forces attempted to take the city of Jolo from Philippine government troops. The devastating battle resulted in the partial destruction of the city. Thousands of people fled Jolo, many going to Zamboanga and others to Bongao and Sitangkai. The continuing conflict on Jolo island in subsequent years caused even more people to abandon the area for the southern islands. Precise figures are unavailable for the actual numbers who moved from Jolo to the south during this period, but they had to be in the many thousands to account for the rapid growth of Tawi-Tawi communities, especially Bongao and Sitangkai.

The separatist conflict was not limited to Jolo, although the greatest fighting in Sulu occurred there. Sporadic fighting in Tawi-Tawi between the Philippine military and Muslim separatists during the 1970s resulted in movements of Sama people from outer settlements to Bongao, where Philippine troops provided a degree of security. A secessionist attempt to capture the air force base on Sanga-Sanga island in 1972 climaxed in heavy bombardment of the island by government forces and the ultimate departure of all its residents, including the Sama Dilaut at Tungkalang and Lu'uk Tulai. Many went to Bongao, but others chose to leave the Philippines for eastern Borneo, especially Sabah, where large

numbers of Sama people from Tawi-Tawi and Sibutu already resided. At about
the same time, the Philippine Navy shelled Simunul Island, seven miles south
of Bongao, to dislodge MNLF members believed to reside there. This, too, resulted
in population movements.

A truce of sorts was eventually established between the national government and the MNLF. Manila promised the Muslim provinces greater autonomy
in governing their territories, as well as economic assistance to help them catch
up with other parts of the Philippines. In Tawi-Tawi, this resulted in funds for
a university, housing projects, hospitals, schools, roads, bridges, water systems,
electricity, and other public works.

The separatist movement in the Muslim provinces is far from resolved.
The Moro Islamic Liberation Front, a splinter group from the MNLF, is still
resisting government troops and demanding complete autonomy from the
Philippines.[1] The ramifications of the separatist conflict are multifaceted, including the displacement of many people as they fled the areas of greatest
conflict. In some places, the movement of such people has drastically altered
the ethnic composition of the islands. Such is the case in Tawi-Tawi where Sama
people, including the Sama Dilaut, have been displaced by invading outsiders,
especially the Tausug.

Within the Sulu archipelago, the Tausug historically dominated the Jolo and
Siasi islands whereas the Sama were scattered throughout the archipelago but
concentrated in the Tawi-Tawi and Sibutu islands. The Tausug were always the
politically dominant group since the establishment of their sultanate in Jolo.
Within the past two-and-a-half decades, however, the traditional settlement
patterns of Sulu, especially in Tawi-Tawi province, have been significantly altered. Several factors account for this alteration, namely: (1) the secessionist
conflict discussed above, (2) the development of the *bakkaw* industry by immigrant Tausug on the northwest coast of Tawi-Tawi island, (3) the introduction of
agalagar aquaculture on the great reefs of Tawi-Tawi and Sibutu, and (4) the
creation of Tawi-Tawi as a separate province with its capital in Bongao.

Small settlements of Tausug have long existed in Tawi-Tawi. Some were
transient groups who came to the area for a few months or years to fish or farm,
and then returned to Jolo or Siasi. Others were families who had lived in Tawi-
Tawi for several generations with no intention of ever returning to Jolo or Siasi.
Their numbers, however, were insignificant compared to the overwhelming
majority of Sama people in the islands.

The earliest significant movement of Tausug into Tawi-Tawi during the
period under consideration began in 1970. At that time several Tausug families
from Jolo moved to the central northwest coast of Tawi-Tawi island to harvest
bakkaw, the bark of the mangrove trees which grow in abundance in that area.

Bakkaw, used in the preparation of leather among other uses, has long been a commercial export of the area. An important by-product of the harvest is the tree itself, which is popular for house piles because of its durability in seawater and for cooking fires because of its slow-burning intense heat. More families joined the first settlers and within a year, a settlement of perhaps 200 Tausug was scattered along the coast. No significant Sama settlements existed there previously and consequently few Sama people were displaced. The lands beyond the mangrove forests were unfarmed, but before long Tausug moved into the forests and carved out farmsteads. Thus, an area of Tawi-Tawi formerly almost uninhabited acquired a Tausug population. The motivations for moving into the area are not clear, but probably lack of economic opportunities at home was the prime mover.

At about the same time, the commercial cultivation of agalagar was introduced to the Sulu archipelago. Varieties of this sea plant are indigenous to the reefs of Sulu, and for some years prior to commercial cultivation, they were collected and sold to Western and Japanese outlets. A research team from the University of Hawaii introduced the aquaculture to the Siasi area in 1970 and then to the Sibutu and central Tawi-Tawi reefs shortly thereafter. For local political reasons, the new crop was initially unsuccessful in Siasi, but within a very short time, it became enormously successful in Tawi-Tawi and Sibutu. Most initial cultivation was in the hands of Sama people who lived near the reefs where it thrived. The success of their plots and the considerable economic rewards for a relatively small amount of work attracted outsiders to the area, especially Tausug from Jolo and Siasi. Meanwhile, the escalating warfare on Jolo island between Muslim separatists and the Philippine military was forcing some Tausug families to seek more peaceful dwelling places. As a result, within a matter of months of the successful introduction of agalagar cultivation, hundreds of Tausug moved into the reefs and villages of central Tawi-Tawi and Sibutu. As more people arrived, competition for growing plots increased, accompanied by quarrels and occasional killings. Before long the aggressive Tausug displaced many of the Sama cultivators and what began as an industry dominated by Sama became an industry dominated by Tausug. What used to be small Sama fishing villages became sizeable towns with large populations of Tausug and Sama from outside the area. Similar movements to Sitangkai, port town of the Sibutu islands, increased its population from 3,400 in 1967 to 34,493 in 1990.

Another factor contributing to population shifts within the Sulu archipelago was the creation of Tawi-Tawi as a separate province in 1973, with its capital in Bongao. The chief reason for establishing Tawi-Tawi province was to provide the resident Sama majority an opportunity to govern themselves rather than live under a Tausug administration in Jolo. Ironically, since the creation of the new province, Tausug from Jolo and Siasi have inundated the area. Many came because of factors already discussed. Others came to fill administrative posts in the government, while still others came to participate in the rapidly expanding economy. As a result, the Tausug are becoming the politically and economically dominant group in Tawi-Tawi.

Large numbers of Christians have also moved to Bongao. Some are former military personnel and their families who decided to remain after their tour of duty ended. Others are military personnel and government bureaucrats, and still others moved to Bongao to participate in the economic boom of the area. No figures are available for the Christian population of Bongao, but estimates given to me in 1997 ranged from one-fifth to one-third of the population. The former is probably the closer estimate. Their growing presence adds to the local Muslims' traditional fear that the national government wants to inundate their lands with Christian settlers.

The population figures from the official Philippines censuses provide some indication of this population shift. The following table reveals the population changes for Tawi-Tawi Province during the period under discussion (*1980 Census of Population and Housing, 1*).

Table 9. Population of Tawi-Tawi Province

1960	1970	1975	1980	1990
78,594	110,196	143,487	194,651	228,204

From 1960 to 1990, the population of Tawi-Tawi almost tripled, and although some of this growth came naturally from within, the bulk was from immigration. The census figures for the municipalities of Bongao and Sitangkai reveal the growth of these port towns during the same period.[2]

Table 10. Population of Bongao and Sitangkai Municipalities

	1960	1970	1980	1990
Bongao	10,822	20,983	27,884	37,932
Sitangkai	10,624	13,738	27,479	34,493

Many Sama have been displaced by this influx of outsiders. In the late 1960s the language of the marketplaces and schools in both Bongao and Sitangkai was Sinama. Now the Tausug language has virtually displaced Sinama in both arenas in both towns. The 1980 Census reports that in the urban areas of Tawi-Tawi (i.e. Bongao and Sitangkai) 67.05 percent of the population spoke Tausug and 21.03 percent spoke Sinama. The number is doubtless greater now. During the 1960s, Tausug speakers probably numbered less than 10 percent in Bongao and less than 5 percent in Sitangkai.

Household census data during the late 1960s revealed a population of about 1,600 Sama Dilaut for the Tawi-Tawi islands. I was unable to conduct a similar census in 1982, but my estimate based on interviews and visits to Sama Dilaut communities was about 600 Sama Dilaut for the Tawi-Tawi islands. The 1980 Census claimed that only 347 households spoke "Badjao" (i.e., Sama Dilaut Sinama) in all of Tawi-Tawi province, 132 in Bongao and 215 in Sitangkai. If Tawi-Tawi Sama Dilaut households still averaged five people, 660 Sama Dilaut lived in the Tawi-Tawi islands in 1980, a figure close to my 1982 estimate. The 1980 census claimed that 1.04 percent (2,024) of Tawi-Tawi province were "Badjao" (Sama Dilaut Sinama) speakers. If Bongao had 660 of this population, then Sitangkai had only 1,364 Sama Dilaut, about half the number who lived there in 1966.

The Sama Dilaut left because of the great influx of outsiders, especially Tausug, onto the reefs of Tawi-Tawi and Sibutu. A peaceful, nonaggressive people, the Sama Dilaut historically fished and collected from these reefs. Although occasionally forced to contribute a share of their catches to local datu, they were for the most part left to the reefs where they lived in relative isolation, an isolation that contributed to the conservative nature of their culture and their peripheral position in the Islam embraced by the rest of Tawi-Tawi. When great numbers of outsiders began to invade their reefs in recent years—whether fleeing from conflict or seeking fortunes in agalagar— the Sama Dilaut reacted in traditional fashion and began moving away. As tensions mounted over fishing grounds and agalagar plots, quarrels and killings occurred. Predictably, those Sama Dilaut least acculturated to Islam left first since they were least culturally equipped to deal with the invading Tausug and Sama Muslims.

In general, the movement of Sama Dilaut has been southwestward. Many Tawi-Tawi Sama Dilaut moved to the Sibutu islands only to find similar problems there. From Sibutu, some moved on to the relative peace of eastern Borneo, especially the Semporna area. Many Sibutu Sama Dilaut also moved to the Semporna area where they have kinsmen.

The Tawi-Tawi Sama Dilaut are not the only Sama Dilaut displaced by recent events in Sulu, and not all fled southward. Many Sama Dilaut left Jolo for Zamboanga and Basilan during the conflicts of recent decades. Others went southward to Siasi, Tawi-Tawi, and Sibutu. Large communities of Siasi and Jolo Sama Dilaut are found in Bongao and the Bilatan islands of central Tawi-Tawi. Sitangkai also has a large Siasi Sama Dilaut community. In addition, many shore-dwelling Sama from throughout the Tawi-Tawi islands have moved to Sibutu and Sabah to escape the violence of the secessionist war and the tensions created by the Tausug invasion of Tawi-Tawi. Also, many Sibutu Sama have left the Sibutu islands for the security of Sabah.

Thus, the southwestward movement of Tausug has created a domino effect. As they moved into Sama areas, many Sama moved further southward, resulting in great numbers of Sama on the eastern shores and islands of Borneo. Meanwhile, the Tausug are rapidly dominating Tawi-Tawi province.

The Growth of Bongao

The growth of Bongao, the capital of Tawi-Tawi, illustrates the dramatic changes that occurred in the province in recent years.

When I first visited Bongao town in 1963, it was a sleepy little port town nestled at the foot of Mount Bongao on the northeast corner of the island. Most of its population of about 5,000 was Sama, with a few Tausug, Chinese, and Christian Filipinos. A small wharf served the three interisland ships that made the weekly roundtrip up and down the archipelago from Zamboanga. Philippine Air Lines was scheduled to arrive twice a week on the grassy air strip on Sanga-Sanga island, where a nearby launch transported passengers to Bongao town. Frequently, however, no planes came for a week or so at a time. The interisland launches that connected Bongao to the rest of Tawi-Tawi moored at Chinese Pier, the bustling marketplace in Bongao that served western Tawi-Tawi. Much interisland travel was by locally built sailboats. Bongao's only street was a half-mile dirt road that led from the wharf behind Chinese Pier to become a trail around the island. An old truck with no engine, left over from World War II, was the island's only vehicle. Cargo was loaded onto the truck, which was then pushed to deposit goods at roadside shops and Chinese Pier.

Bongao hosted a mosque, the largest in western Tawi-Tawi, a small Catholic church, a post office, a telegraph office that seldom operated, a small detachment of Philippine Constabulary, an elementary school, high school, and college operated by the Oblate priests, a public elementary school, retail shops, and a couple dozen *sari-sari* stores. A public health official and a private physician were the only modern medical care available for all of Tawi-Tawi and Sibutu. The nearest hospital was in Jolo, but Catholic nuns opened a small clinic in 1965. A few households had radios, but they were unaffordable luxury items for most residents, and reception was both limited and problematic. Telephones and televisions were unknown. The town had no electricity, although private generators served a few homes and businesses. Rains and brackish wells provided drinking water, but during droughts water was transported from nearby Sanga-Sanga island. The Philippine Air Force maintained a small outpost near the airstrip on Sanga-Sanga island, and an equally small Philippine Navy outpost was stationed at nearby Batu-Batu on Tawi-Tawi island.

Most of Bongao island was rocky, steep, and unsuitable for agriculture, but it hosted a thick undergrowth of indigenous vegetation. Where soil permitted, coconuts, cassava, and fruit trees were cultivated. Other settlements on the island were four small villages scattered along the shore and connected by the footpath that circled the island. Like most Tawi-Tawi villagers, the inhabitants fished the nearby sea and farmed the interior, which was uninhabited.

When I left Tawi-Tawi in May 1967, Bongao had changed little from when I first saw it in 1963. The events of the next three decades, however, brought significant changes to the area. Bongao experienced its greatest changes between 1967 and 1977. The secessionist war was at its height during this period, and agalagar cultivation was introduced. The changes of the next twenty years were continuations of those planted during the previous decade.

In July 1977 I received special permission to visit Tawi-Tawi province for one week during a lull in the secessionist fighting. When I arrived at the Sanga-Sanga airport, I was placed under heavy military escort and after four days I was told I must leave on the next ship since it was uncertain if transportation would be available on my scheduled departure date. So after a quick four-day glimpse of Bongao and Sanga-Sanga island, I left. In the summer of 1982, I returned to Tawi-Tawi for three weeks. A degree of stability had returned to the province and my travel was unrestricted, although I was discouraged from visiting the Bilatan islands. I spent two days in Jolo and the remainder of my stay was divided between Bongao and Sitangkai. In late October 1997, I again visited Tawi-Tawi. The entire twelve days of this visit was spent on Bongao island and Sanga-Sanga island, where I located a few Sama Dilaut families I knew from the 1960s.

The Bongao I returned to in 1997 was hardly recognizable, although my 1977 and 1982 visits prepared me for some of the changes. The population had grown from about 5,000 to approximately thirty-five thousand. On Sanga-Sanga island, a paved runway and modern terminal had replaced the grass airstrip and the little thatched terminal of the 1960s. Commercial airlines provided daily flights to and from Zamboanga while military planes made more sporadic arrivals. The airport was now the Tawi-Tawi International Airport and the tarmac was being extended to accommodate jets from Malaysia and Indonesia. A paved road lined with houses and shops led from the airport to a bridge that connected Sanga-Sanga island to Bongao island. The road continued beyond the bridge to circle Bongao island and climb the slope of Mount Bongao to a new provincial capitol building, an imposing structure inspired by Islamic architecture. Within the town of Bongao where once a dirt road and rickety walkways over the sea served the inhabitants, paved roadways were congested by motorized tricycles, jeepneys and trucks. In 1977, a local policeman told me with thinly disguised pride that three people had died in motor accidents; in 1997, such deaths were so common that no one knew how many had occurred. The settlement around the airport was expanding so rapidly that plans were underway to make it a separate municipality from Bongao. A second bridge connecting Sanga-Sanga island to Tawi-Tawi island was in the final stages of construction, which, when completed, will allow vehicles to travel from Bongao town to Batu-Batu and eventually to other communities of southeastern Tawi-Tawi island

The bridge and roads replaced much water traffic, but water transportation continues to be important in Bongao. Cargo ships, passenger ships, and navy vessels call at the wharf daily. Launches transport goods and passengers throughout the islands, some serving as commuting vessels for people who work in Bongao town but live on nearby islands. Sailboats are noticeably absent. In the 1960s, locally made boats were commonly used to travel among the islands and the Tawi-Tawi waters were always dotted with their sails. I saw only one sailboat during the twelve days I was in Tawi-Tawi in 1997.

Bongao communicates with the world through media unavailable in the 1960s. Cable TV provides news and entertainment channels from around the world. Local telephone service connects Bongao to some of the outer Tawi-Tawi islands, and long-distance service allows contact with the rest of the world. Cellular phones are common, as are personal computers with e-mail. Many Bongao homes have VCRs and in the outer islands, battery-powered VCRs serve wealthier residents who charge admission to others who wish to watch their videos. Radios are found in most homes and their reception includes Australia, Indonesia, Sabah, and the Philippines, as well as the local radio station in Bongao. In 1963, I was in Bilatan on a fishing trip and did not learn of President John Kennedy's assassination until a week after it happened. Such an event would be known immediately throughout Tawi-Tawi today.

The town of Bongao provides other services to its residents. A Catholic hospital and a public hospital now serve the community's medical needs. In addition to the medical staffs of these hospitals, over a dozen doctors and dentists maintain offices in town. Three high schools and several elementary schools provide education for Bongao's youth. Mindanao State University, located on Sanga-Sanga island, offers advanced education to some 2,000 students. A vocational agricultural school teaches farming techniques to local youth while a private institution provides computer science training. A generator on Sanga-Sanga island supplies electricity to the municipality, and the perennial problem of water shortage has been solved by water piped to Bongao from wells on

Sanga-Sanga island. Two movie theaters feature the latest Tagalog and some-times American films.

The ethnic composition of Bongao has changed considerably. In the 1960s the municipality was primarily Sama, with a handful of Tausug, Chinese, and Christian Filipinos. No figures are available for the current ethnic mix, and opinions vary greatly among residents. The Tausug language now dominates the marketplace and is widely used for school instruction. As previously noted, Christians account for perhaps one- fifth of the total population. In the 1960s, a total of eighty Christians lived in Bongao. The Chinese population is still relatively small, but as in the past, has a strong hold on the economy. The outer islands are still predominately Sama with large numbers of Tausug in the areas of intensive agalagar cultivation.

Islamic fundamentalism has reached Bongao. A few days prior to my arrival, several hundred members of a fundamentalist Muslim sect from throughout Southeast Asia, India, and Pakistan convened in Bongao for several days of meeting and worship. Other fundamentalist Muslim groups also have missionaries in Bongao. The costumes of local Muslims reflects an increasing identity with the larger Islamic world. Many men and women now wear garments of Middle Eastern design, and some women wear full purdah in public. An official Muslim calendar is used throughout Tawi-Tawi to insure that all holy days are celebrated at the same time. In the past, different imams read the stages of the moon differently and thus commu-nities celebrated holy days on different days. Muslim holy days are now recognized as national holidays, and schools, government offices, and busi-nesses are closed throughout the Muslim provinces.

The military presence was greatly reduced from my earlier visits. A detach-ment of 400 marines remained in the area, as well as a small air force unit on Sanga-Sanga and a small navy base at Batu-Batu. Philippine Constabulary were scattered throughout the province.

A string of hamlets now encircles Bongao island. Tausug and Christian Filipinos who, unlike the native Sama people, have a tradition of living inland, now populate the formerly uninhabited interior. Land is reserved on the south side of the island for a public park near the path that leads to Mount Bongao, the summit of which has been designated a provincial park.

More tourists visit Bongao now than in the past, and when the interna-tional airport is completed, even more visitors will arrive. A comfortable airconditioned hotel on the eastern side of the island is currently the most luxurious accommodation in Bongao. Plans are underway to expand the hotel to fifty rooms with amenities such as a bowling alley, golf course, and karaoke bar. An even larger resort complex is planned for a nearby site, and discussion is underway for a third resort near Banaran island in eastern Tawi-Tawi. Tourism promoters are advertising Tawi-Tawi as the "last paradise in the Philippines" and a public relations campaign has posted signs throughout the municipality that state: "In Tawi-Tawi, Peace is the Language of our Hearts."

The expansion of the community has taken a heavy toll on the environment. Virtually all beaches on Bongao island are gone, the sand removed for concrete construction. Concrete walls fight further erosion where beaches once kept the sea at bay. The coral exposed by the sand removal is also being harvested for construction, as is live coral from nearby reefs. All undergrowth is gone from the island, much of it cut away by the military after several of their vehicles were ambushed by secessionists hiding in bushes along the roadways. Some was also cut for firewood and house construction. Litter is accumulating throughout the settlements, especially in the heavily populated sections. Air pollution from motorized vehicles is a problem in downtown Bongao, as is the din of noisy vehicles. Bongao has no sewer system and most waste is dumped into the sea, to the detriment of marine life. Inland settlements have outhouses, and areas of concentration suffer the smell of accumulated human waste.

Bongao has other problems, too. During my twelve-day visit in 1997, six murders occurred. Many people complained about the prevalence of drugs, especially mephamphetamines (known locally as *shabu*), and I encountered several individuals obviously on drugs. Sexually transmitted diseases are widespread, as well as a virulent strain of malaria that seems immune to traditional treatment. Many blame the drugs and diseases on the formerly large military presence.

The few Tawi-Tawi Sama Dilaut remaining in the area have been affected in varying degrees by the changes in Bongao.

The Tawi-Tawi Sama Dilaut Today

Sama Dilaut Communities The Sama Dilaut who lived in Tawi-Tawi during the 1960s were members of a single community scattered among five moorages connected by a web of kinship ties. That is no longer the case. In the fall of 1997, I was able to locate only three small groups of Sama Dilaut from the community I knew in the 1960s. Six extended family households lived at Lu'uk Bangka at the edge of Bongao town, seventeen households resided at the old moorage of Tungkalang near the bridge that now connects Sanga-Sanga island to Bongao island, and about six households reportedly lived at Tungbangkao near Bilatan island.

In the 1960s, Lu'uk Bangka was an uninhabited inlet near unoccupied land owned by the Oblate priests.[3] When I visited the site in the summer of 1977, it was a moorage of some forty-seven houseboats, refugees from the fighting on nearby Sanga-Sanga island. The Sama Dilaut moorage at Tungkalang was abandoned in 1972 and all the houses were later burned as the military combed Sanga-Sanga island for secessionist troops. The Sama Dilaut moorage at Lu'uk Tulai on the northwest tip of Tawi-Tawi island was also abandoned at this time as residents fled to Lu'uk Bangka. Many Sama Dilaut also left the Bilatan moorages of Tungbangkao and Lioboran for the relative security of Lu'uk Bangka. Located near the hospital of the Medical Mission Sisters and the convento of the Oblate priests, Lu'uk Bangka provided a sanctuary for the Sama Dilaut who some years previously were befriended by the two Catholic orders. No Tawi-Tawi Sama Dilaut lived at the former moorage of Lamiun at the edge of Bongao town, but twelve Sama Dilaut houseboats were moored near Pahot, a small land village on Bongao island across the channel from Tungkalang. If the Bajau houseboat still averaged five people, then the Sama Dilaut population of Bongao was only about 300 in 1977.[4]

When I returned to Bongao in the summer of 1982, Lu'uk Bangka had become a village of some forty houses, a joint project of the national government and the Oblate priests to house the displaced Tawi-Tawi Sama Dilaut. In addition to the houses, six houseboats also moored there. Perhaps ten households were Sibutu Sama and Siasi Sama Dilaut, but the bulk of the population was from the Tawi-Tawi Sama Dilaut community I knew in the 1960s. Three women from the community were married to Muslim Sama men and two others were married to Christians. The community elected its first barrio captain shortly before my arrival, the first time to my knowledge that the Tawi-Tawi Sama Dilaut participated in an election. The barrio captain and a few other Sama Dilaut men attended a Sama mosque on nearby Bongao island.

In 1982, twenty-four houseboats had returned to Tungkalang, and two families lived in houses. Most of these families had resided there in the 1960s. No Tawi-Tawi Sama Dilaut lived at Lamiun, which had been swallowed by the expansion of Bongao town.

I was unable to visit the Bilatan area, but I learned that both Tungbangkao and Lioboran were large communities of Tausug and Muslim Sama who tended agalagar on the surrounding reefs. I was told few Sama Dilaut lived there.

In 1997, I was able to locate only four households of Tawi-Tawi Sama Dilaut in Lu'uk Bangka, a total of about thirty people. The rest of the community, which had grown by some twenty houses, consisted of Sama Dilaut from Siasi and Jolo, and Sama from Sibutu and Sanga-Sanga (fig. 73). The Tawi-Tawi Sama Dilaut were almost totally displaced from the community that began as a special project to house them.

Fig. 73 Lu'uk Bangka, Bongao island, 1997

In 1997, Tungkalang was a small village of seventeen houses with a population of about 100 people, part of the sprawling community around the airport and Mindanao State University. The houses were poorly constructed—one man told me it was a waste of money to build a good house when you might have to abandon it. The construction of the bridge between Sanga-Sanga island and Bongao island closed the mouth of the Tungkalang bay and prevented the flow of tidal currents; consequently, the water around and beneath the houses was filled with debris, such as plastic, glass, tin cans, and other jetsam (fig. 74). Most villagers or their parents had lived at Tungkalang in the 1960s. Some had moved to Sabah in the late 1980s, but became homesick and returned to Tungkalang in the early 1990s.

The remaining Tawi-Tawi Sama Dilaut population I discovered lived at Tungbangkao, which in the 1960s was a Sama Dilaut community of some 400 residents, plus a handful of Muslim Sama from eastern Tawi-Tawi. In 1990, Tungbangkao had a population of 2,718 according to the official census. Nearby Lioboran was a Sama Dilaut moorage of about 100 people in the 1960s. According to the 1990 Census, it had a population of 2,532. Both places are doubtless larger now, but I could find no current population figures for either community. The reefs surrounding Tungbangkao and Lioboran are intensely cultivated in agalagar. In 1997 I learned of six households of Tawi-Tawi Sama Dilaut who still lived at Tungbangkao. I was told they were all agalagar farmers. I was also told no Sama Dilaut currently lived at Lioboran.

Fig. 74 Tungkalang, Sanga-Sanga island, 1997

The Tawi-Tawi Sama Dilaut at Lu'uk Bangka have been integrated into the surrounding community. Their children attend school and members of all four households occasionally attend the village mosque. Members of all households have intermarried with Muslim Sama. The Sama Dilaut at Tungkalang are more isolated. Physically separated from the nearby land community, they appear to have little social interaction outside their village. To my knowledge, none of them attend a mosque and none of their children attend school. I was unable to visit the Sama Dilaut at Tungbangkao, but they probably interact regularly with the neighboring Muslim Sama, as many of them did in the 1960s. I was told that some of them worship at a mosque in the community.

I did not conduct any household surveys among the Tawi-Tawi Sama Dilaut I visited in 1997, but the ones I visited all lived in extended family households. I encountered no boat-dwelling families and was repeatedly told that none exist anymore in Tawi-Tawi.

The total population of the Tawi-Tawi Sama Dilaut I located in 1997 is probably no more than 225. In the 1960s, their population was about 1,600. What happened to the others? Some of them died in the secessionist conflicts and some went to Sabah where they established a village at Kampung Halo near Semporna (Sather 1997, 84).[5] Others went to the Sibutu islands, which never experienced the violence of the Bongao-Sanga-Sanga area. And still others have probably disappeared into the large community of displaced Sama Dilaut from Siasi and Jolo who now reside in Tawi-Tawi.

Material Culture Perhaps the most significant change among the Tawi-Tawi Sama Dilaut is the disappearance of their boats. As discussed in chapter 3, the Sama Dilaut traditionally lived in three different houseboats and used a variety of fishing boats. Today no Sama Dilaut in Tawi-Tawi are boat dwellers, and many families do not even own fishing boats. None of the Tawi-Tawi Sama Dilaut families at Lu'uk Bangka have boats. At Tungkalang, a few families have boggo', the simple dugout traditionally used for fishing and moving about the moorage, and three brothers owned two motorized launches. No Sama Dilaut owned such launches in the 1960s. I did not visit the community at Tungbangkao, but I was told only boggo' are used there for occasional fishing and cultivating agalagar; other transportation needs are met by the many motorized launches that connect Tungbangkao to other parts of Tawi-Tawi. I was consistently told houseboats are no longer built, a sharp contrast to the 1960s, when most families lived in houseboats and had at least one fishing boat. The families at Lu'uk Bangka need no boats since they no longer fish, and their houses, although built over the water, are connected by walkways to Bongao island. A few boats at Tungkalang are used for fishing, but they are unnecessary for transportation since the houses are connected to Sanga-Sanga island and the nearby bridge to Bongao provides easy access to that island.

Economics During the 1960s, fishing, boatbuilding, and farming were the main economic activities of the Tawi-Tawi Sama Dilaut. Today none of these activities is important to the people I met. Most adult males in the households at Lu'uk Bangka work as stevedores at the Bongao wharf. At Tungkalang, the two Sama Dilaut launches that operate throughout Tawi-Tawi provide jobs for six men. Three other men sometimes work as stevedores in Bongao and two old men occasionally fish for subsistence needs. In Tungbangkao, the families depend on agalagar farms for income, with occasional fishing for subsistence needs. I learned of no families who still garden, probably because the land on Sanga-Sanga island that was cultivated by Sama Dilaut families in the 1960s is now occupied by the airport, the marine base and Mindanao State University. Many women at Lu'uk Bangka (including some Tawi-Tawi Sama Dilaut) weave mats for sale. Tawi-Tawi Sama Dilaut women wove such mats only for domestic use during the 1960s.

Religion Of the two groups of Tawi-Tawi Sama Dilaut I visited in 1997, those living at Lu'uk Bangka were most influenced by Islam. A mosque is located in Lu'uk Bangka and members from all six households of Tawi-Tawi Sama Dilaut living there attended the mosque occasionally. Tawi-Tawi Sama Dilaut women in four of the households were married to Muslim Sama men from Siasi and Sibutu. The traditional religion was still practiced by a very old djin I knew during my research in the 1960s. He wore djin clothes and lived in a special room of his house where he kept his djin paraphernalia. He was highly respected as a curer, and in addition to serving his own people he treated many non-Sama Dilaut.

The nearby cemetery revealed the coexistence of Islam and traditional Sama Dilaut religion. The Tawi-Tawi Sama Dilaut graves were low rectangular walls filled with sand, the traditional graves of the Muslim people of Tawi-Tawi. However, within the enclosures were small green and white flags, empty perfume bottles, and other offerings typical of traditional Sama Dilaut ceremonies. A few had simple gravemarkers reminiscent of the traditional ones. A large nunuk tree nearby was believed inhabited by a saitan. Green, white, and yellow flags, traditional offerings to spirits, surrounded its base. I was told that both imams and djin held ceremonies at the tree, and even a Protestant Sama missionary once visited to offer prayers to the saitan.

The Sama Dilaut at Tungkalang do not have a mosque in their village and do not attend the nearby mosque on Sanga-Sanga island. One young woman was married to a Muslim man from Siasi, but they did not worship at the mosque although they both claimed to be Muslims. Three old women (two sisters and their cousin) are djin and attend to some of the healing needs of the community. Many of these people, however, as well as many at Lu'uk Bangka, visit the Catholic hospital in Bongao for their medical needs.

I did not visit the Tawi-Tawi Sama Dilaut families at Tungbangkao, but I was told several families there attend the community mosque.

Many Muslims of Bongao believe the Oblate priests converted many Sama Dilaut to Catholicism. To my knowledge, however, no Sama Dilaut were converted to Catholicism. The local belief probably stems from the many charitable acts and gifts provided the Sama Dilaut by the priests and the Medical Mission Sisters. Few Sama Dilaut are attracted to Christianity, and most have always considered themselves Muslims even though their Muslim neighbors did not regard them as such. By becoming Christians, the Sama Dilaut would only add to their peripheral position in Tawi-Tawi society, but by being Muslims, they are more acceptable to their Muslim neighbors.

Arts During the 1960s, the Tawi-Tawi Sama Dilaut had a rich artistic tradition especially manifested in songs and carvings. By 1997 those traditions were virtually gone. As noted, boatbuilding is now almost nonexistent among the Sama Dilaut, and with its demise went boat carvings. Grave art has almost disappeared too. During the disruptions in the 1970s, many Sama Dilaut left the Bilatan area where their cemeteries were located for the relative security of Bongao. Fearful of returning to Bilatan for burials, they began burying their dead in a plot near Lu'uk Bangka provided by the Oblate priests. The gravemarkers for these graves were very simple, probably because the site was considered temporary. As the community at Lu'uk Bangka became increasingly permanent, the graveyard expanded and was also used by Muslim Sama whose grave art was considerably simpler than that of the Tawi-Tawi Sama Dilaut. During this period, the Tawi-Tawi Sama Dilaut were increasingly influenced by Islam, which discouraged the representation of human and animal figures in art. The result was the deterioration of grave art.

The song traditions of the Sama Dilaut were also altered by recent changes. Tapedecks, radios, television, and movies brought outside music traditions to the Sama Dilaut. The pop music of the rest of the world is now the preferred music of Sama Dilaut youths who have forgotten their traditional music. The demise of fishing and sailing has brought an end to the traditional songs associated with those activities. The influence of modern medicine has diminished the use of kata-kata chants for curing, and Islam has discouraged the traditional mourning songs at funerals. The only traditional Sama Dilaut songs I heard during my 1997 visit were lullabies.

The dances and instrumental music traditionally performed at Sama Dilaut ceremonies have changed also. Today it is fashionable to hire a band to play pop music at weddings and superincision ceremonies. Young people dance pop dances to band music while the older generation watches television rented for the occasion. The bride wears a Western-style wedding gown and the groom is dressed in Middle Eastern garb. The facial make-up of the bride is Western while the groom's facial adornment is usually limited to sunglasses.

Mat making remains intact among the Tawi-Tawi Sama Dilaut; in fact, the mats made today by Sama Dilaut women are superior to those made traditionally. In the past, all women of the Sulu Islands wove mats. Tawi-Tawi Sama Dilaut women also made mats, but compared to others, they were crudely woven with wide strips and unimaginative patterns and colors. During the dislocations of the 1970s, when the Sama Dilaut could no longer visit their fishing grounds in Bilatan, the Oblate priests of Bongao encouraged new sources of income for them, including mat making. The priests loaned the Sama Dilaut a parcel of land planted to pandan, the plant that provides leaves for mat making, and encouraged the women to sell their mats to the small, but growing tourist traffic in Bongao. During this period, Sama Dilaut from Siasi moved to Lu'uk Bangka with their superior mats. To compete with them, the Tawi-Tawi Sama Dilaut women had to improve their product. They did so, and current mats woven by Tawi-Tawi Sama Dilaut women are thus superior to those made traditionally and provide an important supplemental income to the households at both Lu'uk Bangka and Tungkalang.

Survivors

Most of the Sama Dilaut I knew from the 1960s had either left Tawi-Tawi or were dead. I was, however, able to locate a few people from those days and they told me the stories of their lives since we last met.

Palasia was still beautiful. As a ten-year-old child when I knew her in the 1960s, she was one of the most exquisitely beautiful people I had ever seen. She lived with her family in a houseboat and her father was one of my best friends. In 1997 Palasia lived in a house at Lu'uk Bangka. She proudly told me she was married to a Muslim and that her five children were Muslims also. Two attended the local college and the others were in elementary school. She showed me pictures of her children at birthdays, circumcisions and graduations. Without my asking, she told me her present life was far superior to the old boat-dwelling way of life. She was glad her children had opportunities she never had.

Hadjulani was blind now. In the 1960s, he was one of the finest boatbuilders at Tungkalang. He regretted the changes that had come to his world. He and his family fled Tungkalang in 1972, when Sanga-Sanga was bombed, and they lived for a while at Lu'uk Bangka. Hadjulani did not like the outsiders from Jolo and Siasi at Lu'uk Bangka, so he went to Semporna with his extended family. They lived there for two years, but they never fit in and were always homesick. When peace returned to Tawi-Tawi, they returned to Tungkalang. The once isolated moorage was now a slum community near the bridge that connects Sanga-Sanga and Bongao and only a stone's throw from Mindanao State University. It is almost engulfed by the commercial sector of Sanga-Sanga and its location is too valuable for Sama Dilaut to live there much longer. Hadjulani said he and his wife have no money since he can no longer work, and both are dependent on their children. They live in a tiny, rickety house above the flotsam and jetsam of Tungkalang. I remembered his independent spirit and the beautiful lepa he once built.

Mastarani was ten when I knew him in the 1960s. A big smile always spread across his face and he could charm your boots off with his genuine sweetness. He was one of the few children who attended school at Tungkalang, where he learned English. When I met him again, he owned two launches with his two younger brothers. He and one of his brothers were married to Muslims although they did not attend mosque. He claimed his children were Muslims. His launch business was prosperous and made runs with goods and passengers throughout the Tawi-Tawi waters. He felt that too many outsiders lived in Tawi-Tawi now—especially Tausug—but for the most part, he believed his life was better than that of his father's generation. People respected him more than they respected his father, he said.

Old Pandia was a relic from the past. He was an old man when I knew him in the 1960s. Now he seemed ancient. He is still a djin as he was in the 1960s. He lives with his daughter and her Muslim husband. He has a special room in the house where all his djin paraphernalia are kept. He stays there most of the time by himself, and the saitan frequently visit him. He says they are his old friends, most of his human friends are dead. He wears his green and white djin clothes all the time. Pandia is considered the most powerful djin in the community and has clients from all ethnic groups that reside there. He does not think about the changed times. Things are different, he says—some are better, some are worse. But the saitan are the same and they are his chief concern in his old age.

Hadjira's sweet smile still lights her face. She is tinier than I remember, almost miniscule. She lives at Tungkalang with her blind husband Hadjulani. Times are very bad, she says, but what can you do? You have to keep living. She is now a djin. Her mother was one of the most powerful djin in Tungkalang in the 1960s. Hadjira is not a powerful djin, but she helps people with their illnesses and makes a little money that way. She would rather live in a house-boat like in the old days, but those days are gone. A stray bullet killed one of her sons during the fighting of the early 1970s. She tries not to think about the old days, she says. They were good, but they are gone forever. People shared things then. Now people are selfish and do not share. But there isn't much to share anyway.

Tampi lived with his wife in a tiny house at the edge of Tungkalang. They had moved there from Sitangkai only a few months before my arrival. Tampi was a teenager when I knew him in the 1960s. He married his childhood sweet-heart and they moved to Sitangkai during the conflicts of the 1970s. He did well in Sitangkai, but his oldest son became addicted to shabu. They tried everything they could to help him, but to no avail. Finally, to get away from his demands and violence, they left Sitangkai and returned to Tungkalang. Tampi was having trouble finding work and he felt badly about abandoning his son. But there was nothing he could do. He often wished for the old days when his people lived by themselves in boats. He fondly reminisced about our fishing trips in the Bilatan waters when lots of fish were available for everyone. Now fish are few because of the dynamiting, and they are too expensive. He and his wife some-times go several days with no fish to eat.

Conclusion

The events in the Sulu archipelago during the past few decades are singular but their consequences are not. The displacement and absorption of Sama people by outsiders is an old theme in Sulu history and dates back to at least the arrival of the Tausug in Jolo. Pallesen's linguistic study (1985) and other documentation (Nimmo 1986, 32–33) reveal that many Sama groups were absorbed into Tausug culture. Others were not absorbed by the Tausug, but they were significantly altered when they embraced Islam. In many respects, the story of the Tawi-Tawi Sama Dilaut during the past three decades is the story of many Sama groups before them. The details differ, but the patterns are similar.

Unlike some minorities of the world, the Tawi-Tawi Sama Dilaut are not destined to live a pariah existence at the periphery of a society they can never join. Like other Sama before them, the Tawi-Tawi Sama Dilaut will become part of the Islamic Sama culture of the southern Sulu islands and eastern Sabah. Few linguistic and physical differences distinguish them from other Sama groups and they share many pre-Islamic cultural patterns with them. Within a generation or two, most of them will lose their Sama Dilaut boat-dwelling past and become part of Muslim Sama cultures.

When the Tawi-Tawi Sama Dilaut abandoned their boats, they relinquished their traditional method of preserving their culture. In the past they escaped in their boats from places, people, and events that threatened them. Now those few who remain in Tawi-Tawi have no boats and they cannot escape forces of change. Those who fled in their boats to Sabah have retained their traditional culture for the time being, but they, too, will ultimately lose their distinctive cultural identity and become part of the larger Sama culture. It is unnecessary to go far into the past to observe this process. Prior to World War II, virtually all the Sitangkai Sama Dilaut were non-Muslim boat dwellers. After the war, they began moving to houses and embracing Islam to become a variant of Sulu Islamic culture (Nimmo 1972). They are currently becoming further absorbed into Muslim culture as other Muslim Sama and Tausug inundate their home territory. The Sama of Tabauan island in eastern Tawi-Tawi appear to have a similar history. Several cultural features of these people suggest they, too, were once boat dwellers from the Sibutu Islands.[6] Today they have retained enough of their past to make them distinctive within eastern Tawi-Tawi, but they are house dwellers and as Muslim as the other Sama of Tawi-Tawi. A study of other Sama communities would probably reveal other boat-dwelling pasts absorbed by Muslim groups.

When I lived with the Tawi-Tawi Sama Dilaut in the 1960s, I frequently accompanied them to their cemetery islands in Bilatan. Near the Bunabuna'an graves was an abandoned cemetery with distinctively different gravemarkers. When I asked the Sama Dilaut who it belonged to, they replied "the people of old." At the time, I thought some day someone would visit Bunabuna'an and see the Sama Dilaut graves long after the Sama Dilaut themselves were gone and would be told the graves belonged to "the people of old." But now I know that will not happen. During the events of recent years, Bunabuna'an was raided by grave robbers who stole the gravemarkers as well as the contents of the graves, probably for antique shops in Manila. No graves are witness to the Sama Dilaut past, a past remembered only in Tawi-Tawi oral traditions and a few increasingly dusty tomes of anthropology.

The Tawi-Tawi Sama Dilaut still magosaha, but their search for sustenance has taken them to new currents very different from their past. These currents are without boats and are flowing toward an uncertain future that will test the survival skills they learned as boat dwellers. Their unique boat-dwelling culture is now part of the realm of the mbo', or ancestors. The loss of that culture is a loss for Tawi-Tawi, the Philippines, Southeast Asia, and ultimately humankind. For each culture offers a unique view of the world, a special way of creating and interpreting reality, and when that uniqueness is lost, humankind's vision and understanding are reduced. But hopefully, the descendants of the boat-dwelling Sama Dilaut will retain some of those special perspectives to create a unique subculture within the larger Muslim culture of Tawi-Tawi.

APPENDIX

KATA-KATA

Chanted by Salbaiyani

Introduction

The woman I am going to tell about lives at the end of the world.

Since he was small, like a young coconut, a certain man was in love with this woman.

Text

Datu Amilebangsa ordered his followers to prepare food in preparation for a long journey.

The followers asked: "Where are we going?"

Datu Amilebangsa said: "We are going to visit a special place. Even if we drift, we will be able to locate the place. You prepare the food while I go to my mother and father to ask permission to make this voyage. If they grant permission, we shall leave; if not, we shall not leave."

The followers finished preparing the food.

The name of their boat was *Galila*.

Datu Amilebangsa went to his parents' house to request permission to leave.

He said to them: "As you know, the female child usually stays at home, but the male child often leaves home and travels. I want to travel."

His full name was Datu Amilebangsa Sahaia.

His parents said: "If you are seeking a wife, you cannot leave since you already have a betrothed in this place. Her name is Gimbaiansampakan-Tapanggan-Bangan-Sampaka."

Datu Amilebangsa said: "I am not seeking a wife since I already have a fiancée here."

Datu Amilebangsa's followers came to him and said: "When will we leave?"

Datu Amilebangsa said: "We will leave now. My parents have granted me permission to go, so long as I am not seeking a wife."

After they began to sail, Datu Amilebangsa said to his followers: "Where do you prefer to go, a nearby place or a faraway place?"

His followers said: "Let us go to a faraway place. If we are going to a nearby place, we do not want to go."

Datu Amilebangsa said: "There is no wind, but if you want to leave now, put up the mast."

Datu Amilebangsa then spoke to the wind and asked it to blow.

He said: "If my mother and father have power, the strong winds will now blow."

The winds began to blow immediately. His boat sailed swiftly through the sea like a kris cutting the water.

Datu Amilebangsa told his followers he would sleep. He said: "When we reach our destination, do not go near the shore because a woman there will use her magic to cast a spell on you."

Datu Amilebangsa then went to sleep. The boat sailed for three days and three nights until it finally reached its destination.

When Datu Amilebangsa awakened, he saw many men and women collecting shells on shore.

Eva-Eva Denda and Misahela, two women, were surprised to see the boat and said: "Whose boat is that? It looks like the boat of Datu Amilebangsa."

Misahela said: "Oh you, in that boat. Who is your leader?"

Datu Amilebangsa's followers said: "Our leader is inside the boat."

The two women said: "That is the boat of Datu Amilebangsa."

The followers of Datu Amilebangsa said: "You are right. This is the boat of Datu Amilebangsa, but he is not here."

Eva-Eva Denda told Misahela they should board the boat and see if the men were telling the truth.

The two women boarded the boat without an invitation from the men.

They did not see Datu Amilebangsa on deck. Eva-Eva Denda told her companion to go below deck and see if anyone was there.

When Misahela went below deck, she saw Datu Amilebangsa sleeping.

Eva-Eva Denda and Misahela said: "Why are you sleeping?"

When Datu Amilebangsa awakened and saw the two women, he was surprised and said: "Why did we anchor at this shore?"

The two women said: "Why do you speak like that? If you came here in search of women, you will find no women better than we."

Datu Amilebangsa said: "Since I left the womb of my mother, I have never seen such wanton women. I hope you will not be angry with me, but I did not come here to seek women. I already have a fiancée in my home place. Her name is Gimbaiansampakan-Tapanggan-Bangan-Sampaka."

The two women said: "You cannot fool us with such talk. We know you came here to find women. You will find no other women around here like us."

Datu Amilebangsa said: "You are very wanton women. Do you want to live or die?"

The two women said: "You make it very difficult for us to entice you."

Datu Amilebangsa said to his followers: "Give me my kris."

When he drew his kris, the two women left the boat crying. They said: "It is very difficult to tempt Datu Amilebangsa."

After sailing three nights and three days, the boat reached another island. The people on the island saw the boat approaching and were curious about whose boat it might be. Soon Datu Amilebangsa appeared on the deck.

Datu Amilebangsa asked the people: "Where is the house of Babo-Putlih-Lihaumata?"

The people said: "Who are you? Why are you asking for Babo-Putlih-Lihaumata? Her house is directly in front of your boat."

Babo-Putlih-Lihaumata came to the window of her house and saw Datu Amilebangsa asking for her. She wanted to go to the boat of Datu Amilebangsa.

Datu Amilebangsa said: "Do not come to my boat. I will come to your house."

Babo-Putlih-Lihaumata said: "I am very flattered that you have traveled so far to visit me."

Datu Amilebangsa went into her house. She ordered her family to cook food for him. They put the dishes of food in place. Babo-Putlih-Lihaumata invited Datu Amilebangsa to eat. She said: "After you eat, we will converse."

Datu Amilebangsa said: "You should not have prepared so much food. We have plenty of food on the boat. But since you have gone to so much trouble, I will eat a few bites."

Datu Amilebangsa ate only a few bites and was soon satiated.

After she ate, Babo-Putlih-Lihaumata said: "Forgive me for asking, but why did you come here?"

Datu Amilebangsa said: "I came here because I want to go to Bailan-Asaha."

Babo-Putlih-Lihaumata said: "If you want to go to Bailan-Asaha, you can walk there. You will find thieves there who have come to kidnap people. You will find a place of many crossroads. Do not take the north or west path. Do not take the path to the south or the path to the northeast. Only the east path will lead you to Bailan-Asaha."

Datu Amilebangsa began walking and reached the crossroads. He said to himself: "Babo-Putlih-Lihaumata told me not to go south, west, north or northeast, but take the eastern path."

He began to walk eastward. Halfway there, the countryside became very open. He met Manar-Bangsahaia at the place where the thieves were supposed to be. Manar-Bangsahaia said: "Who is that datu coming here to Bailan-Asaha? I am the kidnapper-thief."

Datu Amilebangsa said: "I did not come here to fight you. I came here for recreation."

Manar-Bangsahaia said: "I do not believe you. You came here to fight. I do not want to fight you, but if you remain here, we will fight."

They began to fight. The fight lasted not for days or months, but for years.

Manar-Bangsahaia said: "We have fought for years. Now you may continue your journey."

Datu Amilebangsa continued on his way. He sensed he was near the end of his journey. The path led into the forest. Beyond the forest was the sea and across a narrow channel was another island.

Manar-Bangsahaia climbed to the top of a tall tree. He said: "By the power of my parents, I order the channel separating those two islands to become very deep with a strong current."

Datu Amilebangsa soon reached the channel. He said: "It will be very difficult to reach the other side." He stood for a long time trying to figure out how he could reach the other side. He removed his clothing, tied his kris tightly in its scabbard and began to wade across the channel. The water became deeper and he had to swim. He almost drowned and became exhausted from swimming so he returned to the shallow water. He lay on the shore. His stomach was bloated with seawater and water drained from his mouth and anus.

As he was resting, he said: "It is very difficult to go to Bailan-Asaha."

After resting he again waded into the sea and began to swim. He again almost drowned. He returned to shore and again the water drained from his mouth and anus. When his clothes dried and he was recovered, he put on his shoes, pants, shirt, and turban. He secured his kris around his waist.

He said: "If my parents have strong power, they will send me a *kurah sambailani* to carry me across."[1]

After he spoke, the horse arrived complete with gear. He mounted the horse, and it swam across the channel.

Manar-Bangsahaia was still watching from the treetop. He said: "Never in my life have I seen such a determined person. He is certainly determined to go to Bailan-asaha."

Datu Amilebangsa dismounted the horse and began to walk. Soon he saw a big house. The house was shiny like a bright moon. It was so bright he could not look directly at it.

Datu Amilebangsa said: "The woman in this house is the most beautiful woman in the world."

When he reached the house, he said: "You people inside, open the door so I can come in for a few minutes."

Ma'ajarat-Tornorka, the woman in the house, said: "Who is that datu who is telling us to open the door? I would not even open the door for my former lover, Datu Ahsarakar-Tantu, if I did not care to admit him."

Datu Amilebangsa said again: "Open the door. I want to come inside."

Ma'ajarat-Tornorka again said: "Who is this datu who insists that I open my door? Even my former lover would not be allowed in my house if I did not feel like admitting him."

Datu Amilebangsa said to himself: "It is very difficult to enter this house."

Datu Amilebangsa said: "By the power of my parents, I will break down this door." He then broke the lock and kicked in the door. He entered but found no one inside. He said: "Where are the people who were here a few minutes ago?"

He looked around and passed through seven curtains. No one was behind the curtains. He approached an eighth curtain, pulled it aside and saw a woman lying on a bed. He was so excited by her beauty that he went to her immediately.

Datu Amilebangsa said: "Your beauty is famous throughout the world."

Ma'ajarat-Tornorka said: "Where is this datu from? He behaves like a thief."

She then said to the bird Bulung-Kakak: "Go to Datu Ahsarakar-Tantu and tell him this datu has invaded my house."

The bird flew to Pangih-Nor-Hamdu, the home of Datu Ahsarakar-Tantu, and said: "You must come immediately, your betrothed has been approached by another datu."

Datu Ahsarakar-Tantu said: "If my parents have power, they will send me a kurah sambailani to take me to the house of my betrothed."

The horse immediately appeared.

He rode the horse to the house of Ma'ajarat-Tornorka. He said to the bird: "Give me my kris immediately." The bird gave him his kris.

Datu Ahsarakar-Tantu said to Datu Amilebangsa: "Why have you come here to steal my treasure? Let us fight."

Datu Amilebangsa said: "How shall we fight? Shall we take turns attacking one another or shall we fight together at the same time?"

Datu Ahsarakar-Tantu said: "It is up to you."

Datu Amilebangsa said: "If you are allowed to stab first, I might die. If I am allowed to stab first, you might die. It is better if we attack at the same time, then we both have a chance."

They began to fight. As they hit each other, the marks of the kris left wavy imprints on their bodies. The imprints shone brightly like the sun.

After fighting a long time, Datu Amilebangsa was driven under a log. Datu Ahsarakar-Tantu told Datu Amilebangsa to stay under the log and admit defeat. He then went into the house with his betrothed.

Datu Amilebangsa said: "If my mother and father have power, I will escape from under this log." Then, like a centipede, he came from under the log.

Datu Amilebangsa mounted his horse and chased Datu Ahsarakar-Tantu. When he reached him, they immediately began to fight again. Before long, Datu Ahsarakar-Tantu drove Datu Amilebangsa under a big stone.

Datu Ahsarakar-Tantu said: "You should stay under the stone." He rode away with his betrothed.

Datu Amilebangsa said: "If my mother and father have power, I will escape from under this stone." He then came out from under the stone as agilely as a crab.

Datu Amilebangsa again mounted his horse and pursued Datu Ahsarakar-Tantu. When they met, they immediately began to fight. Datu Amilebangsa fell into a deep hole, more than 1000 fathoms deep. Datu Ahsarakar-Tantu rode away on his horse with Ma'ajarat-Tornorka.

Datu Amilebangsa said: "If my mother and father have power, I will escape from this hole." Then, like a snake, he emerged from the hole.

He rode on his horse and chased Datu Ahsarakar-Tantu.

Datu Amilebangsa said: "I was placed under a log, under a rock and into a hole because Datu Ahsarakar-Tantu has much practice in such tricks. If I had not pitied you in the beginning and not attacked you directly, you would be dead by now."

They fought again. Datu Amilebangsa kicked Datu Ahsarakar-Tantu into the air. When Datu Ahsarakar-Tantu fell, all his bones were broken.

Ma'ajarat-Tornorka cried when Datu Ahsarakar-Tantu's bones were broken. She said: "I would like to help you, Datu Ahsarakar-Tantu, but you are a man, and I am only a woman."

Datu Amilebangsa placed Ma'ajarat-Tornorka on his horse. After they rode a while, they were halfway to Bailan-Asaha.

Ma'ajarat-Tornorka said: "You came here to Bailan-Asaha to see me."

After they talked, Datu Amilebangsa rode on with Ma'ajarat-Tornorka. They soon reached her house.

As they approached the house, people from other houses saw them and said: "Now we know why Datu Amilebangsa came here. He wanted Ma'ajarat-Tornorka."

Ma'ajarat-Tornorka said to Babau-Putlih-Lihaumata: "I told you to stay on shore so you could warn me of approaching men. But you did not. Instead you told Datu Amilebangsa where he could find me."

Babau-Putlih-Lihaumata said: "Datu Amilebangsa told me he was going to Bailan-Asaha for recreation. Even Manar-Bangsahaia, who you stationed midway between your place and the shore, could not defeat Datu Amilebangsa. So how could a mere woman like me stop him? Besides you are already with Datu Amilebangsa."

END OF PART I

Introduction to Part II

People who gossip about others will be punished.
People who lie will also be punished.

Text

After she finished talking to Babau-Putlih-Lihaumata, Ma'ajarat-Tornorka boarded the *Galila*, and the boat was navigated toward the home of Datu Amilebangsa. A gong was hung on the boat. The name of the gong was Sigtagbanuamakadjag-Djag-Dagaha.[2] The crew struck the gong slowly as they sailed on the low tide current.

The people from the houses on shore gossiped and said: "Now we know why Datu Amilebangsa came here. He came to get Ma'ajarat-Tornorka. His gong has a beautiful sound."

At home, Datu Amilebangsa's parents were afraid their son was lost at sea.

Gimbaiansampakan-Tapanggan-Bangan-Sampaka said to Datu Amilebangsa's parents: "I was reluctant to stop him when he left because I did not want him to think I am a possessive woman. I knew he was looking for a woman."

Datu Amilebangsa's mother said: "Do not think he left here to seek a woman. You are his betrothed. He asked our permission to see new places, not to seek a woman."

Gimbaiansampakan-Tapanggan-Bangan-Sampaka said: "I cannot argue with you since you are older than I. If I did not respect your age, I would argue that Datu Amilebangsa has a new lover. If we were the same age, I would challenge you."

Gimbaiansampakan-Tapanggan-Bangan-Sampaka called to her bird Manuk-Bulan-Kakak. She told the bird to fly to Datu Amilebangsa with her scarf. The bird flew with the scarf. En route the bird saw Datu Amilebangsa's boat returning home. The bird returned and told Gimbaiansampakan-Tapanggan-Bangan-Sampaka that Datu Amilebangsa had a new lover. The bird said: "The name of his new lover is Ma'ajarat-Tornorka."

After hearing this, Datu Amilebangsa's parents became worried. After three nights and three days, Datu Amilebangsa arrived home.

When Datu Amilebangsa arrived, his parents said: "When you left, you said you were not seeking a lover. But now you have brought a lover home with you."

Datu Amilebangsa said: "If you had good luck, would you refuse it? I had the good fortune to meet this woman on my journey, so I brought her home."

His parents said: "Had you told us you were seeking a lover, we would not have given you permission to go."

Gimbaiansampakan-Tapanggan-Bangan-Sampaka said: "Do not discuss it. It is of no matter."

Datu Amilebangsa's parents were worried.

Ma'ajarat-Tornorka said: "Why are you worried?"

Datu Amilebangsa's parents said: "We are worried because we do not know who should receive your bride wealth."

Ma'ajarat-Tornorka said: "Do not worry about the bride wealth. It does not matter if you do not give one."

The parents said: "Do not speak that way. All women should have bridewealth."

Ma'ajarat-Tornorka said: "You do not have to give bridewealth. I was abducted by your son, so there is no need for bridewealth."

The parents said: "Even if our son abducted you, you should be given bridewealth. We are worried because you have no relatives here to whom we can give your bridewealth."

Ma'ajarat-Tornorka said: "Do not worry about it. I have many relatives here to whom you can give the money."

The parents said: "Tell us who your relatives are so we can give them the bridewealth."

Ma'ajarat-Tornorka said: "Do not give me any bridewealth. If I were not abducted by your son, I would be able to get a bridewealth of millions in my home place."

The parents said: "Now that we know the amount of your bridewealth at your home place, we will give it to you."

Ma'ajarat-Tornorka said: "If your son had not abducted me, there would be many relatives to whom you could give the money."

The parents then gave bridewealth for two women, one to Gimbaiansampakan-Tapanggan-Bangan-Sampaka and one to Ma'ajarat-Tornorka.

Three months after the wedding Ma'ajarat-Tornorka was worried. She could not eat even though there was plenty of food.

Datu Amilebangsa said: "Why don't you eat? You have become very thin."

Ma'ajarat-Tornorka said: "I don't know what is wrong with me."

Datu Amilebangsa said: "Why don't you know? Why don't you eat?"

Ma'ajarat-Tornorka said: "Don't ask me anymore. Ask yourself why I am sick. You have brought on my illness."

Datu Amilebangsa said: "Tell me what food you want and I will get it for you."

Ma'ajarat-Tornorka said: "I do not like any of the food in this place."

Datu Amilebangsa said: "Tell me what food you want and I will search for it. If there is none here, I will go away to find it."

Ma'ajarat-Tornorka said: "Even if I tell you the name you will be unable to find it. The only food I like is *bunga-bunga mangih*.[3]

Datu Amilebangsa said: "Had you told me sooner, I would have found it for you."

Datu Amilebangsa went to the forest to look for the fruit. After he was gone a long time, Ma'ajarat-Tornorka said: "Datu Amilebangsa must be lost in the forest."

Datu Amilebangsa could not find the fruit. He stood on top of the mountain in his search for the fruit. As he stood on the mountain, he said: "By the power of my parents, I wish for bunga-bunga-mangih." The fruit immediately appeared before him. Datu Amilebangsa climbed the tree and gathered all the fruit in his turban. After he gathered the fruit, the tree disappeared. He went home immediately.

His wife said: "I thought you were lost."

Datu Amilebangsa said: "It wouldn't matter if I were lost. I had to find the fruit since I caused your illness."

Datu Amilebangsa went into the house and gave his wife the fruit. Ma'ajarat-Tornorka cut the fruit with a sharp knife. As she ate, she called Datu Amilebangsa to eat. He said: "You eat it. We men can eat any fruit, but when you women become pregnant you can eat only certain types of fruit."

Ma'ajarat-Tornorka said: "Even though you are responsible for my condition, there is enough fruit here for both of us."

Datu Amilebangsa joined Ma'ajarat-Tornorka in eating the fruit. Ma'ajarat-Tornorka began to perspire.

During her tenth month of pregnancy, Ma'ajarat-Tornorka again became worried.

Datu Amilebangsa said: "Why are you worried?"

Ma'ajarat-Tornorka said: "I do not know what is worrying me."

Datu Amilebangsa said: "Why do you not know why you are worried? You should know."

Ma'ajarat-Tornorka said: "I am afraid Datu Ahsarakar-Tantu is coming after me."

Datu Amilebangsa said: "Don't worry about him. If he comes, I will challenge him to fight."

Ma'ajarat-Tornorka said: "I would not be worried about a fight between only the two of you, but he has many followers."

Datu Amilebangsa said: "Who are his followers?"

Ma'ajarat-Tornorka said: "His followers are millions of ghosts."

Datu Amilebangsa said: "Don't worry about that. When will they arrive?"

Ma'ajarat-Tornorka said: "In three days they will arrive like a floating island. The ghosts are already on their way."

When Datu Ahsarakar-Tantu arrived with his ghost-followers, they surrounded the entire island. Datu Amilebangsa invited Simataigarulanavidialumtana to assist him.[4]

When the ghosts and Datu Ahsarakar-Tantu arrived, Datu Amilebangsa met them with his kris. He killed millions of ghosts with one sweep of his kris. With another sweep of his kris, he killed more than a thousand ghosts.

Datu Ahsarakar-Tantu said to his ghosts: "I asked you to come with me because I thought you were powerful, but I see now you are useless."

Simataigarulanavidialumtana was killing the ghosts in the air.

When Datu Ahsarakar-Tantu could not defeat Datu Amilebangsa, he departed for home. Datu Amilebangsa said to him: "If you came here for your wife, forget about it because she is already pregnant."

At the end of ten months, Ma'ajarat-Tornorka became worried again.

Datu Amilebangsa said to her: "What is wrong with you?"

Ma'ajarat-Tornorka said: "I do not know what is wrong with me."

Datu Amilebangsa said: "You do not know what is wrong with you, but you knew that ghosts were coming from far away."

Ma'ajarat-Tornorka said: "I am worried because I am ready to deliver my baby. You should call the midwife."

Datu Amilebangsa went to the house of his aunt.

His aunt said: "What do you want?"

Datu Amilebangsa said: "I have come to ask you to help deliver my wife's child."

When the aunt reached the house and felt the stomach of Ma'ajarat-Tornorka, she said: "Your wife will give birth immediately." When she was ready to deliver, Ma'ajarat-Tornorka called to her husband.

Datu Amilebangsa said: "Why do you call me? I am not a midwife. What is wrong with you?"

Ma'ajarat-Tornorka said: "Even though you are not a midwife, come near me."

Datu Amilebangsa went to his wife's side. His tears began to fall. When he reached his wife, he said: "What is wrong with you?"

Ma'ajarat-Tornorka did not answer, but simply clasped the hand of Datu Amilebangsa. Datu Amilebangsa clasped hands with his wife and cried.

The baby was soon delivered and Ma'ajarat-Tornorka died. Datu Amilebangsa gathered all the imams to pray for her.

After his wife was buried, Datu Amilebangsa could not stop thinking of her and became very thin. He was very lonely in his house with only himself and his newborn child. He did not eat. His child said to him: "Father, why do you not eat? Why are you depressed?"

Datu Amilebangsa looked around to see who had spoken. He said: "Who is talking? I see no one but my baby boy wrapped in a blanket."

The child said: "There is no one else here. I am the one talking to you. Why are you depressed? You are like an *amukogmukog-lantai-amontong-amontong-lampid.*"[5]

Datu Amilebangsa was very surprised and said: "You are so young. Your body is still red from your recent birth. How are you able to talk to me? If you are the one who spoke to me a moment ago and told me I look like an amukogmukog-lantai-amontong-amontong-lampid, I will tell you. I am depressed because of your mother's death."

The son said: "That is the reason for your depression?"

Datu Amilebangsa said: "Yes."

The son said: "You are so skinny because you will not eat and you look like an amukogmukog-lantai-amontong-amontong-lampid. If you die, you will be able to see your wife. Even if you do not eat, you will not die if it is not your time to die. After I was born, my mother died and left me here alone. You fought to win my mother and she also went through hardships. But now she is dead, so you should live to care for me. I am the result of your affair with my mother. You should care for me."

Datu Amilebangsa said: "You have many aunts who can care for you. If I do not eat, maybe I will be fortunate enough to die."

The son said: "I do not believe you really want to die. If you do not go to the afterworld, you will be unable to see my mother. If you take good care of me, I will go after my mother."

Datu Amilebangsa said: "How can you go after your mother? You are so small, only newly born. Even I, who made you, cannot go after your mother unless I die."

The son said: "I may not be able to go after my mother, but I shall try."

After three days and three nights passed, the baby disappeared from the house. Datu Amilebangsa searched the house but could not find his son. He became depressed again.

The son had disappeared to Umilkiama, the place between earth and the afterworld. The son went to the place where his ancestors dwelt. The ancestors said: "Why has that tiny baby from earth come here? He is very odorous."[6]

The baby said: "I came here to find my mother. Since my birth, I have been unable to suck the milk of my mother."

The ancestors said: "If that is your reason for coming here, you should go back to earth. If you never had the opportunity to suck the milk of your mother, go to the tree called *Kayu Taobi* and suck the milk of that tree."[7]

The child said: "You are right. That tree has milk for babies, but I want to suck the milk of my mother. I have never tasted the milk of my mother because she died at my birth."

The ancestors said: "If you know the appearance of your mother, you may go to her. But if you do not know her, you must go back to earth."

The child said: "I can recognize my mother by her beautiful body. She has dimples on her cheeks and long hair."

Tuhan said to the ancestors: "Why did you bring that baby here? He is so odorous."

The ancestors replied: "This baby wants to see his mother because he never had a chance to nurse before she died."

Tuhan said: "All babies who have no mother to nurse should suckle from the Kayu Taobi. After he has nursed, send him back to earth."

The child said to Tuhan: "Other babies have tasted the milk of their mothers, but I have not even had one taste. If I cannot taste my mother's milk, I do not want to drink milk from that tree."

Tuhan said: "If you know the appearance of your mother, you can go to her."

The child said: "I do not know the appearance of my mother. You know her so you should tell me what she looks like."

Tuhan said: "You had better return to earth if you do not know your mother."

The child said: "I know my mother's appearance. She has a beautiful body, two dimples and long hair."

Tuhan said: "You have sought your mother because you know her appearance. You had better walk now."

The baby began to walk to heaven. He walked through a plain of grass barren of trees and hills. When he became tired, he stopped and made a hammock from his diaper for sleeping. He came to a post, but it was only a single post with no house nearby. He walked to the post and stopped there. While he was standing there, he saw a *maligai* in the sky.[8] The maligai turned in the sky, and the child turned to watch it.

The maligai was controlled by Munkar, a messenger of Tuhan who investigates peoples' lives to determine whether they should be admitted to heaven. Munkar shouted to the people in the maligai and told them to look at the baby below. The baby looked like an ant to them because they were so high in the sky. All the people in the maligai looked at the baby. The only one who did not look was the child's mother, Ma'ajarat-Tornorka.

The people in the maligai said: "Only you Ma'ajarat-Tornorka are not looking out the window."

Ma'ajarat-Tornorka said: "What are you looking at?"

They said: "Come and see. It looks like an ant."

Ma'ajarat-Tornorka was surprised to see the baby. She called Munkar and told him she wanted to see if the child was her baby.

Munkar said: "Do not lie. Look and see if that is really your child. If he is your child, I will let you go down to see him. If he is not your child, the maligai will not go down."

Ma'ajarat-Tornorka said: "I cannot go down if you will not let me. I gave birth to my child, but I have never seen him. If I were the one guarding this maligai and someone was in it who had never seen her son, I would let her go down to see him."

The baby was still watching the maligai. The wind turned the maligai in all directions as the child watched it.

Munkar said: "Look and see if that is your child. If it is, I'll let you go down. If it is not, I cannot let you go."

Ma'ajarat-Tornorka said to Munkar: "It is your choice. I cannot do anything except what you allow. But I am sure it is my son. I will go down."

Munkar let the maligai descend.

Ma'ajarat-Tornorka was ready to jump from the maligai in her excitement, but it was too high.

Ma'ajarat-Tornorka said: "It is very hard to leave the maligai because of the wind." To her child, she said: "I have not seen you, even when I gave birth to you. If it were not for these glass windows in the maligai, I would jump out in my eagerness to see you."

Munkar said: "What is your business in coming here?"

The child said: "All babies can drink milk from that tree, but I have never tasted the milk of my mother so I want to do so now."

Munkar said: "Do you know who your mother is? If you cannot identify your mother, you cannot see her."

The child said: "She has a beautiful body, dimples on her cheeks and long hair."

The windows of the maligai opened and Ma'ajarat-Tornorka jumped out, grabbed her baby and let it nurse at her breast. She said: "This is our first time to meet."

After the child nursed, the maligai went up into the sky, leaving the mother and child behind.

The child said: "Mother, wrap me in my blanket and put me on your head and let us walk." The mother wrapped him, put him on her head and began walking. After they walked a short distance, they met some people playing a gambling game. They invited the mother and child to play with them.

The mother said to the child: "They asked us to play with them."

The child said: "Ask them if they know us."

The players said: "We do not know you."

The child said: "Then you should not call us. When you were alive, gambling was your game. So now you are playing the same game in the afterworld."

They left the gamblers and met some people carrying coconuts. The carriers said: "Come and help us carry these coconuts."

Ma'ajarat-Tornorka said: "Should we help them carry their coconuts?"

The child said: "Ask them if they know us. If they do, we will go to them."

The carriers said: "We do not know you."

The child said: "Don't call us. You stole coconuts in life, and now in the afterworld you are doing the same thing."

When they left, they met women swimming in blood. The women said: "Come and take a bath in this blood."

Ma'ajarat-Tornorka said: "They called us to take a bath. Should we go?"

The child said: "If they know us we will go, but if they do not know us we will not go. Do not call us to take a bath in the blood. You were midwives in the world who performed abortions and that is why you must now swim in blood."

Next they met some people putting betel leaves in their hair. They called the mother and child to join them.

The mother said: "They have called us to join them."

The child said: "Ask them if they know us."

The people said: "We do not know you."

The child said: "Do not call us. In the real world you stole the betel leaves of others."

They next came to a very deep, dark hole. The child said: "There is a woman in that deep hole and her hair is divided into seven strands."

The mother said: "We cannot go further. This hole is blocking our way."

The hole was so dark they could not see the black hair of the woman.

The child said: "If you cannot walk, put me down." When he was on the ground, he held on to his mother's leg. He said: "We must go through this hole to enter earth, but it is so dark we cannot see."

The child went through the dark hole alone. When he emerged from the hole, he looked down and saw that it was the grave of his mother. He said: "You stay here in the grave. I will go to the house of my father. You are already dead, so you must stay in the grave."

When he approached the house, Datu Amilebangsa ran out and embraced him.

(Salbaiyani 1966)

244

NOTES

Prologue (pages 1–10)

* In 1994, I published *The Songs of Salanda and Other Stories of Sulu*, a semi-fictionalized anthology of stories based on my fieldwork in Tawi-Tawi. The interested reader is referred to that book for a personal account of my research among the Sama Dilaut.

Chapter 1 (pages 11–21)

1. In 1973, the province of Sulu was divided into Sulu and Tawi-Tawi. Sulu includes the islands of Jolo, Siasi, Pangutaran, and Samales. Tawi-Tawi includes the islands of Tawi-Tawi, Sibutu, and Cagayan de Tawi-Tawi.

2. In 1973 Basilan became a separate province.

3. The various spellings of "Bajau" in the literature include Badjao, Bajao, Badjaw, Bajau, and Badjau.

4. Stone (1962) dealt with this complexity by dividing the group into first- and second-class Sama; although this division is a step in the right direction, the Sama population of Sulu is more complex than this. In an early version of a published paper, Arong (1962) suggested the Sama Dilaut be called "*Sama Pala'u*" to identify them as members of the general Sama population and to emphasize their uniqueness within that population. His suggestion was valid, but unfortunately that portion of his paper never saw print.

5. "Sinama" is the name of the language spoken by the Sama people.

6. Earlier writers (such as Arce 1963, Szanton 1963) called the Sama Dilaut "pagans." The term is misleading in that it fails to recognize the great influence of Islam on the Sama Dilaut, and overlooks the fact that most of their villages (excluding the Tawi-Tawi Sama Dilaut) have mosques.

7. Szanton (p. 40) reports "definitely distinguishable" differences between the Sitangkai and Tawi-Tawi grave art. He was, however, able to visit only one cemetery in Tawi-Tawi and the cemetery of the acculturated Sama Dilaut in Sitangkai. Had he visited other cemeteries in both Tawi-Tawi and Sibutu, I think he would have seen fewer differences between the two groups. Recent Sitangkai grave art has become greatly simplified due to Islamic influence, but the older forms as well as early photographs of the art (Taylor 1931) reveal affinities to the Tawi-Tawi Sama Dilaut art.

8. "Bangsa" has sometimes been defined as a bilateral kinship group. I have chosen to define bangsa as "subculture," which is more in keeping with the Tawi-Tawi Sama Dilaut use of the term as a group of closely related people with traditions different from others.

They acknowledge that other Sama groups are related to them, but regard themselves, the Sitangkai Sama Dilaut, and the Semporna Sama Dilaut as a bangsa, or subculture, different from other Sama.

Chapter 2 (pages 22–31)

1. The headman's direct descendants are: Pangalima Ammalawi, Pangalima Alari, Pangalima Agi, Pakasa Bata, Pakasa Ajab, Pakasa Tungbang, Pakasa Pa'og'gon, and Pakasa Unsing. The last-named was allegedly a Sama Dilaut from Johore who settled in Sitangkai.

2. Additional versions of the Johore story are found in Sopher (1985).

3. Pallesen suggests the language be called "Sama-Bajaw," the names most commonly used to identify it.

4. Significantly, many of the origin stories I collected among the Tawi-Tawi and Sitangkai Sama Dilaut mention Zamboanga as their homeland (Nimmo 1968).

5. Pallesen suggested that possibly the Sama movements to southern Sulu displaced Bornean people. Given the proximity of the islands to Borneo, they were most likely inhabited at the time. Spoehr (1973) found evidence of human habitation on Sanga-Sanga island, one of the Tawi-Tawi islands, dating to 7945 BP. He doubts, however, that the early habitation is ancestral to present populations of the area.

Chapter 3 (pages 32–50)

* These population figures are approximate. Each time I visited a moorage I counted the number of houseboats and houses. My population estimates are based on these figures. I was unable to visit all moorages during one day to obtain a more accurate census of the total Tawi-Tawi Sama Dilaut population. But even had I been able to do so, many houseboats would have been away from the moorages for reasons discussed below.

Chapter 4 (pages 51–80)

1. I have no data on the kinds of trees used in boat construction. Spoehr (1971, 118) identifies the trees used in the construction of a vinta in Zamboanga: "The hull is made from a tree locally called red *lauan* (*Shorea negrosensis*), which is easy to work. The thwarts and the dowels used to secure the gunwale and side planks to the keel are *bakauan* or mangrove (*Rhizophora sp.*), a strong and tough wood." Probably the Tawi-Tawi Sama Dilaut use these same trees, as well as others I am unable to identify.

2. Kurais (1975, 83) reports that among some Tawi-Tawi Sama the position of the felled tree determines which sections will be used for the different parts of the boat: "The bottom of the boat would be the side that struck the ground; the hull the upward side; the prow is towards the root, and stern towards the treetop." I learned of no such tradition among the Tawi-Tawi Sama Dilaut.

3. Sather (1985, 194) identifies the gelum tree as *Osbornia octadonata*.

4. In my first published paper on the Tawi-Tawi Sama Dilaut (Nimmo 1965, 425), based on my first field trip, I reported they had eight different types of boats. Subsequent field research revealed seven additional types.

5. Several of the terms used by Kurais (1975) for boats built by Sama (presumably in eastern Tawi-Tawi) are used by the Tawi-Tawi Sama Dilaut for different types of boats.

6. I called this boat *pidlas* in an early publication (1965), but subsequently learned it is more commonly known as lepa among the Sama Dilaut. Kurais (1975, 123) claims the proper spelling of this boat is "*pedlas*" and not "pidlas." He acknowledges variant pronunciations

of the word in eastern Tawi-Tawi, and quite possibly the pronunciation I recorded (Nimmo 1965, 425) is a variant in western Tawi-Tawi.

7. Taylor's articles (1930a, 1930b, 1931) on the Sitangkai Sama Dilaut have pictures of the lepa which he describes as one of three boats built by these Sama Dilaut. In his book (1936), based on the same visit to Sitangkai, he claims the Sama Dilaut sometimes bought their lepa from boatbuilders in Borneo. Thus, it would appear the lepa was firmly established in Sitangkai by 1930.

8. The name djenging appears elsewhere in the literature. In describing the boats of the Sama Dilaut of the Darvel Bay area of Sabah, James Warren writes: "Among the most common were the *jengeng*, often called *dupong*, an elaborately carved, double out-riggered canoe used primarily in fishing . . ." (1971, 10). In Tawi-Tawi, these names refer to two different types of boats. Kurais (1975, 97) claims *depang* is the Tausug name for the pilang, and I was told *dapang* is the Tausug name for the pilang. Kurais (1975, 97) provides a brief description of the djenging, which he spells "*zing-nging.*"

9. Pala'u is also the name many land dwellers use when referring to the Sama Dilaut; it is, however, considered pejorative by some Sama Dilaut.

10. "Vinta" is a name apparently introduced to Sulu from the northern Philippines. The Sama Dilaut call this boat pilang while the Tausug call it dapang. Kurais (1975, 97) reports that the Sama call it *pelang* and the Tausug call it *depang.*

11. Agta-agta is probably a cognate of *naga*, an art motif found among the Maranao of the Lake Lanao region of Mindanao. David Baradas (1981, 177) describes naga as a "Serpent figure in the shape of the letter S" and believes it is related to Sulu art motifs (p. 181). Several Sama Dilaut told me the agta-agta motif represented an animal, but most said they did not know what kind of animal. One man told me it represented a crocodile, and another said it was a fish; none mentioned the serpent as its inspiration.

12. The boats of the Sulu Archipelago have been documented over the years. David Szanton's survey (1963, 42–47) of the arts of Sulu includes a brief discussion of Sama Dilaut boat art (which confuses boat-types) accompanied by several photos of boats. Alexander Spoehr (1971) published a descriptive account of a Sama vinta in Zamboanga, a boat related to the Tawi-Tawi Sama Dilaut pilang. Edwin Doran, Jr. also discussed the Sama vinta of Bongao in a study of Austronesian canoe origins (1981), in a study of boats and culture history (1973), and in a comparative study of the sailing efficiency of three different boats (1976). James Warren (1981, 256–58) has a brief, but good description of three boats that were important in Sulu during the trading and piracy activities of the nineteenth century. Alain Martenot (1981) published an excellent description of the lepa, the boggo' and the balutu of the Sitangkai Sama Dilaut. An article by Muhammad Kurais II (1975) contains much information about Sama boatbuilding, boats, and sailing in Tawi-Tawi. His data come from Sama traditions and his personal observations and experiences. The article is an important addition to the literature on Sulu boats, not only because of the wealth of information it contains, but also because it is written from a Sama perspective. Clifford Sather (1997) has good descriptions, accompanied by photographs, of the lepa and boggo' of the Sama Dilaut of Semporna, a people closely related to the Sitangkai Sama Dilaut. In addition to these academic publications, various other books and articles published over the years contain pictures of indigenous Sulu watercraft. Photographs and sketches of Sulu boats appear in Worcester (1898, 181), Brownell (1905, 980), Orosa (1970 [1923], 2, 3, 24, 60, 63, 68, 84, 87), Taylor (1930a, 158, 159; 1930b, 290, 291; 1931, 476, 477, 480, 481; 1936, 46, 47, 60, 61), Follett (1945, 10, 11, 130, 131), Dacanay (1967, 150), Nimmo (1971) and de Henning Singh (1976).

Although the accompanying descriptions are sometimes brief, misleading or non-existent, the pictures nonetheless provide important documentation.

Chapter 5 (pages 81–103)

1. Sections of the reefs are identified more specifically by islets, sand bars, and other geographic features. Fishing grounds are not "owned" by anyone; however, those who arrive first to fish are given priority by those who arrive later.

2. This was a popular fishing ground during my first field trip in 1963. However, when I returned in 1965, few Sama Dilaut fished there because of intimidating encounters with Tausug.

3. Sather (1997, 117) reports that the Semporna Sama Dilaut make two sizes of linggi and four sizes of salibut. The Tawi-Tawi Sama Dilaut also make different sizes of each net, but I do not have names for them.

4. In Sitangkai, women usually weave fishing nets. These house-dwelling Sama Dilaut are much more sedentary than the Tawi-Tawi Sama Dilaut and women do not usually participate extensively in fishing. Apparently as a result of their greater free time, they have assumed the responsibility of making and maintaining nets. Older Sitangkai Sama Dilaut told me men made and maintained the nets when the community lived as boat dwellers.

5. "Aneba" means to strike the water with a paddle or pole. "To'going" is a type of fish that feeds on the Bilatan reefs. "Aneba to'going" involves striking the water with paddles and poles to drive the fish into nets.

6. This type of fishing is called *magambit* in Sitangkai and Semporna. In Tawi-Tawi, magambit is used more generally for any type of fish drive with or without nets.

7. The magambit groups in Sitangkai are much larger and cover greater territories than the aneba groups in Tawi-Tawi. I was once with a Sitangkai magambit that stayed out ten days.

8. Sama Dilaut always divide their catches equally among all participants. At the beginning of my fieldwork, before I convinced them otherwise, the Sama Dilaut insisted I take a share of the catch when I accompanied them fishing even though my contribution was minimal, if not nil. Children are early taught the value of sharing. One time at Tungbangkao, three preteen boys came home from an afternoon of fishing with a dozen fish. A quarrel ensued when two of the boys insisted they caught the fish and should keep them all. The other said he assisted and deserved a share of the catch. Parents of two of the boys and the grandmother of the third overheard the disagreement and soundly scolded the boys, telling them the catch must be divided among all three regardless who actually caught the fish.

9. Sather (1997, 123) identifies tua as *Derris elliptica*.

10. Spoehr (1980, 81) reports that he did not observe liftnet fishing in Tawi-Tawi or Sibutu during his visits in 1966, 1967, and 1969, and doubts the method was in use. It was, however, occasionally practiced in Tawi-Tawi and was widely practiced in Sibutu during the time of my fieldwork in 1965, 1966, and 1967.

11. Twenty (nineteen percent) of 106 boat dwelling families and thirty-one (47 percent) of eighty-eight house dwelling families surveyed had gardened at one time.

Chapter 6 (pages 104–138)

1. The Sama Dilaut claim polygyny is permissible among them, but I never encountered a case or discovered one from genealogical data. Although not common, polygyny is practiced among the land-dwelling Sama and the Tausug.

2. Differences in household composition, residence patterns, marriage patterns, and divorce patterns between the boat-dwelling Sama Dilaut and the house-dwelling Sama Dilaut of Tawi-Tawi are insignificant. Sather (1997) reported the same for the boat-dwelling and house-dwelling Sama Dilaut (Bajau Laut) of Semporna. However, I found significant differences between the house-dwelling Sama Dilaut of Sitangkai and the boat-dwelling Sama Dilaut of Tawi-Tawi. At Sitangkai, uxorilocality and uxorilocal extended family households are more common. First-cousin marriages are less common at Sitangkai and divorce rates are higher. Kinship terminology has become more classificatory as nuclear family terms are extended to other members of the extended family household (Nimmo 1972, 56–87). These differences are probably partly due to the more sedentary nature of the Sitangkai community and its longer tradition of house living. It is also possible some of the patterns were present in their boat-dwelling past.

3. Sather (1997, 178) reports that among the Bajau Laut of Semporna adoption involves a formal verbal agreement between the biological and adoptive parents sealed with a payment of cash and goods to the biological parents. Adoption is much more informal among the Tawi-Tawi Sama Dilaut. The adopted child is usually a nephew or niece and is given to a childless couple by a couple who already have a sizeable family. Sometimes the adopted child has been orphaned and is raised by an uncle or aunt.

4. The casual sleeping habits of the Sama Dilaut are probably responsible for the stories about Sama Dilaut incest told by Muslim land dwellers whose unmarried youth always sleep in segregated sections of the household. Although incest probably does occur occasionally, I learned of none among the Sama Dilaut.

Chapter 7 (pages 139–82)

1. Sather suggests that the Bajau Laut djin of Semporna are more appropriately called "spirit-mediums" rather than "shaman" because they do not "undertake spiritual journeys while in trance nor send out his or her soul on healing missions into the cosmos" (1997, 303). I met djin among the Tawi-Tawi Sama Dilaut who took spiritual journeys while in a trance to discover sources of illness. One old woman described a trip to Borneo undertaken by her spirit to find the whereabouts of her grandson.

2. Such personal saitan are important in the curing ceremonies of the Sitangkai Sama Dilaut. They are frequently named and have been in families for generations. The Sitangkai Sama Dilaut have a much more elaborate cult of shamanism than that practiced by the Tawi-Tawi Sama Dilaut.

3. Throughout the Tawi-Tawi Islands, certain graves are associated with important Muslims from the early days of Islam. Among the best known of these are the graves atop Mount Bongao, but others are found on islets or in well-tended groves on larger islands. Often they are covered by a pile of white sand, perhaps ringed by stones, with receptacles for offerings. Usually called tempat (the same name the Sama Dilaut use for places where saitan reside), these sites are important in the religious lives of the Muslim people of Tawi-Tawi. They are much less important to the Sama Dilaut, although occasionally they visit them to leave offerings if spirits have directed them to do so.

4. Kata-kata are also found among the Sama Dilaut of Semporna, where they are also used for curing (Sather 1979, 304). Martenot and Maceda (1980) report that kata-kata are not used for curing in Sitangkai. This was not the case, however, during the time of my fieldwork in Sitangkai. I saw a sick man go into a trance when a kata-kata was recited in his presence, and I witnessed two other ceremonies where kata-kata were used for curing. I also heard kata-kata recited for entertainment in Sitangkai.

5. Malud is the annual celebration of Prophet Mohammed's birthday.

6. I was consistently told that seawater is used in ceremonies simply because it is more available than fresh water and has no special significance.

7. Discussions of life-cycle ceremonies for other groups in the Sulu Archipelago are found in Ewing (1958) for the Tausug; Ducommun (1962) for the Siasi Sama Dilaut; Wulff (1964) for the Yakan; Kiefer (1972) for the Tausug; Casino (1974) for the Jama Mapun; Allison (1984) for the Sibutu Sama; Teo (1989) for the Siasi Sama Dilaut; and Bottignolo (1995) for the Tawi-Tawi Sama Dilaut.

8. Most burials take place in the early morning, but I attended some in the afternoon. Burial time is determined not by tradition but by the time the funeral entourage arrives at the cemetery island.

9. Sather (1997, 283) reports that among the Semporna Bajau Laut, if the deceased is female a white banner is flown from the stern of the boat, and if the deceased is male a white banner is flown from the bow. I did not observe this tradition among the Tawi-Tawi Sama Dilaut.

Chapter 8 (pages 183–211)

1. The recording by Martenot and Maceda (1980), "Sama de Sitangkai," includes both instrumental and vocal selections of Sitangkai Sama Dilaut music. Although some differences are evident between Sitangkai and Tawi-Tawi, the Sitangkai music is very similar to Tawi-Tawi Sama Dilaut music and the interested reader is referred to that recording.

2. I regret that I have no Sinama language texts for these songs. The songs were collected incidental to my research on Sama Dilaut social organization. When I recorded them I was primarily interested in their cultural content and they were translated directly into English from the tapes. Some of the original tapes were lost in a storm at sea, and because of the limited tapes I had, others were recorded over for interviews. I intended to return to Tawi-Tawi to record the songs of the Sama Dilaut, but for reasons that are explained in the final chapter of this book that never happened.

3. The Tamuk gong is central to the superincision ceremony. The youth sits astride the gong, places his penis on the central knob and the djin cuts the incision.

4. The dances of the Sitangkai Sama Dilaut djin are much more complex than those of the Tawi-Tawi Sama Dilaut djin. Sitangkai has an elaborate cult of shamanism, which demands that all djin come together every three months under the full moon to dance until possessed. At these ceremonies I saw the most beautiful and technically sophisticated dances of all the dances I witnessed in the course of my fieldwork.

Epilogue (pages 212–33)

1. There is a large literature on the Muslim secessionist movement in the Philippines. Among the important books on the subject are: *Muslim Rulers and Rebels* (1998) by Thomas M. McKenna; *Roots of Conflict: Muslims, Christians, and the Mindanao Struggle* (1997) by Rosalita Tolibas-Nuñez; *Liberalism and the Quest for Islamic Identity in the Philippines* (1991) by Kenneth E. Bauzon; *The Contemporary Muslim Movement in the Philippines* (1985) by Cesar Adib Majul; and *Revolt in Mindanao* (1980) by T. J. S. George. The many articles on the subject are too numerous to list, but one of the best summaries of the conflict is "Appreciating Islam in the Muslim Philippines: Authority, Experience, and Identity in Cotabato" by Thomas M. McKenna (1997). The interested reader is referred to the bibliographies of these books for other articles.

2. "Municipality" is an administrative unit that includes the *poblacion* (the central town) and the surrounding *barangay* (barrios) to which it is connected.

3. Talib Sangogot (1980) refers to Lu'uk Bangka as "Nalil," a name apparently used for the moorage in 1979-80, the time of his research. Today "Nalil" is the name of the community surrounding the agricultural college west of Bongao town.

4. The population may have been even smaller. Talib Sangogot (1980, 76) discovered during his research among the Tawi-Tawi Sama Dilaut in 1979–80 that the average number of children per household was only two. During the time of my research in the 1960s, the average number of children per household was three.

5. I learned of fifteen Sama Dilaut deaths during the unrest of the 1970s and 1980s.

6. The Tabauan Sama practice maggambit fish drives, celebrate mbo'pai baha'o, and at one time wove fishing nets. All of these cultural features are, or were, found among the Tawi-Tawi and Sitangkai Sama Dilaut, but not among other Sama groups of the southern Sulu islands.

Appendix (pages 234–44)

1. Kurah sambailani – A horse sent from heaven, a common figure in Tawi-Tawi Muslim traditions.

2. Sigtagbanuamakadjag-Djag-Dagaha – The literal translation of the name of the gong is: "The sound of the gong will make you jump as if you were frightened."

3. Bunga-bunga mangih – A type of fruit.

4. Simataigarulanavidialumtana – "A prophet from the ground."

5. Amukogmukog-lantai-amontong-amontong-lampid – A very thin, flat fish.

6. In Tawi-Tawi Muslim tradition, it is believed that living people who go to the afterworld are unclean and, therefore, offensive to the spirits who reside there.

7. Kayu Taobi – A tree in the afterworld where infants suckle throughout eternity.

8. Maligai – A small, houselike structure containing foods used in various ceremonies. Variations of the maligai are found in many Tawi-Tawi Muslim traditions, as in this story where it is a flying house.

Selected Bibliography

This bibliography includes all works cited in the text as well as other significant writings about the Sama Dilaut of the Sulu Islands.

Allison, Karen J. 1982. *A view from the islands: The Samal of Tawi-Tawi.* Dallas: International Museum of Cultures.

Arce, Wilfredo F. 1963. Social organization of the Muslim peoples of Sulu. In *Sulu's people and their art*, edited by Frank Lynch, 1–25. Quezon City: Ateneo de Manila University Press.

Arong, Jose R. 1962. The Badjaw of Sulu. *Philippine Sociological Review* 10 (3–4): 134–47.

Baradas, David B. 1981. Some implications of the okir motif in Lanao and Sulu art. In *The Muslim Filipinos*, edited by Nagasura T. Madale, 172–209. Quezon City: Alemar-Phoenix.

Bauzon, Kenneth E. 1991. *Liberalism and the quest for Islamic identity in the Philippines.* Quezon City: Ateneo de Manila University Press.

Bottignolo, Bruno. 1995. *Celebrations with the sun: An overview of religious phenomena among the Badjaos.* Quezon City: Ateneo de Manila University Press.

Brownell, Atherton. 1905. A Moro experiment. *Outlook* 81 (12): 975–85.

Casiño, Eric. 1974. Folk-Islam in the life cycle of the Jama Mapun. In *The Muslim Filipinos*, edited by Peter G. Gowing and Robert D. McAmis, 165–81. Manila: Solidaridad Publishing House.

Cloman, Sydney A. 1923. *Myself and a few Moros.* Garden City: Doubleday, Page and Company.

Combes, Franciso. 1904. The natives of the southern islands. In *The Philippine islands, 1493–1898*, edited by Emma H. Blair and James A. Robertson, 40: 99–182. Cleveland: Arthur H. Clark.

Dacanay, Julian E., Jr. 1967. The o*kil* in Muslim art: A view from the drawing board. In *Brown heritage: Essays on Philippine cultural tradition and literature*, edited by Antonio G. Manuud, 149–61. Quezon City: Ateneo de Manila University Press.

De Henning Singh, Anne. 1976. The sea gypsies of the Philippines. *National Geographic* 149 (5): 659–77.

Doran, Edwin, Jr. 1973. *Nao, junk, and vaka: Boats and culture history.* College Station: Texas A and M University.

_____. 1976. Wa, vinta, and trimaran. In *Pacific navigation and voyaging*, edited by Ben R. Finney, 29–45. Wellington: The Polynesian Society.

_____. 1981. *Wangka: Austronesian canoe origins.* College Station: Texas A and M University Press.

Ducommun, Dolores. 1962. Sisangat: A Sulu fishing community. *Philippine Sociological Review* 10 (3–4): 91–107.

Eslao, Nena. 1962. Child–rearing among the Samal of Manubul, Siasi, Sulu. *Philippine Sociological Review* 10 (3–4): 80–91.

Ewing, Franklin. 1958. Some rites of passage among the Tawsug of the Philippines. *Anthropological Quarterly* 31 (2): 33–41.

Follet, Helen. 1945. *Men of the Sulu sea.* New York: Charles Scribner's Sons.

George, T. J. S. 1980. *Revolt in Mindanao. The rise of Islam in Philippine politics.* Kuala Lumpur: Oxford University Press.

Herre, Abert W. C. T. 1926. The Sibutu islands. *Proceedings of the Third Pan-Pacific Science Congress* 3: 2357–64.

Horvatich, Patricia. 1993. Keeping up with the Hassans: Tradition, change, and rituals of death in Tawi-Tawi, Philippines. *Pilipinas: A Journal of Philippine Studies* 21:51–71.

_____. 1994. Ways of knowing Islam. *American Ethnologist* 21 (4): 807–20.

_____. 1997. The Ahmadiyya movement in Simunul: Islamic reform in one remote and unlikely place. In *Islam in an era of nation-states,* edited by Robert W. Hefner and Patricia Horvatich, 183–206. Honolulu: University of Hawaii Press.

Kiefer, Thomas M. 1972. *The Tausug: Violence and law in a Philippine Moslem society.* New York: Holt, Rinehart and Winston.

Kiefer, Thomas M. and Clifford Sather. 1970. Gravemarkers and the repression of sexual symbolism: The case of two Philippine-Borneo Muslim societies. *Bijdragen Tot de Taal-, Land- en Volkenkunde* 126: 75–90.

Kurais, Muhammed II. 1975. Boatbuilding of the Sama. *Mindanao Journal* 1 (4): 421–39.

Landor, A. Henry Savage. 1904. *The gems of the east.* New York: Harper and Brothers Publishers.

Lapian, Adrian B. and Nagatsu Kazufumi. 1996. Research on Bajau communities: Maritime people in Southeast Asia. *Asian research trends: A humanistic social science research review.* Tokyo: The Center for East Asian Cultural Studies for UNESCO.

Maceda, Jose and Alain Martenot. 1980. *Sama de Sitangkai.* Societe d'Etudes Linguistiques et Anthropologiques de France.

Majul, Cesar Adib. 1985. *The contemporary Muslim movement in the Philippines.* Berkeley: Mizan Press.

Martenot, Alain. 1981. Bateaux Sama de Sitangkai. *Archipel* 22: 183–207.

Martenot, Alain and Jose Maceda. 1980. *Sama de Sitangkai.* LP recording. Paris: Office de la Recherche Scientifique et Technique Outre-Mer.

McKenna, Thomas M. 1997. Appreciating Islam in the Muslim Philippines: Authority, experience, and identity in Cotobato. In *Islam in an era of nation-states,* edited by Robert W. Hefner and Patricia Horvatich, 43–73. Honolulu: University of Hawaii Press.

_____. 1998. *Muslim rulers and rebels: Everyday politics and armed separatism in the southern Philippines.* Berkeley: University of California Press.

Nimmo, H. Arlo. 1965a. Social organization of the Tawi-Tawi Badjaw. Master's thesis, University of Hawaii.

_____. 1965b. Social organization of the Tawi-Tawi Badjaw. *Ethnology* 4 (4): 421–39.

_____. 1966. Themes in Badjaw dreams. *Philippine Sociological Review* 14 (1): 49–56.

_____. 1967. Book Review: *The sea nomads* by David Sopher. *Philippine Studies* 25 (1): 209–12.

_____. 1968a. Reflections on Bajau history. *Philippine Studies* 16 (1): 32–59.

_____. 1968b. Songs of the Sulu sea. *ETC.* 25 (4): 489–94.

_____. 1968c. The Bajau of Sulu—fiction and fact. *Philippine Studies* 16 (4): 771–75.

_____. 1969. The structure of Bajau society. Ph.D. diss., University of Hawaii.

_____. 1970a. Posong, trickster of Sulu. *Western Folklore* 29 (3): 185–91.

_____. 1970b. Bajau sex and reproduction. *Ethnology* 9 (3): 251–62.

_____. 1971. Bajau: Gentle boat-dwellers of the Philippines. In *Nomads of the world*, edited by Robert L. Breeden, 72–91. Washington, D. C.: National Geographic Society.

_____. 1972a. *The sea people of Sulu*. San Francisco: The Chandler Press.

_____. 1972b. You will remember us because we have sung for you. *Philippine Studies* 20 (2): 299–322.

_____. 1972c. Bajau communities in southeastern Sulawesi, Indonesia. *Borneo Research Bulletin* 4 (2): 42–43.

_____. 1973a. *The Bajau of the Philippines*. HRAFlex Volume #EOOA8–001. New Haven: Human Relations Area Files.

_____. 1973b. A tribe of ancient mariners comes ashore. *Natural History* 82 (10): 334–45.

_____. 1975. The shamans of Sulu. *Asian and Pacific Quarterly* 7 (1): 1–9.

_____. 1976a. A functional interpretation of Bajau songs. In *Directions in Pacific traditional literature*, edited by Adrienne L. Kaeppler and H. Arlo Nimmo, 289–309. Honolulu: Bishop Museum Press.

_____. 1976b. Film Review: *People of the current. American Anthropologist* 78: 717–18.

_____. 1977a. Bajoe: A Sama community at Watampone, Sulawesi. *Borneo Research Bulletin* 9 (2): 102–5.

_____. 1977b. The Bajau of Sulu. In *Filipino heritage: The making of a nation*, edited by Alfredo R. Roces, 1: 261–65.

_____. 1978. The relativity of sexual deviance: A Sulu example. *Papers in Anthropology* 19 (1): 91–98.

_____. 1984. Bajau. In *Muslim peoples*, edited by Richard V. Weekes, 1: 75–80. Westport: Greenwood Press.

_____. 1986. Recent population movements in the Sulu archipelago: Implications to Sama culture history. *Archipel* 32: 25–38.

_____. 1987. Film Review: *The Bajao: Seagoing nomads. American Anthropologist* 8 (1): 254–55.

_____. 1990a. Religious beliefs of the Tawi-Tawi Bajau. *Philippine Studies* 38 (1): 3–17.

_____. 1990b. Religious rituals of the Tawi-Tawi Bajau. *Philippine Studies* 38 (2): 166–98.

_____. 1990c. The boats of the Tawi-Tawi Bajau, Sulu archipelago, Philippines. *Asian Perspectives* 29 (1): 51–88.

_____. 1994. *The songs of Salanda*. Quezon City: Ateneo de Manila University Press.

_____. 1995. The relativity of sexual deviance. In *Human sexuality*, edited by Andrei Simic, Patricia A. Omidian and Alan J. Almquist, 234–39. Dubuque: Kendall/Hunt Publishing Company.

_____. 1999. Book Review: *The Bajau Laut: Adaptation, history, and fate in a maritime fishing society of south-eastern Sabah* by Clifford Sather. *American Anthropologist* 101 (2): 461–62.

1960 Census of the Philippines. Population and housing. Sulu. Manila: Bureau of the Census and Statistics.

1970 Census of population and housing. Sulu. Manila: National Census and Statistics Office.

1980 Census of population and housing. Tawi-Tawi. Manila: National Census and Statistics Office.

1990 Census of population and housing. Report No. 2–960. Population by city, municipality and barangay. Tawi-Tawi. Manila: National Statistics Office.

Orosa, Sixto. 1923. *The Sulu archipelago and its people*. New York: World Books and Company.

Pallesen, A. Kemp. 1972. Reciprocity in Samal marriage. *Sulu Studies* 1: 123–42.

_____. 1985. *Culture contact and language convergence.* Manila: Linguistic Society of the Philippines.

Pigafetta, Antonio. 1906. *Magellan's voyage around the world,* edited by James Alexander Robertson. Cleveland: Arthur H. Clark Company.

Saleeby, Najeeb M. 1963. *The history of Sulu.* Manila: Carmelo and Bauerman, Inc.

Sangogot, Talib L. 1980. Socio-economic-religious status and school attendance rate of the Badjaos (Tawi-Tawi): Implications for educational policies, curricula and management practices revisions. Master's thesis, Marikina Institute of Science and Technology.

Sather, Clifford. 1965a. Bajau riddles. *Sarawak Museum Journal* 12 (25–26): 162.

_____. 1965b. Bajau numbers and adjectives of quantity. *Sabah Society Journal* 2 (4): 194–97.

_____. 1966. A Bajau prawn snare. *Sabah Society Journal* 3 (1): 42–44.

_____. 1967. Social rank and marriage payments in an immigrant Moro community in Malaysia. *Ethnology* 6: 97–102.

_____. 1968a. Some notes concerning Bajau Laut phonology and grammar. *Sabah Society Journal* 3 (4): 205–24.

_____. 1968b. A note on Bajau gravemarkers from the Semporna district of Sabah. *Sarawak Museum Journal* 16: 103–6.

_____. 1971a. Book Review: *The North Borneo chartered company's administration of the Bajau, 1879–1909: The pacification of a maritime nomadic people* by James F. Warren. *Sarawak Museum Journal* 19: 381–82.

_____. 1971b. Bajau pottery-making in the Semporna district. *Borneo Research Bulletin* 3 (1): 10–11.

_____. 1971c. Bajau villages in the Lesser Sunda islands, Indonesia. *Borneo Research Bulletin* 3 (1): 11–12.

_____. 1971d. Sulu's political jurisdiction over the Bajau Laut. *Borneo Research Bulletin* 3 (2): 58–62.

_____. 1971e. Marriage and domestic relations among the Bajau Laut of northeastern Borneo. Ph.D. diss., Harvard University.

_____. 1974. Cultural affiliations in eastern Sabah and Sulu province. *Borneo Research Bulletin* 6 (1): 15–16.

_____. 1975a. Bajau Laut. In *Ethnic groups of insular Southeast Asia,* edited by Frank M. LeBar, 2: 9–12. New Haven: Human Relations Area Files Press.

_____. 1975b. Literary form in Bajau Laut riddles. *Sarawak Museum Journal* 23: 187–95.

_____. 1975c. There was a boy: A Bajau Laut prose narrative tale from Sabah. *Sarawak Museum Journal* 23: 197–206.

_____. 1975d. Seven fathoms: Bajau Laut narrative tales from the Semporna district of Sabah. *Brunei Museum Journal* 3 (3): 30–40.

_____. 1976. Kinship and contiguity: Variation in social alignments among the Semporna Bajau Laut. In *The societies of Borneo,* edited by George N. Appell, 40–65. Washington, D.C.: American Anthropological Association.

_____. 1978. The Bajau Laut. In *Essays on Borneo societies,* edited by V. T. King, 172–92. Hull Monographs on Southeast Asia, no. 7. London: Oxford University Press.

_____. 1984. Sea and shore: Ethnicity and ethnic interaction in Southeastern Sabah. *Contributions to Southeast Asian Ethnography* 3: 3–27.

_____. 1985. Boat crews and fishing fleets: The social organization of maritime labour among the Bajau Laut of southeastern Sabah. *Contributions to Southeast Asian Ethnography* 4: 165–214.

_____. 1993a. Bajau. In *Encyclopedia of world cultures*, edited by David Levinson, 5: 30–35. Boston: G. K. Hall and Company.

_____. 1993b. Samal. In *Encyclopedia of world cultures*, edited by David Levinson, 5: 217–21. Boston: G. K. Hall and Company.

_____. 1995. Sea nomads and rainforest hunter-gatherers: Foraging adaptations in the Indo-Malaysian archipelago. In *The Austronesians: Historical and comparative perspectives*, edited by Peter Bellwood, James J. Fox, and Darrell Tryon, 229–68. Camberra: The Australian National University.

_____. 1997. *The Bajau Laut: Adaptation, history, and fate in a maritime fishing society of south-eastern Sabah.* Kuala Lumpur: Oxford University Press.

Sopher, David. 1977 [1965]. *The sea nomads.* Singapore: National Museum.

Spoehr, Alexander. 1973. *Zamboanga and Sulu: An archaeological approach to ethnic diversity.* Pittsburgh: Department of Anthropology, University of Pittsburgh.

_____. 1980. *Protein from the sea.* Pittsburgh: Department of Anthropology, University of Pittsburgh.

Stone, Richard L. 1962. Intergroup relations among the Taosug, Samal and Badjaw of Sulu. *Philippine Sociological Review* 10 (3–4): 107–33.

Szanton, David E. 1963. Art in Sulu: A survey. In *Sulu's people and their art*, edited by Frank Lynch, 29–66. Quezon City: Ateneo de Manila University Press.

Taylor, Carl. 1930a. The Bajaos—children of the sea. *Philippine Magazine* 27 (3): 158–59, 176.

_____. 1930b. The Bajaos—children of the sea. *Philippine Magazine* 27 (5): 290–91, 322, 324, 326, 328, 330.

_____. 1931. The sea gypsies of Sulu. *Asia* 31: 8, 477–83, 534–55.

_____. 1932. Sailing the Sulu sea with the Moros. *Travel* 60 (1): 7–12, 41.

_____. 1936. *Odyssey of the islands.* New York: Charles Scribner's Sons.

Teo, Saladin S. 1989. *The life-style of the Badjaos: A study of education and culture.* Manila: Centro Escolar University Research and Development Center.

Tolibas-Nunez, Rosalita. 1997. *Roots of conflict: Muslims, Christians, and the Mindanao struggle.* Makati City: Asian Institute of Management.

U. S. Naval Oceanographic Office. 1956. *Sailing directions for the Philippine Islands 3.* Washington, D.C.: Government Printing Office.

Warren, James. 1971. *The North Borneo Chartered Company's administration of the Bajau, 1878–1909: The pacification of a maritime nomadic people.* Athens: Ohio University Center for International Studies.

_____. 1981. *The Sulu zone, 1768–1898.* Singapore: Singapore University Press.

Whitmarsh, Phelps. 1900. The Sulu archipelago. *The Outlook* 66 (10): 578–87.

Wilkes, Charles. 1844. *Narrative of the United States exploring expeditions during the years 1838, 1839, 1840, 1841, 1842.* Philadelphia.

Worcester, Dean C. 1899. *The Philippine Islands and their people.* London: Macmillan.

Wulff, Inger. 1964. Features of Yakan culture. *Folk* 6:53–72.

INDEX